FOURTH EDITION ▪ FOR HIGH SCHOOLS

# "THEY SAY / I SAY"

## The Moves That Matter in Academic Writing

### GERALD GRAFF

### CATHY BIRKENSTEIN

*both of the University of Illinois at Chicago*

*Foreword by*
### JIM BURKE
*Burlingame High School, California*

W·W· NORTON & COMPANY

NEW YORK | LONDON

W. W. Norton & Company has been independent since its founding in 1923, when William Warder Norton and Mary D. Herter Norton first published lectures delivered at the People's Institute, the adult education division of New York City's Cooper Union. The firm soon expanded its program beyond the Institute, publishing books by celebrated academics from America and abroad. By mid-century, the two major pillars of Norton's publishing program—trade books and college texts—were firmly established. In the 1950s, the Norton family transferred control of the company to its employees, and today—with a staff of four hundred and a comparable number of trade, college, and professional titles published each year—W. W. Norton & Company stands as the largest and oldest publishing house owned wholly by its employees.

**ISBN 978-0-393-64328-2**

W. W. Norton & Company, Inc., 500 Fifth Avenue, New York, NY 10110
wwnorton.com

W. W. Norton & Company Ltd., 15 Carlisle Street, London W1D 3BS

1 2 3 4 5 6 7 8 9 0 20 19 18

For
Aaron David

For
Karin Ford

# BRIEF CONTENTS

# CONTENTS

# CONTENTS

# Contents

# FOREWORD

## *An Invitation to the Conversation*

———

The best academic writing has one underlying feature: it is deeply
engaged in some way with other people's views.

> Gerald Graff and Cathy Birkenstein,
> "*They Say / I Say*"

Have you ever had the experience of not understanding
what you were supposed to write, or not knowing how your
teacher wanted you to write it? Have you ever been asked to
read, watch, or listen to something to determine the author's
argument and respond to it—but had no idea how to read or
write in the way your teacher wanted? Have you ever gone from
thinking you were rather capable to feeling totally incompe-
tent when asked to write in a style or about a complex subject
that was completely foreign to you? Or was there ever a paper
you got halfway written then suddenly ran out of ideas, with
nothing else to say no matter how hard you tried? You've had
experiences like these, right? I sure did, all through high school
and into my first year at college.

At some point, every student I teach in my high school
English classes, including Advanced Placement classes, has

such experiences, especially as I begin to assign longer, more complex papers. I remember one senior, a great student who was accepted early to Stanford, who tried to convince me that a paragraph he wrote about *Crime and Punishment* was so perfect, so complete, that adding anything to it would be shameful. And he was sincere. More to the point, though, whether he was aware of it or not, he had found his limit: he had no idea how to fully develop an argument. It was *"They Say / I Say"* that showed him how to do that.

We all need guidance doing things we have never done before or have not done well. No one is born knowing how to do academic writing. Myself, I earned a D- in English my senior year of high school and was placed in a remedial writing class my first year of college. It was then (and there) that I discovered that academic writing is a craft that can be learned.

*"They Say / I Say"* takes the mystery out of the academic writing required in high school and prepares you for what you will need to do in college and beyond. Much like a GPS application, this book will guide you through the often confusing passages of the texts you will read, write about, and discuss (and help you avoid potential obstacles), whether you study poetry or political science, biology or business. Most important, it will give you templates to help you construct arguments of your own—and to analyze arguments you read, hear, or watch someone make during a speech or presentation.

To demystify academic writing in general and argumentative writing in particular, this book:

- *Shows you how to read with a critical eye so* you can identify and understand what others are saying (and why) before you respond with arguments of your own.

- *Guides you through the process of constructing and supporting an argument* that engages others, explaining why your argument matters and how it differs from other positions on the same topic.
- *Teaches you how to listen to and enter sophisticated conversations* with others, both in-class and online, including those whose views you may not share, and to respond respectfully with arguments of your own.
- *Provides a variety of tools and techniques, including templates,* to help you generate and organize your argument, elaborate on it even when you feel like you have nothing more to say, and revise and finalize it.

These and other lessons in this book will help you to write effectively in response to an SAT, college-application, or Advanced Placement prompt. Thanks to this book, my students are now less intimidated by such prompts than they used to be, realizing that they are not all that different from the prompts we use in class. Whether they are interpreting a work of literature, analyzing a scientific theory, or critiquing an online article, my students have learned to craft arguments that present their position—their "I say"—as a response to what others have said to incorporate the views of naysayers, to explain why their argument matters, and more.

For research papers, the book is especially useful. Each chapter corresponds with a phase in the research process, a benefit my students find tremendously helpful when writing their big research paper at the end of the year. Such projects inevitably begin with a "they say"; thus students must establish their own motivation by explaining who or what they are responding to and why others should care. The book then guides them through the process of agreeing, disagreeing, or doing a bit of both as they respond to others' arguments with arguments of their own. In the past, my students often got lost in the labyrinth of putting together research papers, but the final section of this book never fails to help them find their way. They can then apply these skills to virtually any other academic writing assignment, since all such writing requires us to respond to the views of others.

Students often enter my class writing in predictable, even formulaic ways, as though there were only one way to write a paper or write about a topic. In these situations, the source of the problem is often rather simple: they don't have any idea about what a different approach would look or sound like. Again, in such a situation, *"They Say / I Say"* proves invaluable as we move in and out of it over the course of the year, trying on the different moves the book shows them how to make. As we study these moves in the context of writing, however, they begin to read more rhetorically, noticing how an author such as Michelle Alexander, in one of the new readings included here, "introduces an ongoing debate" or "plants a naysayer." In other words, while the book teaches you how to *write* papers by examining what "they say," it also teaches you how to *read* texts for what "they say," a move we all need to work hard to master in today's world.

When trying to figure out what to say about our own writing or the writing of authors we study, students often lack the language they need to enter such conversations. As a philosopher once said, we cannot enter a world (or a conversation) for which we do not have the language. One of the features of this book my students and I find especially helpful is the language it gives us as we begin to examine and discuss writing. While Graff and Birkenstein emphasize their efforts to "demystify academic conversation," it is often the small phrases that introduce each chapter—"Her Point Is," "Yes / No / Okay, But" and "Skeptics May Object" to name a few examples—that really demystify writing and give you the language you need to make that move or discuss it with your classmates or your teacher. It is, in other words, difficult to ask for help or try to make some move as a writer if you don't know what to call it or how to describe it. Graff and Birkenstein simply tell us what the move is called by using everyday language.

In recent years, my students have begun to rely more and more on computers as an essential tool for writing, researching, and reading. This new edition of *"They Say / I Say"* offers new help in these areas where my students and I struggled for some time, through such chapters as "Entering Online Conversations" and the interactive online tutorials available through the companion website. While reading articles about such potentially contentious topics as "the differences that divide us" poses many challenges to those in college, they are all the more difficult to discuss in a high-school class such as mine where thirty-five very different young adults gather each day. Students need the guidance these templates offer, for they give students the language they need to make the thoughtful moves such discussions require if they are to enter into and contribute to the conversation about those topics that all too often divide, scare, challenge, and confuse us.

The world is, indeed, made of arguments. Our ability to understand, think about, and make arguments of our own is essential to our success as students, workers, and citizens. Once you read this book and start to listen closely to what "they say," you will begin to ask yourself, "What do *I say?*" This book and your teachers will help you answer that question in your own words—and your own voice.

Welcome to the conversation.

Jim Burke

# PREFACE
# TO THE FOURTH EDITION

———◲———

SINCE IT WAS FIRST PUBLISHED OVER A DECADE AGO, this book has been dedicated to the idea that our own views are most thoughtfully formed in conversation with the views of others, including views that differ from our own. As the twenty-first century unfolds, however, the increasingly polarized state of our society is making it harder to listen to those who see things differently and to summarize their views in ways that our templates encourage. The wider the divisions become, the harder it can be to find anyone who is willing to seriously consider viewpoints that oppose their own. The tendency can be either to avoid difficult discussions altogether or to talk mainly with like-minded people, who often reinforce our preexisting assumptions and insulate us from serious challenge. It is our hope that the guidance and templates in our book will help student writers see the value in seeking out other perspectives and will give students strategies for incorporating the ideas of others into their own academic writing.

In this fourth edition of our book, therefore, we double down in a variety of ways on our emphasis on engaging with the views of others:

**New guidelines in the introduction** offer advice for listening carefully to what others say ("they say") and for treating our own ideas (what "I say") not as uncontestable givens but as entries in a conversation or a debate in which participants may agree, agree up to a point, or disagree.

**A new chapter on entering online conversations** underscores the importance of referencing what "they say" in online discussions. In this chapter, which offers more practical advice on how to write than the more theoretical chapter it replaces, we show how the rhetorical moves taught in this book can help students contribute clearly and respectfully to conversations on class discussion boards and in other digital spaces. We provide explicit suggestions and templates for fostering genuine online conversations, including guidance on linking to and embedding the views of others.

**A substantially revised chapter on academic language now called "You Mean I Can Just Say It That Way?"** encourages students to draw on, not set aside, their everyday voices in their academic writing and to use everyday language as a tool for thinking and discovery as well. This chapter shows how "translating" academic claims into everyday language can help clarify academic arguments.

**Many new model examples**—fifteen in all—from a wide range of authors, including Rebecca Goldstein, Deborah Tannen, Charles Murray, Nicholas Carr, and Michelle Alexander, among others, highlight the many different contexts for academic conversations.

**A substantially revised and updated chapter on writing in the social sciences** reflects a broader range of writing assignments, with examples from academic publications in sociology, psychology, and political sciences.

**New documented readings from two different fields**—an essay by the computer scientist Michael Littman and a selection from *The New Jim Crow* by the legal scholar Michelle Alexander—show how the rhetorical moves taught in this book work across disciplines.

Even as we have revised and added to *"They Say / I Say,"* our basic goals remain unchanged: to demystify academic reading and writing by identifying the key moves of persuasive argument and representing those moves in forms that students can put into practice. We hope this fourth edition will get us even closer to these goals, equipping students with the writing skills they need to enter the academic world and beyond.

### WHAT'S ONLINE

**Online tutorials.** New tutorials give students hand-on practice recognizing and using the rhetorical moves that matter. Each tutorial helps students read a full essay with an eye toward the rhetorical moves and then respond to a writing prompt using templates from the book.

*They Say / I Blog.* Updated monthly, this blog provides up-to-the-minute readings on the issues covered in the book, along with questions that prompt students to literally join the conversations. Check it out at **theysayiblog.com**.

**A Teacher's Companion.** Features advice from Jim Burke on using *"They Say / I Say"* in the high school classroom. Each chapter includes teaching tools and activities, including academic writing and reading activities that engage students in applying the rhetorical moves outlined in the textbook, tools for introducing key terms and concepts essential to understanding each chapter's objectives, multimedia activities to help students further explore the concepts, and supplements activities for English learners.

**Ebook.** Searchable, portable, and interactive. The complete textbook for a fraction of the price. Students can interact with the text—take notes, bookmark, search, and highlight. The ebook can be viewed on—and synced between—all computers and mobile devices.

**InQuizitive for Writers.** Adaptive, game-like exercises help students practice editing so they're better prepared to find and fix common errors in their writing.

**Coursepack.** Easily add high-quality Norton resources to your online, hybrid, or lecture course—all at no cost. Norton Coursepacks work within your existing learning management system; there's no new system to learn, and access is free and easy. Customizable resources include assignable writing prompts from theysayiblog.com, quizzes on grammar and documentation, documentation guides, model student papers, and more.

Find it all at **digital.wwnorton.com/theysay4hs** or contact your Norton representative for more information.

# "THEY SAY / I SAY"

*The Moves That Matter
in Academic Writing*

# INTRODUCTION

## *Entering the Conversation*

———◻———

THINK ABOUT AN ACTIVITY that you do particularly well: cooking, playing the piano, shooting a basketball, even something as basic as driving a car. If you reflect on this activity, you'll realize that once you mastered it you no longer had to give much conscious thought to the various moves that go into doing it. Performing this activity, in other words, depends on your having learned a series of complicated moves—moves that may seem mysterious or difficult to those who haven't yet learned them.

The same applies to writing. Often without consciously realizing it, accomplished writers routinely rely on a stock of established moves that are crucial for communicating sophisticated ideas. What makes writers masters of their trade is not only their ability to express interesting thoughts but their mastery of an inventory of basic moves that they probably picked up by reading a wide range of other accomplished writers. Less experienced writers, by contrast, are often unfamiliar with these basic moves and unsure how to make them in their own writing. Hence this book, which is intended as a short, user-friendly guide to the basic moves of academic writing.

One of our key premises is that these basic moves are so common that they can be represented in *templates* that you can use right away to structure and even generate your own writing. Perhaps the most distinctive feature of this book is its presentation of many such templates, designed to help you successfully enter not only the world of academic thinking and writing, but also the wider worlds of civic discourse and work.

Instead of focusing solely on abstract principles of writing, then, this book offers model templates that help you put those principles directly into practice. Working with these templates will give you an immediate sense of how to engage in the kinds of critical thinking you are required to do at the college level and in the vocational and public spheres beyond.

Some of these templates represent simple but crucial moves like those used to summarize some widely held belief.

▶ **Many Americans assume that _____.**

Others are more complicated.

▶ **On the one hand, _____. On the other hand, _____.**

▶ **Author X contradicts herself. At the same time that she argues _____, she also implies _____.**

▶ **I agree that _____.**

▶ **This is not to say that _____.**

It is true, of course, that critical thinking and writing go deeper than any set of linguistic formulas, requiring that you question assumptions, develop strong claims, offer supporting reasons and evidence, consider opposing arguments, and so on. But these deeper habits of thought cannot be put into practice unless you have a language for expressing them in clear, organized ways.

## STATE YOUR OWN IDEAS AS A
## RESPONSE TO OTHERS

The single most important template that we focus on in this book is the "they say _____ ; I say _____" formula that gives our book its title. If there is any one point that we hope you will take away from this book, it is the importance not only of expressing your ideas ("I say") but of presenting those ideas as a *response to some other person or group* ("they say"). For us, the underlying structure of effective academic writing—and of responsible public discourse—resides not just in stating our own ideas but in listening closely to others around us, summarizing their views in a way that they will recognize, and responding with our own ideas in kind. Broadly speaking, academic writing is argumentative writing, and we believe that to argue well you need to do more than assert your own position. You need to enter a conversation, using what others say (or might say) as a launching pad or sounding board for your own views. For this reason, one of the main pieces of advice in this book is to write the voices of others into your text.

In our view, then, the best academic writing has one underlying feature: it is deeply engaged in some way with other people's views. Too often, however, academic writing is taught as a process of saying "true" or "smart" things in a vacuum, as if it were possible to argue effectively without being in conversation *with* someone else. If you have been taught to write a traditional five-paragraph essay, for example, you have learned how to develop a thesis and support it with evidence. This is good advice as far as it goes, but it leaves out the important fact that in the real world we don't make arguments without being provoked. Instead, we make arguments because someone has said or done something (or perhaps *not* said or done

3

something) and we need to respond: "I can't see why you like the Lakers so much"; "I agree: it was a great film"; "That argument is contradictory." If it weren't for other people and our need to challenge, agree with, or otherwise respond to them, there would be no reason to argue at all.

## "WHY ARE YOU TELLING ME THIS?"

To make an impact as a writer, then, you need to do more than make statements that are logical, well supported, and consistent. You must also find a way of entering into conversation with the views of others, with something "they say." The easiest and most common way writers do this is by *summarizing* what others say and then using it to set up what they want to say.

"But why," as a student of ours once asked, "do I always need to summarize the views of others to set up my own view? Why can't I just state my own view and be done with it?" Why indeed? After all, "they," whoever they may be, will have already had their say, so why do you have to *repeat* it? Furthermore, if they had their say in print, can't readers just go and read what was said themselves?

The answer is that if you don't identify the "they say" you're responding to, your own argument probably won't have a point. Readers will wonder what prompted you to say what you're saying and therefore motivated you to write. As the figure on the following page suggests, without a "they say," *what* you are saying may be clear to your audience, but *why* you are saying it won't be.

Even if we don't know what film he's referring to, it's easy to grasp what the speaker means here when he says that its characters are very complex. But it's hard to see why the speaker feels the need to say what he is saying. "Why," as one member

4

of his imagined audience wonders, "is he telling us this?" So the characters are complex—so what?

Now look at what happens to the same proposition when it is presented as a response to something "they say":

We hope you agree that the same claim—"the characters in the film are very complex"—becomes much stronger when presented as a response to a contrary view: that the film's characters "are sexist stereotypes." Unlike the speaker in the first cartoon, the speaker in the second has a clear goal or mission: to correct what he sees as a mistaken characterization.

## THE AS-OPPOSED-TO-WHAT FACTOR

To put our point another way, framing your "I say" as a response to something "they say" gives your writing an element of contrast without which it won't make sense. It may be helpful to think of this crucial element as an "as-opposed-to-what factor" and, as you write, to continually ask yourself, "Who says otherwise?" and "Does anyone dispute it?" Behind the audience's "Yeah, so?" and "Why is he telling us this?" in the first cartoon above lie precisely these types of "As opposed to what?" questions. The speaker in the second cartoon, we think, is more satisfying because he answers these questions, helping us see his point that the film presents complex characters *rather than* simple sexist stereotypes.

## HOW IT'S DONE

Many accomplished writers make explicit "they say" moves to set up and motivate their own arguments. One famous example is Martin Luther King Jr.'s "Letter from Birmingham Jail," which consists almost entirely of King's eloquent responses to a public statement by eight clergymen deploring the civil rights protests

6

he was leading. The letter—which was written in 1963, while King was in prison for leading a demonstration against racial injustice in Birmingham—is structured almost entirely around a framework of summary and response, in which King summarizes and then answers their criticisms. In one typical passage, King writes as follows.

> You deplore the demonstrations taking place in Birmingham. But your statement, I am sorry to say, fails to express a similar concern for the conditions that brought about the demonstrations.
>
> MARTIN LUTHER KING JR., "Letter from Birmingham Jail"

King goes on to agree with his critics that "It is unfortunate that demonstrations are taking place in Birmingham," yet he hastens to add that "it is even more unfortunate that the city's white power structure left the Negro community with no alternative." King's letter is so thoroughly conversational, in fact, that it could be rewritten in the form of a dialogue or play.

King's critics:
King's response:
Critics:
Response:

Clearly, King would not have written his famous letter were it not for his critics, whose views he treats not as objections to his already-formed arguments but as the motivating source of those arguments, their central reason for being. He quotes not only what his critics have said ("Some have asked: 'Why didn't you give the new city administration time to act?'"), but also things they *might* have said ("One may well ask: 'How can you advocate breaking some laws and obeying others?'")—all to set the stage for what he himself wants to say.

A similar "they say / I say" exchange opens an essay about American patriotism by the social critic Katha Pollitt, who uses her own daughter's comment to represent the patriotic national fervor after the terrorist attacks of September 11, 2001.

> My daughter, who goes to Stuyvesant High School only blocks from the former World Trade Center, thinks we should fly the American flag out our window. Definitely not, I say: the flag stands for jingoism and vengeance and war. She tells me I'm wrong—the flag means standing together and honoring the dead and saying no to terrorism. In a way we're both right. . . .
>
> KATHA POLLITT, "Put Out No Flags"

As Pollitt's example shows, the "they" you respond to in crafting an argument need not be a famous author or someone known to your audience. It can be a family member like Pollitt's daughter, or a friend or classmate who has made a provocative claim. It can even be something an individual or a group might say—or a side of yourself, something you once believed but no longer do, or something you partly believe but also doubt. The important thing is that the "they" (or "you" or "she") represent some wider group with which readers might identify—in Pollitt's case, those who patriotically believe in flying the flag. Pollitt's example also shows that responding to the views of others need not always involve unqualified opposition. By agreeing and disagreeing with her daughter, Pollitt enacts what we call the "yes and no" response, reconciling apparently incompatible views.

See Chapter 4 for more on agreeing, but with a difference.

While King and Pollitt both identify the views they are responding to, some authors do not explicitly state their views but instead allow the reader to infer them. See, for instance, if you can identify the implied or unnamed "they say" that the following claim is responding to.

> I like to think I have a certain advantage as a teacher of literature because when I was growing up I disliked and feared books.
>
> GERALD GRAFF, "Disliking Books at an Early Age"

In case you haven't figured it out already, the phantom "they say" here is the common belief that in order to be a good teacher of literature, one must have grown up liking and enjoying books.

## COURT CONTROVERSY, BUT...

As you can see from these examples, many writers use the "they say / I say" format to challenge standard ways of thinking and thus to stir up controversy. This point may come as a shock to you if you have always had the impression that in order to succeed academically you need to play it safe and avoid controversy in your writing, making statements that nobody can possibly disagree with. Though this view of writing may appear logical, it is actually a recipe for flat, lifeless writing and for writing that fails to answer what we call the "so what?" and "who cares?" questions. "William Shakespeare wrote many famous plays and sonnets" may be a perfectly true statement, but precisely because nobody is likely to disagree with it, it goes without saying and thus would seem pointless if said.

But just because controversy is important doesn't mean you have to become an attack dog who automatically disagrees with everything others say. We think this is an important point to underscore because some who are not familiar with this book have gotten the impression from the title that our goal is to train writers simply to disparage whatever "they say."

## DISAGREEING WITHOUT BEING DISAGREEABLE

There certainly are occasions when strong critique is needed. It's hard to live in a deeply polarized society like our current one and not feel the need at times to criticize what others think. But even the most justified critiques fall flat, we submit, unless we really listen to and understand the views we are criticizing:

▶ While I understand the impulse to _____, my own view is _____.

Even the most sympathetic audiences, after all, tend to feel manipulated by arguments that scapegoat and caricature the other side.

Furthermore, genuinely listening to views we disagree with can have the salutary effect of helping us see that beliefs we'd initially disdained may not be as thoroughly reprehensible as we'd imagined. Thus the type of "they say / I say" argument that we promote in this book can take the form of agreeing up to a point or, as the Pollitt example above illustrates, of both agreeing and disagreeing simultaneously, as in:

▶ While I agree with X that _____, I cannot accept her overall conclusion that _____.

▶ While X argues _____, and I argue _____, in a way we're both right.

Agreement cannot be ruled out, however:

▶ I agree with _____ that _____.

## THE TEMPLATE OF TEMPLATES

There are many ways, then, to enter a conversation and respond to what "they say." But our discussion of ways to do so would be incomplete were we not to mention the most comprehensive way that writers enter conversations, which incorporates all the major moves discussed in this book:

▶ In recent discussions of _____, a controversial issue has been whether _____. On the one hand, some argue that _____. From this perspective, _____. On the other hand, however, others argue that _____. In the words of _____, one of this view's main proponents, "_____." According to this view, _____. In sum, then, the issue is whether _____ or _____.

My own view is that _____. Though I concede that _____, I still maintain that _____. For example, _____. Although some might object that _____, I would reply that _____. The issue is important because _____.

This "template of templates," as we like to call it, represents the internal DNA of countless articles and even entire books. Writers commonly use a version of it not only to stake out their "they say" and "I say" at the start of their manuscript, but—just as important—to form the overarching blueprint that structures what they write over the entire length of their text.

Taking it line by line, this master template first helps you open your text by identifying an issue in some ongoing conversation or debate ("In recent discussions of _____, a controversial issue has been _____"), and then to map some of the voices in this controversy (by using the "on the one hand / on the other hand" structure). The template then helps you introduce a quotation ("In the words of"), to explain the quotation in your own words ("According to this view"), and—in a new paragraph—to state your own argument ("My own view is that"), to qualify your argument ("Though I concede that"), and then to support your argument with evidence ("For example"). In addition, the template helps you make one of the most crucial moves in argumentative writing, what we call "planting a naysayer in your text," in which you summarize and then answer a likely objection to your own central claim ("Although it might be objected that _____, I reply _____"). Finally, this template helps you shift between general, over-arching claims ("In sum, then") and smaller-scale, supporting claims ("For example").

Again, none of us is born knowing these moves, especially when it comes to academic writing. Hence the need for this book.

## BUT ISN'T THIS PLAGIARISM?

"But isn't this plagiarism?" at least one student each year will usually ask. "Well, is it?" we respond, turning the question around into one the entire class can profit from. "We are, after all, asking you to use language in your writing that isn't your own—language that you 'borrow' or, to put it less delicately, steal from other writers."

Often, a lively discussion ensues that raises important questions about authorial ownership and helps everyone better understand the frequently confusing line between plagiarism and the legitimate use of what others say and how they say it. Students are quick to see that no one person owns a conventional formula like "on the one hand . . . on the other hand. . . ." Phrases like "a controversial issue" are so commonly used and recycled that they are generic—community property that can be freely used without fear of committing plagiarism. It *is* plagiarism, however, if the words used to fill in the blanks of such formulas are borrowed from others without proper acknowledgment. In sum, then, while it is not plagiarism to recycle conventionally used formulas, it is a serious academic offense to take the substantive content from others' texts without citing the author and giving him or her proper credit.

## "OK—BUT TEMPLATES?"

Nevertheless, if you are like some of our students, your initial response to templates may be skepticism. At first, many of our students complain that using templates will take away their originality and creativity and make them all sound the same. "They'll turn us into writing robots," one of our students insisted. "I'm in college now," another student asserted; "this is third-grade-level stuff."

In our view, however, the templates in this book, far from being "third-grade-level stuff," represent the stock-in-trade of sophisticated thinking and writing, and they often require a great deal of practice and instruction to use successfully. As for the belief that pre-established forms undermine creativity, we think it rests on a very limited vision of what creativity is all about. In our view, the templates in this book will actually help your writing become *more* original and creative, not less. After all, even the most creative forms of expression depend on established patterns and structures. Most songwriters, for instance, rely on a time-honored verse-chorus-verse pattern, and few people would call Shakespeare uncreative because he didn't invent the sonnet or the dramatic forms that he used to such dazzling effect. Even the most avant-garde, cutting-edge artists like improvisational jazz musicians need to master the basic forms that their work improvises on, departs from, and goes beyond, or else their work will come across as uneducated child's play. Ultimately, then, creativity and originality lie not in the avoidance of established forms but in the imaginative use of them.

Furthermore, these templates do not dictate the *content* of what you say, which can be as original as you can make it, but only suggest a way of formatting *how* you say it. In addition, once you begin to feel comfortable with the templates in this book, you will be able to improvise creatively on them to fit new situations and purposes and find others in your reading. In other words, the templates offered here are learning tools to get you started, not structures set in stone. Once you get used to using them, you can even dispense with them altogether, for the rhetorical moves they model will be at your fingertips in an unconscious, instinctive way.

But if you still need proof that writing templates need not make you sound stiff and artificial, consider the following opening to an essay on the fast-food industry that we've included at the back of this book.

If ever there were a newspaper headline custom-made for Jay Leno's monologue, this was it. Kids taking on McDonald's this week, suing the company for making them fat. Isn't that like middle-aged men suing Porsche for making them get speeding tickets? Whatever happened to personal responsibility?

I tend to sympathize with these portly fast-food patrons, though. Maybe that's because I used to be one of them.

DAVID ZINCZENKO, "Don't Blame the Eater"

Although Zinczenko relies on a version of the "they say / I say" formula, his writing is anything but dry, robotic, or uncreative. While Zinczenko does not explicitly use the words "they say" and "I say," the template still gives the passage its underlying structure: "*They say* that kids suing fast-food companies for making them fat is a joke; but *I say* such lawsuits are justified."

## PUTTING IN YOUR OAR

Though the immediate goal of this book is to help you become a better writer, at a deeper level it invites you to become a certain type of person: a critical, intellectual thinker who, instead of sitting passively on the sidelines, can participate in the debates and conversations of your world in an active and empowered way. Ultimately, this book invites you to become a critical thinker who can enter the types of conversations described eloquently by the philosopher Kenneth Burke in the following widely cited passage. Likening the world of intellectual exchange to a never-ending conversation at a party, Burke writes:

> You come late. When you arrive, others have long preceded you, and they are engaged in a heated discussion, a discussion too heated

for them to pause and tell you exactly what it is about. . . . You
listen for a while, until you decide that you have caught the tenor
of the argument; then you put in your oar. Someone answers; you
answer him; another comes to your defense; another aligns himself
against you. . . . The hour grows late, you must depart. And you do
depart, with the discussion still vigorously in progress.

KENNETH BURKE, *The Philosophy of Literary Form*

What we like about this passage is its suggestion that stating an
argument (putting in your oar) can only be done in conversation with others; that entering the dynamic world of ideas must
be done not as isolated individuals but as social beings deeply
connected to others.

This ability to enter complex, many-sided conversations
has taken on a special urgency in today's polarized, Red State /
Blue State America, where the future for all of us may depend
on our ability to put ourselves in the shoes of those who think
very differently from us. The central piece of advice in this
book—that we listen carefully to others, including those who
disagree with us, and then engage with them thoughtfully
and respectfully—can help us see beyond our own pet beliefs,
which may not be shared by everyone. The mere act of crafting a sentence that begins "Of course, someone might object
that _____" may not seem like a way to change the world;
but it does have the potential to jog us out of our comfort
zones, to get us thinking critically about our own beliefs, and
even to change minds, our own included.

*Exercises*

1. Write a short essay in which you first summarize our rationale
   for the templates in this book and then articulate your own

position in response. If you want, you can use the template below to organize your paragraphs, expanding and modifying it as necessary to fit what you want to say.

In the Introduction to *"They Say / I Say": The Moves That Matter in Academic Writing,* Gerald Graff and Cathy Birkenstein provide templates designed to _____. Specifically, Graff and Birkenstein argue that the types of writing templates they offer _____. As the authors themselves put it, "_____." Although some people believe _____, Graff and Birkenstein insist that _____. In sum, then, their view is that _____.

I [agree/disagree/have mixed feelings]. In my view, the types of templates that the authors recommend _____. For instance, _____. In addition, _____. Some might object, of course, on the grounds that _____. Yet I would argue that _____. Overall, then, I believe _____ —an important point to make given _____.

2. Read the following paragraph from an essay by Emily Poe, a student at Furman University. Disregarding for the moment what Poe says, focus your attention on the phrases she uses to structure what she says (italicized here). Then write a new paragraph using Poe's as a model but replacing her topic, vegetarianism, with one of your own.

The term "vegetarian" tends to be synonymous with "tree-hugger" in many people's minds. *They see* vegetarianism as a cult that brainwashes its followers into eliminating an essential part of their daily diets for an abstract goal of "animal welfare." *However,* few vegetarians choose their lifestyle just to follow the crowd. *On the contrary,* many of these supposedly brainwashed people are actually independent thinkers, concerned citizens, and compassionate human beings. *For the truth is* that there are many very good reasons for giving up meat. Perhaps the best reasons are to improve the environment, to encourage humane treatment of livestock, or to enhance one's own health. *In this essay, then,* closely examining a vegetarian diet as compared to a meat-eater's diet will show that vegetarianism is clearly the better option for sustaining the Earth and all its inhabitants.

# ONE

# "THEY SAY"

## *Starting with What Others Are Saying*

———

NOT LONG AGO we attended a talk at an academic conference where the speaker's central claim seemed to be that a certain sociologist—call him Dr. X—had done very good work in a number of areas of the discipline. The speaker proceeded to illustrate his thesis by referring extensively and in great detail to various books and articles by Dr. X and by quoting long passages from them. The speaker was obviously both learned and impassioned, but as we listened to his talk we found ourselves somewhat puzzled: the argument—that Dr. X's work was very important—was clear enough, but why did the speaker need to make it in the first place? Did anyone dispute it? Were there commentators in the field who had argued against X's work or challenged its value? Was the speaker's interpretation of what X had done somehow novel or revolutionary? Since the speaker gave no hint of an answer to any of these questions, we could only wonder why he was going on and on about X. It was only after the speaker finished and took questions from the audience that we got a clue: in response to one questioner, he referred to several critics who had

The hypothetical audience in the figure on p. 5 reacts similarly.

vigorously questioned Dr. X's ideas and convinced many sociologists that Dr. X's work was unsound.

This story illustrates an important lesson: that to give writing the most important thing of all—namely, a point—a writer needs to indicate clearly not only what his or her thesis is, but also what larger conversation that thesis is responding to. Because our speaker failed to mention what others had said about Dr. X's work, he left his audience unsure about why he felt the need to say what he was saying. Perhaps the point was clear to other sociologists in the audience who were more familiar with the debates over Dr. X's work than we were. But even they, we bet, would have understood the speaker's point better if he'd sketched in some of the larger conversation his own claims were a part of and reminded the audience about what "they say."

This story also illustrates an important lesson about the *order* in which things are said: to keep an audience engaged, a writer needs to explain what he or she is responding to—either before offering that response or, at least, very early in the discussion. Delaying this explanation for more than one or two paragraphs in a very short essay or blog entry, three or four pages in a longer work, or more than ten or so pages in a book reverses the natural order in which readers process material—and in which writers think and develop ideas. After all, it seems very unlikely that our conference speaker first developed his defense of Dr. X and only later came across Dr. X's critics. As someone knowledgeable in his field, the speaker surely encountered the criticisms first and only then was compelled to respond and, as he saw it, set the record straight.

Therefore, when it comes to constructing an argument (whether orally or in writing), we offer you the following advice: remember that you are entering a conversation and therefore need to start with "what others are saying," as the title of this chapter recommends, and then introduce your own ideas as a response. Specifically, we suggest that you summarize what "they say" as soon as you can in your text, and remind readers of it at strategic points as your text unfolds. Though it's true that not all texts follow this practice, we think it's important for all writers to master it before they depart from it.

This is not to say that you must start with a detailed list of everyone who has written on your subject before you offer your own ideas. Had our conference speaker gone to the opposite extreme and spent most of his talk summarizing Dr. X's critics with no hint of what he himself had to say, the audience probably would have had the same frustrated "why-is-he-going-on-like-this?" reaction. What we suggest, then, is that as soon as possible you state your own position and the one it's responding to *together*, and that you think of the two as a unit. It is generally best to summarize the ideas you're responding to briefly, at the start of your text, and to delay detailed elaboration until later. The point is to give your readers a quick preview of what is motivating your argument, not to drown them in details right away.

Starting with a summary of others' views may seem to contradict the common advice that writers should lead with their own thesis or claim. Although we agree that you shouldn't keep readers in suspense too long about your central argument, we also believe that you need to present that argument as part of some larger conversation, indicating something about the arguments of others that you are supporting, opposing, amending, complicating, or qualifying. One added benefit of summarizing others' views as soon as you can: you let those others do some of the work of framing and clarifying the issue you're writing about.

Consider, for example, how George Orwell starts his famous essay "Politics and the English Language" with what others are saying.

Most people who bother with the matter at all would admit that the English language is in a bad way, but it is generally assumed that we cannot by conscious action do anything about it. Our civilization is decadent and our language—so the argument runs—must inevitably share in the general collapse. . . .

[But] the process is reversible. Modern English . . . is full of bad habits . . . which can be avoided if one is willing to take the necessary trouble.

GEORGE ORWELL, "Politics and the English Language"

Orwell is basically saying, "Most people assume that we cannot do anything about the bad state of the English language. But I say we can."

Of course, there are many other powerful ways to begin. Instead of opening with someone else's views, you could start with an illustrative quotation, a revealing fact or statistic, or— as we do in this chapter—a relevant anecdote. If you choose one of these formats, however, be sure that it in some way illustrates the view you're addressing or leads you to that view directly, with a minimum of steps.

In opening this chapter, for example, we devote the first paragraph to an anecdote about the conference speaker and then move quickly at the start of the second paragraph to the misconception about writing exemplified by the speaker. In the following opening, from an opinion piece in the *New York Times Book Review*, Christina Nehring also moves quickly from an anecdote illustrating something she dislikes to her own claim—that book lovers think too highly of themselves.

"I'm a reader!" announced the yellow button. "How about you?" I looked at its bearer, a strapping young guy stalking my town's Festival of Books. "I'll bet you're a reader," he volunteered, as though we were two geniuses well met. "No," I replied. "Absolutely not," I wanted to yell, and fling my Barnes & Noble bag at his feet. Instead, I mumbled something apologetic and melted into the crowd.

There's a new piety in the air: the self-congratulation of book lovers.

CHRISTINA NEHRING, "Books Make You a Boring Person"

Nehring's anecdote is really a kind of "they say": book lovers keep telling themselves how great they are.

## TEMPLATES FOR INTRODUCING WHAT "THEY SAY"

There are lots of conventional ways to introduce what others are saying. Here are some standard templates that we would have recommended to our conference speaker.

▸ **A number of sociologists have recently suggested <u>that X's work has several fundamental problems.</u>**

▸ **It has become common today to dismiss _____.**

▸ **In their recent work, Y and Z have offered harsh critiques of _____ for _____.**

## TEMPLATES FOR INTRODUCING "STANDARD VIEWS"

The following templates can help you make what we call the "standard view" move, in which you introduce a view that has become so widely accepted that by now it is essentially the conventional way of thinking about a topic.

▶ Americans have always believed that <u>individual effort can triumph over circumstances</u>.

▶ Conventional wisdom has it that _____.

▶ Common sense seems to dictate that _____.

▶ The standard way of thinking about topic X has it that _____.

▶ It is often said that _____.

▶ My whole life I have heard it said that _____.

▶ You would think that _____.

▶ Many people assume that _____.

These templates are popular because they provide a quick and efficient way to perform one of the most common moves that writers make: challenging widely accepted beliefs, placing them on the examining table, and analyzing their strengths and weaknesses.

## TEMPLATES FOR MAKING WHAT "THEY SAY" SOMETHING *YOU* SAY

Another way to introduce the views you're responding to is to present them as your own. That is, the "they say" that you respond to need not be a view held by others; it can be one that you yourself once held or one that you are ambivalent about.

▶ I've always believed that <u>museums are boring</u>.

▶ When I was a child, I used to think that _____.

- ▸ Although I should know better by now, I cannot help thinking that _____.

- ▸ At the same time that I believe _____, I also believe _____.

## TEMPLATES FOR INTRODUCING
## SOMETHING IMPLIED OR ASSUMED

Another sophisticated move a writer can make is to summarize a point that is not directly stated in what "they say" but is implied or assumed.

- ▸ Although none of them have ever said so directly, my teachers have often given me the impression that <u>education will open doors</u>.

- ▸ One implication of X's treatment of _____ is that _____.

- ▸ Although X does not say so directly, she apparently assumes that _____.

- ▸ While they rarely admit as much, _____ often take for granted that _____.

These are templates that can help you think analytically—to look beyond what others say explicitly and to consider their unstated assumptions, as well as the implications of their views.

## TEMPLATES FOR INTRODUCING
## AN ONGOING DEBATE

Sometimes you'll want to open by summarizing a debate that presents two or more views. This kind of opening demonstrates your awareness that there are conflicting ways to look at your subject, the clear mark of someone who knows the subject and therefore is likely to be a reliable, trustworthy guide. Furthermore, opening with a summary of a debate can help you explore the issue you are writing about before declaring your own view. In this way, you can use the writing process itself to help you discover where you stand instead of having to commit to a position before you are ready to do so.

Here is a basic template for opening with a debate.

> ▸ In discussions of X, one controversial issue has been _____. On the one hand, _____ argues _____. On the other hand, _____ contends _____. Others even maintain _____. My own view is _____.

The cognitive scientist Mark Aronoff uses this kind of template in an essay on the workings of the human brain.

> Theories of how the mind/brain works have been dominated for centuries by two opposing views. One, rationalism, sees the human mind as coming into this world more or less fully formed—preprogrammed, in modern terms. The other, empiricism, sees the mind of the newborn as largely unstructured, a blank slate.
>
> MARK ARONOFF, "Washington Slept Here"

A student writer, Michaela Cullington, uses a version of this template near the beginning of an essay to frame a debate over online writing abbreviations like "LOL" ("laughing out loud") and to indicate her own position in this debate.

> Some people believe that using these abbreviations is hindering the writing abilities of students, and others argue that texting is

actually having a positive effect on writing. In fact, it seems likely that texting has no significant effect on student writing.

MICHAELA CULLINGTON, "Does Texting Affect Writing?"

Another way to open with a debate involves starting with a proposition many people agree with in order to highlight the point(s) on which they ultimately disagree.

▸ **When it comes to the topic of _____, most of us will readily agree that _____. Where this agreement usually ends, however, is on the question of _____. Whereas some are convinced that _____, others maintain that _____.**

The political writer Thomas Frank uses a variation on this move.

That we are a nation divided is an almost universal lament of this bitter election year. However, the exact property that divides us—elemental though it is said to be—remains a matter of some controversy.

THOMAS FRANK, "American Psyche"

## KEEP WHAT "THEY SAY" IN VIEW

We can't urge you too strongly to keep in mind what "they say" as you move through the rest of your text. After summarizing the ideas you are responding to at the outset, it's very important to continue to keep those ideas in view. Readers won't be able to follow your unfolding response, much less any complications you may offer, unless you keep reminding them what claims you are responding to.

In other words, even when presenting your own claims, you should keep returning to the motivating "they say." The longer and more complicated your text, the greater the chance that readers will forget what ideas originally motivated it—no matter how clearly you lay them out at the beginning. At strategic moments throughout your text, we recommend that you include what we call "return sentences." Here is an example.

> ▸ In conclusion, then, as I suggested earlier, defenders of _____ can't have it both ways. Their assertion that _____ is contradicted by their claim that _____.

We ourselves use such return sentences at every opportunity in this book to remind you of the view of writing that our book questions—that good writing means making true or smart or logical statements about a given subject with little or no reference to what others say about it.

By reminding readers of the ideas you're responding to, return sentences ensure that your text maintains a sense of mission and urgency from start to finish. In short, they help ensure that your argument is a genuine response to others' views rather than just a set of observations about a given subject. The difference is huge. To be responsive to others and the conversation you're entering, you need to start with what others are saying and continue keeping it in the reader's view.

*Exercises*

1. The following is a list of arguments that lack a "they say." Like the speaker in the cartoon on page 5 who declares that the film presents complex characters, these one-sided

arguments fail to explain what view they are responding to—what view, in effect, they are trying to correct, add to, qualify, complicate, and so forth. Your job in this exercise is to provide each argument with such a counterview. Feel free to use any of the templates in this chapter that you find helpful.

    a. Our experiments suggest that there are dangerous levels of chemical X in the Ohio groundwater.
    b. Material forces drive history.
    c. Proponents of Freudian psychology question standard notions of "rationality."
    d. Male students often dominate class discussions.
    e. The film is about the problems of romantic relationships.
    f. I'm afraid that templates like the ones in this book will stifle my creativity.

2. Below is a template that we derived from the opening of David Zinczenko's "Don't Blame the Eater" (p. 245). Use the template to structure a passage on a topic of your own choosing. Your first step here should be to find an idea that you support that others not only disagree with but actually find laughable (or, as Zinczenko puts it, worthy of a Jay Leno monologue). You might write about one of the topics listed in the previous exercise (the environment, gender relations, the meaning of a book or movie) or any other topic that interests you.

If ever there was an idea custom-made for a Jay Leno monologue, this was it: _____. Isn't that like _____? Whatever happened to _____?

    I happen to sympathize with _____, though, perhaps because _____.

# TWO

# "HER POINT IS"

## *The Art of Summarizing*

—◻—

IF IT IS TRUE, as we claim in this book, that to argue persuasively you need to be in dialogue with others, then summarizing others' arguments is central to your arsenal of basic moves. Because writers who make strong claims need to map their claims relative to those of other people, it is important to know how to summarize effectively what those other people say. (We're using the word "summarizing" here to refer to any information from others that you present in your own words, including that which you paraphrase.)

Many writers shy away from summarizing—perhaps because they don't want to take the trouble to go back to the text in question and wrestle with what it says, or because they fear that devoting too much time to other people's ideas will take away from their own. When assigned to write a response to an article, such writers might offer their own views on the article's *topic* while hardly mentioning what the article itself argues or says. At the opposite extreme are those who do nothing *but* summarize. Lacking confidence, perhaps, in their own ideas, these writers so overload their texts with summaries of others' ideas that their own voice gets lost. And since these summaries are not animated by the writers' own interests, they often read like mere lists of things that X thinks or Y says—with no clear focus.

As a general rule, a good summary requires balancing what the original author is saying with the writer's own focus. Generally speaking, a summary must at once be true to what the original author says while also emphasizing those aspects of what the author says that interest you, the writer. Striking this delicate balance can be tricky, since it means facing two ways at once: both outward (toward the author being summarized) and inward (toward yourself). Ultimately, it means being respectful of others but simultaneously structuring how you summarize them in light of your own text's central argument.

## ON THE ONE HAND,
## PUT YOURSELF IN *THEIR* SHOES

To write a really good summary, you must be able to suspend your own beliefs for a time and put yourself in the shoes of someone else. This means playing what the writing theorist Peter Elbow calls the "believing game," in which you try to inhabit the world-view of those whose conversation you are joining—and whom you are perhaps even disagreeing with—and try to see their argument from their perspective. This ability to temporarily suspend one's own convictions is a hallmark of good actors, who must convincingly "become" characters whom in real life they may detest. As a writer, when you play the believing game well, readers should not be able to tell whether you agree or disagree with the ideas you are summarizing.

If, as a writer, you cannot or will not suspend your own beliefs in this way, you are likely to produce summaries that are so obviously biased that they undermine your credibility with readers. Consider the following summary.

> David Zinczenko's article "Don't Blame the Eater" is nothing more than an angry rant in which he accuses the fast-food companies of an evil conspiracy to make people fat. I disagree because these companies have to make money. . . .

If you review what Zinczenko actually says (pp. 245–47), you should immediately see that this summary amounts to an unfair distortion. While Zinczenko does argue that the practices of the fast-food industry have the *effect* of making people fat, his tone is never "angry," and he never goes so far as to suggest that the fast-food industry conspires to make people fat with deliberately evil intent.

Another telltale sign of this writer's failure to give Zinczenko a fair hearing is the hasty way he abandons the summary after only one sentence and rushes on to his own response. So eager is this writer to disagree that he not only caricatures what Zinczenko says but also gives the article a hasty, superficial reading. Granted, there are many writing situations in which, because of matters of proportion, a one- or two-sentence summary is precisely what you want. Indeed, as writing professor Karen Lunsford (whose own research focuses on argument theory) points out, it is standard in the natural and social sciences to summarize the work of others quickly, in one pithy sentence or phrase, as in the following example.

> Several studies (Crackle, 2012; Pop, 2007; Snap, 2006) suggest that these policies are harmless; moreover, other studies (Dick, 2011; Harry, 2007; Tom, 2005) argue that they even have benefits.

But if your assignment is to respond in writing to a single author, like Zinczenko, you will need to tell your readers enough about his or her argument so they can assess its merits on their own, independent of you.

When a writer fails to provide enough summary or to engage in a rigorous or serious enough summary, he or she often falls prey to what we call "the closest cliché syndrome," in which what gets summarized is not the view the author in question has actually expressed but a familiar cliché that the writer *mistakes* for the author's view (sometimes because the writer believes it and mistakenly assumes the author must too). So, for example, Martin Luther King Jr.'s passionate defense of civil disobedience in "Letter from Birmingham Jail" might be summarized not as the defense of political protest that it actually is but as a plea for everyone to "just get along." Similarly, Zinczenko's critique of the fast-food industry might be summarized as a call for overweight people to take responsibility for their weight.

Whenever you enter into a conversation with others in your writing, then, it is extremely important that you go back to what those others have said, that you study it very closely, and that you not confuse it with something you already believe. A writer who fails to do this ends up essentially conversing with imaginary others who are really only the products of his or her own biases and preconceptions.

## ON THE OTHER HAND, KNOW WHERE *YOU* ARE GOING

Even as writing an effective summary requires you to temporarily adopt the worldview of another person, it does not mean ignoring your own view altogether. Paradoxically, at the same time that summarizing another text requires you to represent fairly what it says, it also requires that your own response exert a quiet influence. A good summary, in other words, has a focus or spin that allows the summary to fit with your own agenda while still being true to the text you are summarizing.

Thus if you are writing in response to the essay by Zinczenko, you should be able to see that an essay on the fast-food industry in general will call for a very different summary than will an essay on parenting, corporate regulation, or warning labels. If you want your essay to encompass all three topics, you'll need to subordinate these three issues to one of Zinczenko's general claims and then make sure this general claim directly sets up your own argument.

For example, suppose you want to argue that it is parents, not fast-food companies, who are to blame for children's obesity. To set up this argument, you will probably want to compose a summary that highlights what Zinczenko says about the fast-food industry *and parents*. Consider this sample.

In his article "Don't Blame the Eater," David Zinczenko blames the fast-food industry for fueling today's so-called obesity epidemic, not only by failing to provide adequate warning labels on its high-calorie foods but also by filling the nutritional void in children's lives left by their overtaxed working parents. With many parents working long hours and unable to supervise what their children eat, Zinczenko claims, children today are easily victimized by the low-cost, calorie-laden foods that the fast-food chains are all too eager to supply. When he was a young boy, for instance, and his single mother was away at work, he ate at Taco Bell, McDonald's, and other chains on a regular basis, and ended up overweight. Zinczenko's hope is that with the new spate of lawsuits against the food industry, other children with working parents will have healthier choices available to them, and that they will not, like him, become obese.

In my view, however, it is the parents, and not the food chains, who are responsible for their children's obesity. While it is true that many of today's parents work long hours, there are still several things that parents can do to guarantee that their children eat healthy foods. . . .

The summary in the first paragraph succeeds because it points in two directions at once—both toward Zinczenko's own text *and* toward the second paragraph, where the writer begins to establish her own argument. The opening sentence gives a sense of Zinczenko's general argument (that the fast-food chains are to blame for obesity), including his two main supporting claims (about warning labels and parents), but it ends with an emphasis on the writer's main concern: parental responsibility. In this way, the summary does justice to Zinczenko's arguments while also setting up the ensuing critique.

This advice—to summarize authors in light of your own agenda—may seem painfully obvious. But writers often summarize a given author on one issue even though their text actually focuses on another. To avoid this problem, you need to make sure that your "they say" and "I say" are well matched. In fact, aligning what they say with what you say is a good thing to work on when revising what you've written.

Often writers who summarize without regard to their own agenda fall prey to what might be called "list summaries," summaries that simply inventory the original author's various points but fail to focus those points around any larger overall claim. If you've ever heard a talk in which the points were connected only by words like "and then," "also," and "in addition," you

**THE EFFECT OF A TYPICAL LIST SUMMARY**

know how such lists can put listeners to sleep—as shown in the figure above. A typical list summary sounds like this.

> The author says many different things about his subject. *First* he says. . . . *Then* he makes the point that. . . . *In addition* he says. . . . *And then* he writes. . . . *Also* he shows that. . . . *And then* he says. . . .

It may be boring list summaries like this that give summaries in general a bad name and even prompt some instructors to discourage their students from summarizing at all.

Not all lists are bad, however. A list can be an excellent way to organize material—but only if, instead of being a miscellaneous grab bag, it is organized around a larger argument that informs each item listed. Many well-written summaries, for instance, list various points made by an author, sometimes itemizing those points ("First, she argues . . . ," "Second, she argues . . . ," "Third . . ."), and sometimes even itemizing those points in bullet form.

Many well-written arguments are organized in a list format as well. In "The New Liberal Arts," Sanford J. Ungar lists what he sees as seven common misperceptions that discourage college students from majoring in the liberal arts, the first of which begin:

> Misperception No. 1: A liberal-arts degree is a luxury that most families can no longer afford. . . .
>
> Misperception No. 2: College graduates are finding it harder to get good jobs with liberal-arts degrees. . . .
>
> Misperception No. 3: The liberal arts are particularly irrelevant for low-income and first-generation college students. They, more than their more-affluent peers, must focus on something more practical and marketable.
>
> SANFORD J. UNGAR, "The New Liberal Arts"

What makes Ungar's list so effective, and makes it stand out in contrast to the type of disorganized lists our cartoon parodies, is that it has a clear, overarching goal: to defend the liberal arts. Had Ungar's article lacked such a unifying agenda and instead been a miscellaneous grab bag, it almost assuredly would have lost its readers, who wouldn't have known what to focus on or what the final "message" or "takeaway" should be.

In conclusion, writing a good summary means not just representing an author's view accurately, but doing so in a way that fits what you want to say, the larger point you want to make. On the one hand, it means playing Peter Elbow's believing game and doing justice to the source; if the summary ignores or misrepresents the source, its bias and unfairness will show. On the other hand, even as it does justice to the source, a summary has to have a slant or spin that prepares the way for your own claims. Once a summary enters your text, you should think of it as joint property—reflecting not just the source you are summarizing, but your own perspective or take on it.

## SUMMARIZING SATIRICALLY

Thus far in this chapter we have argued that, as a general rule, good summaries require a balance between what someone else has said and your own interests as a writer. Now, however, we want to address one exception to this rule: the satiric summary, in which a writer deliberately gives his or her own spin to someone else's argument in order to reveal a glaring shortcoming in it. Despite our previous comments that well-crafted summaries generally strike a balance between heeding what someone else has said and your own independent interests, the satiric mode can at times be a very effective form of critique because it lets the summarized argument condemn itself without overt editorializing by you, the writer.

One such satiric summary can be found in Sanford J. Ungar's essay "The New Liberal Arts," which we just mentioned. In his discussion of the "misperception," as he sees it, that a liberal arts education is "particularly irrelevant for low-income and first-generation college students," who "must focus on something more practical and marketable," Ungar restates this view as "another way of saying, really, that the rich folks will do the important thinking, and the lower classes will simply carry out their ideas." Few who would dissuade disadvantaged students from the liberal arts would actually state their position in this insulting way. But in taking their position to its logical conclusion, Ungar's satire suggests that this is precisely what their position amounts to.

## USE SIGNAL VERBS THAT FIT THE ACTION

In introducing summaries, try to avoid bland formulas like "she says" or "they believe." Though language like this is sometimes serviceable enough, it often fails to reflect accurately what's been said. In some cases, "he says" may even drain the passion out of the ideas you're summarizing.

We suspect that the habit of ignoring the action when summarizing stems from the mistaken belief we mentioned earlier that writing is about playing it safe and not making waves, a matter of piling up truths and bits of knowledge rather than a dynamic process of doing things to and with other people. People who wouldn't hesitate to *say* "X totally misrepresented," "attacked," or "loved" something when chatting with friends will in their writing often opt for far tamer and even less accurate phrases like "X said."

But the authors you summarize at the college level seldom simply "say" or "discuss" things; they "urge," "emphasize," and "complain about" them. David Zinczenko, for example, doesn't just *say* that fast-food companies contribute to obesity; he *complains* or *protests* that they do; he *challenges*, *chastises*, and *indicts* those companies. The Declaration of Independence doesn't just *talk about* the treatment of the colonies by the British; it *protests against* it. To do justice to the authors you cite, we recommend that when summarizing— or when introducing a quotation—you use vivid and precise signal verbs as often as possible. Though "he says" or "she believes" will sometimes be the most appropriate language for the occasion, your text will often be more accurate and lively if you tailor your verbs to suit the precise actions you're describing.

## TEMPLATES FOR INTRODUCING SUMMARIES AND QUOTATIONS

▸ She advocates <u>a radical revision of the juvenile justice system</u>.

▸ They celebrate the fact that _____.

▸ _____, he admits.

## VERBS FOR INTRODUCING SUMMARIES AND QUOTATIONS

### VERBS FOR MAKING A CLAIM

| | |
|---|---|
| argue | insist |
| assert | observe |
| believe | remind us |
| claim | report |
| emphasize | suggest |

### VERBS FOR EXPRESSING AGREEMENT

| | |
|---|---|
| acknowledge | endorse |
| admire | extol |
| agree | praise |

**VERBS FOR EXPRESSING AGREEMENT**

| | |
|---|---|
| celebrate the fact that | reaffirm |
| corroborate | support |
| do not deny | verify |

**VERBS FOR QUESTIONING OR DISAGREEING**

| | |
|---|---|
| complain | qualify |
| complicate | question |
| contend | refute |
| contradict | reject |
| deny | renounce |
| deplore the tendency to | repudiate |

**VERBS FOR MAKING RECOMMENDATIONS**

| | |
|---|---|
| advocate | implore |
| call for | plead |
| demand | recommend |
| encourage | urge |
| exhort | warn |

## Exercises

1. To get a feel for Peter Elbow's "believing game," write a summary of some belief that you strongly disagree with. Then write a summary of the position that you actually hold on this topic. Give both summaries to a classmate or two, and see if they can tell which position you endorse. If you've succeeded, they won't be able to tell.

2. Write two different summaries of David Zinczenko's "Don't Blame the Eater" (pp. 245–47). Write the first one for an essay arguing that, contrary to what Zinczenko claims, there *are* inexpensive and convenient alternatives to fast-food restaurants. Write the second for an essay that questions whether being overweight is a genuine medical problem rather than a problem of cultural stereotypes. Compare your two summaries: though they are about the same article, they should look very different.

# THREE

# "AS HE HIMSELF PUTS IT"
## *The Art of Quoting*

——◻——

A KEY PREMISE OF THIS BOOK is that to launch an effective argument you need to write the arguments of others into your text. One of the best ways to do so is by not only summarizing what "they say," as suggested in Chapter 2, but by quoting their exact words. Quoting someone else's words gives a tremendous amount of credibility to your summary and helps ensure that it is fair and accurate. In a sense, then, quotations function as a kind of proof of evidence, saying to readers: "Look, I'm not just making this up. She makes this claim, and here it is in her exact words."

Yet many writers make a host of mistakes when it comes to quoting, not the least of which is the failure to quote enough in the first place, if at all. Some writers quote too little— perhaps because they don't want to bother going back to the original text and looking up the author's exact words, or because they think they can reconstruct the author's ideas from memory. At the opposite extreme are writers who so overquote that they end up with texts that are short on commentary of their own—maybe because they lack confidence in their ability to comment on the quotations, or because they don't fully understand what they've quoted and therefore have trouble explaining what the quotations mean.

But the main problem with quoting arises when writers assume that quotations speak for themselves. Because the meaning of a quotation is obvious to *them*, many writers assume that this meaning will also be obvious to their readers, when often it is not. Writers who make this mistake think that their job is done when they've chosen a quotation and inserted it into their text. They draft an essay, slap in a few quotations, and whammo, they're done.

Such writers fail to see that quoting means more than simply enclosing what "they say" in quotation marks. In a way, quotations are orphans: words that have been taken from their original contexts and that need to be integrated into their new textual surroundings. This chapter offers two key ways to produce this sort of integration: (1) by choosing quotations wisely, with an eye to how well they support a particular part of your text, and (2) by surrounding every major quotation with a frame explaining whose words they are, what the quotation means, and how the quotation relates to your own text. The point we want to emphasize is that quoting what "they say" must always be connected with what *you* say.

## QUOTE RELEVANT PASSAGES

Before you can select appropriate quotations, you need to have a sense of what you want to do with them—that is, how they will support your text at the particular point where you insert them. Be careful not to select quotations just for the sake of demonstrating that you've read the author's work; you need to make sure they support your own argument.

However, finding relevant quotations is not always easy. In fact, sometimes quotations that were initially relevant to your argument, or to a key point in it, become less so as your text changes during the process of writing and revising. Given the evolving and messy nature of writing, you may sometimes think that you've found the perfect quotation to support your argument, only to discover later on, as your text develops, that your focus has changed and the quotation no longer works. It can be somewhat misleading, then, to speak of finding your thesis and finding relevant quotations as two separate steps, one coming after the other. When you're deeply engaged in the writing and revising process, there is usually a great deal of back-and-forth between your argument and any quotations you select.

## FRAME EVERY QUOTATION

Finding relevant quotations is only part of your job; you also need to present them in a way that makes their relevance and meaning clear to your readers. Since quotations do not speak for themselves, you need to build a frame around them in which you do that speaking for them.

Quotations that are inserted into a text without such a frame are sometimes called "dangling" quotations for the way they're left dangling without any explanation. One teacher we've worked with, Steve Benton, calls these "hit-and-run" quotations, likening them to car accidents in which the driver speeds away and avoids taking responsibility for the dent in your fender or the smashed taillights, as in the figure that follows.

## DON'T BE A HIT-AND-RUN QUOTER.

What follows is a typical hit-and-run quotation by a student responding to an essay by Deborah Tannen, a linguistics professor and prominent author, who complains that academics value opposition over agreement.

> Deborah Tannen writes about academia. Academics believe "that intellectual inquiry is a metaphorical battle. Following from that is a second assumption that the best way to demonstrate intellectual prowess is to criticize, find fault, and attack."
>
> I agree with Tannen. Another point Tannen makes is that . . .

Since this student fails to introduce the quotation adequately or explain why he finds it worth quoting, readers will have a hard time reconstructing what Tannen argued. First, the student simply gives us the quotation from Tannen without telling us who Tannen is or even indicating that the quoted words are hers. In addition, the student does not explain what he takes Tannen to be saying or how her claims connect with his own. Instead, he simply abandons the quotation in his haste to zoom on to another point.

To adequately frame a quotation, you need to insert it into what we like to call a "quotation sandwich," with the statement introducing it serving as the top slice of bread and the explanation following it serving as the bottom slice. The introductory or lead-in claims should explain who is speaking and set up what the quotation says; the follow-up statements should explain why you consider the quotation to be important and what you take it to say.

### TEMPLATES FOR INTRODUCING QUOTATIONS

▸ X states, "<u>Not all steroids should be banned from sports.</u>"

▸ As the prominent philosopher X puts it, "_____."

▸ According to X, "_____."

▸ X himself writes, "_____."

▸ In her book, _____, X maintains that "_____."

▸ Writing in the journal *Commentary*, X complains that "_____."

▸ In X's view, "_____."

▸ X agrees when she writes, "_____."

▸ X disagrees when he writes, "_____."

▸ X complicates matters further when she writes, "_____."

### TEMPLATES FOR EXPLAINING QUOTATIONS

The one piece of advice about quoting that our students say they find most helpful is to get in the habit of following every major quotation by explaining what it means, using a template like one of the ones below.

▸ Basically, X is warning <u>that the proposed solution will only make the problem worse</u>.

▸ In other words, X believes _____.

▸ In making this comment, X urges us to _____.

▸ X is corroborating the age-old adage that _____.

▸ X's point is that _____.

▸ The essence of X's argument is that _____.

When offering such explanations, it is important to use language that accurately reflects the spirit of the quoted passage. It is often serviceable enough in introducing a quotation to write "X states" or "X asserts," but in most cases you can add precision to your writing by introducing the quotation in more vivid terms. Since, in the example above, Tannen is clearly alarmed by the culture of "attack" that she describes, it would be more accurate to use language that reflects that alarm: "Tannen is alarmed that," "Tannen is disturbed by," "Tannen deplores," or (in our own formulation here) "Tannen complains."

See pp. 40–41 for a list of action verbs for summarizing what other say.

Consider, for example, how the earlier passage on Tannen might be revised using some of these moves.

Deborah Tannen, a prominent linguistics professor, complains that academia is too combative. Rather than really listening to others, Tannen insists, academics habitually try to prove one another wrong. As Tannen herself puts it, "We are all driven by our ideological assumption that intellectual inquiry is a metaphorical battle," that "the best way to demonstrate intellectual prowess is to criticize, find fault, and attack." In short, Tannen objects that academic communication tends to be a competition for supremacy in which loftier values like truth and consensus get lost.

Tannen's observations ring true to me because I have often felt that the academic pieces I read for class are negative and focus on proving another theorist wrong rather than stating a truth . . .

This revision works, we think, because it frames or nests Tannen's words, integrating them and offering guidance about how they should be read. Instead of launching directly into the quoted words, as the previous draft had done, this revised version identifies Tannen ("a prominent linguistics professor") and clearly indicates that the quoted words are hers ("as Tannen herself puts it"). And instead of being presented without explanation as it was before, the quotation is now presented as an illustration of Tannen's point that, as the student helpfully puts it, "academics habitually try to prove one another wrong" and compete "for supremacy." In this way, the student explains the quotation while restating it in his own words, thereby making it clear that the quotation is being used purposefully instead of having been stuck in simply to pad the essay or the works-cited list.

## BLEND THE AUTHOR'S WORDS
## WITH YOUR OWN

This new framing material also works well because it accurately represents Tannen's words while giving those words the student's own spin. Instead of simply repeating Tannen word for word, the follow-up sentences echo just enough of her language while still moving the discussion in the student's own direction. Tannen's "battle," "criticize," "find fault," and "attack," for instance, get translated by the student into claims about how "combative" Tannen thinks academics are and how she thinks they "habitually try to prove one another wrong." In this way, the framing creates a kind of hybrid mix of Tannen's words and those of the writer.

## CAN YOU OVERANALYZE A QUOTATION?

But is it possible to overexplain a quotation? And how do you know when you've explained a quotation thoroughly enough? After all, not all quotations require the same amount of explanatory framing, and there are no hard-and-fast rules for knowing how much explanation any quotation needs. As a general rule, the most explanatory framing is needed for quotations that may be hard for readers to process: quotations that are long and complex, that are filled with details or jargon, or that contain hidden complexities.

And yet, though the particular situation usually dictates when and how much to explain a quotation, we will still offer one piece of advice: when in doubt, go for it. It is better to risk being overly explicit about what you take a quotation to mean than to leave the quotation dangling and your readers in doubt. Indeed, we encourage you to provide such explanatory framing even when writing to an audience that you know to be familiar with the author being quoted and able to interpret your quotations on their own. Even in such cases, readers need to see how *you* interpret the quotation, since words—especially those of controversial figures—can be interpreted in various ways and used to support different, sometimes opposing, agendas.

Your readers need to see what you make of the material you've quoted, if only to be sure that your reading of the material and theirs are on the same page.

## HOW *NOT* TO INTRODUCE QUOTATIONS

We want to conclude this chapter by surveying some ways *not* to introduce quotations. Although some writers do so, you should not introduce quotations by saying something like "Orwell asserts an idea that" or "A quote by Shakespeare says." Introductory phrases like these are both redundant and misleading. In the first example, you could write either "Orwell asserts that" or "Orwell's assertion is that," rather than redundantly combining the two. The second example misleads readers, since it is the writer who is doing the quoting, not Shakespeare (as "a quote by Shakespeare" implies).

The templates in this book will help you avoid such mistakes. Once you have mastered templates like "as X puts it" or "in X's own words," you probably won't even have to think about them—and will be free to focus on the challenging ideas that templates help you frame.

*Exercises*

1. Find a published piece of writing that quotes something that "they say." How has the writer integrated the quotation into his or her own text? How has he or she introduced the quotation, and what, if anything, has the writer said to explain it and tie it to his or her own text? Based on what you've read in this chapter, are there any changes you would suggest?

2. Look at something you have written for one of your classes.
   Have you quoted any sources? If so, how have you integrated
   the quotation into your own text? How have you introduced it? explained what it means? indicated how it relates
   to *your* text? If you haven't done all these things, revise your
   text to do so, perhaps using the Templates for Introducing
   Quotations (p. 47) and Explaining Quotations (pp. 47–48).
   If you've not written anything with quotations, try revising
   some academic text you've written to do so.

# FOUR

# "YES / NO / OKAY, BUT"
## Three Ways to Respond

———🔲———

THE FIRST THREE CHAPTERS of this book discuss the "they say" stage of writing, in which you devote your attention to the views of some other person or group. In this chapter we move to the "I say" stage, in which you offer your own argument as a response to what "they" have said.

Moving to the "I say" stage can be daunting in academia, where it often may seem that you need to be an expert in a field to have an argument at all. Many students have told us that they have trouble entering some of the high-powered conversations that take place in college or graduate school because they do not know enough about the topic at hand or because, they say, they simply are not "smart enough." Yet often these same students, when given a chance to study in depth the contribution that some scholar has made in a given field, will turn around and say things like "I can see where she is coming from, how she makes her case by building on what other scholars have said. Perhaps had I studied the situation longer *I* could have come up with a similar argument." What these students come to realize is that good arguments are based not on knowledge that only a special class of experts has access to, but on everyday habits of mind that can be isolated, identified, and used by almost anyone. Though there's certainly no substitute for expertise and for knowing as much as possible about one's topic, the arguments that finally win the day are built, as the title of this chapter suggests, on some very basic rhetorical patterns that most of us use on a daily basis.

There are a great many ways to respond to others' ideas, but this chapter concentrates on the three most common and recognizable ways: agreeing, disagreeing, or some combination of both. Although each way of responding is open to endless variation, we focus on these three because readers come to any text needing to learn fairly quickly where the writer stands, and they do this by placing the writer on a mental map consisting of a few familiar options: the writer agrees with those he or she is responding to, disagrees with them, or presents some combination of both agreeing and disagreeing.

When writers take too long to declare their position relative to views they've summarized or quoted, readers get frustrated, wondering, "Is this guy agreeing or disagreeing? Is he *for* what this other person has said, *against* it, or what?" For this reason, this chapter's advice applies to reading as well as to writing. Especially with difficult texts, you need not only to find the position the writer is responding to—the "they say"—but also to determine whether the writer is agreeing with it, challenging it, or some mixture of the two.

## ONLY *THREE* WAYS TO RESPOND?

Perhaps you'll worry that fitting your own response into one of these three categories will force you to oversimplify your argument or lessen its complexity, subtlety, or originality. This is certainly a serious concern for academics who are rightly skeptical of writing that is simplistic and reductive. We would argue, however, that the more complex and subtle your argument is, and the more it departs from the conventional ways people think, the more your readers will need to be able to place it on their mental map in order to process the complex details you present. That is, the complexity, subtlety, and originality of your response are more likely to stand out and be noticed if readers have a baseline sense of where you stand relative to any ideas you've cited. As you move through this chapter, we hope you'll agree that the forms of agreeing, disagreeing, and both agreeing and disagreeing that we discuss, far from being simplistic or one-dimensional, are able to accommodate a high degree of creative, complex thought.

It is always a good tactic to begin your response not by launching directly into a mass of details but by stating clearly whether you agree, disagree, or both, using a direct, no-nonsense formula such as: "I agree," "I disagree," or "I am of two minds. I agree that _____ , but I cannot agree that _____." Once you have offered one of these straightforward statements (or one of the many variations discussed below), readers will have a strong grasp of your position and then be able to appreciate the complications you go on to offer as your response unfolds.

See p. 21 for suggestions on previewing where you stand.

Still, you may object that these three basic ways of responding don't cover all the options—that they ignore interpretive or analytical responses, for example. In other words, you might think that when you interpret a literary work you don't necessarily agree or disagree with anything but simply explain the work's meaning, style, or structure. Many essays about literature and the arts, it might be said, take this form—they interpret a work's meaning, thus rendering matters of agreeing or disagreeing irrelevant.

We would argue, however, that the most interesting interpretations in fact tend to be those that agree, disagree, or
both—that instead of being offered solo, the best interpretations take strong stands relative to other interpretations. In fact,
there would be no reason to offer an interpretation of a work
of literature or art unless you were responding to the interpretations or possible interpretations of others. Even when you
point out features or qualities of an artistic work that others
have not noticed, you are implicitly disagreeing with what
those interpreters have said by pointing out that they missed
or overlooked something that, in your view, is important. In
any effective interpretation, then, you need not only to state
what you yourself take the work of art to mean but to do so
relative to the interpretations of other readers—be they professional scholars, teachers, classmates, or even hypothetical
readers (as in, "Although some readers might think that this
poem is about _____, it is in fact about _____").

## DISAGREE—AND EXPLAIN WHY

Disagreeing may seem like one of the simpler moves a writer
can make, and it is often the first thing people associate with
critical thinking. Disagreeing can also be the easiest way to
generate an essay: find something you can disagree with in what
has been said or might be said about your topic, summarize
it, and argue with it. But disagreement in fact poses hidden
challenges. You need to do more than simply assert that you
disagree with a particular view; you also have to offer persuasive
reasons *why* you disagree. After all, disagreeing means more
than adding "not" to what someone else has said, more than
just saying, "Although they say women's rights are improving,

I say women's rights are *not* improving." Such a response merely contradicts the view it responds to and fails to add anything interesting or new. To turn it into an argument, you need to give reasons to support what you say: because another's argument fails to take relevant factors into account; because it is based on faulty or incomplete evidence; because it rests on questionable assumptions; or because it uses flawed logic, is contradictory, or overlooks what you take to be the real issue. To move the conversation forward (and, indeed, to justify your very act of writing), you need to demonstrate that you have something to contribute.

You can even disagree by making what we call the "duh" move, in which you disagree not with the position itself but with the assumption that it is a new or stunning revelation. Here is an example of such a move, used to open an essay on the state of American schools.

> According to a recent report by some researchers at Stanford University, high school students with college aspirations "often lack crucial information on applying to college and on succeeding academically once they get there."
>
> Well, duh. . . . It shouldn't take a Stanford research team to tell us that when it comes to "succeeding academically," many students don't have a clue.
>
> GERALD GRAFF, "Trickle-Down Obfuscation"

Like all of the other moves discussed in this book, the "duh" move can be tailored to meet the needs of almost any writing situation. If you find the expression "duh" too brash to use with your intended audience, you can always dispense with the term itself and write something like "It is true that _____; but we already knew that."

## TEMPLATES FOR DISAGREEING, WITH REASONS

▸ X is mistaken because she overlooks <u>recent fossil discoveries in the South</u>.

▸ X's claim that _____ rests upon the questionable assumption that _____.

▸ I disagree with X's view that _____ because, as recent research has shown, _____.

▸ X contradicts herself/can't have it both ways. On the one hand, she argues _____. On the other hand, she also says _____.

▸ By focusing on _____, X overlooks the deeper problem of _____.

You can also disagree by making what we call the "twist it" move, in which you agree with the evidence that someone else has presented but show through a twist of logic that this evidence actually supports your own, contrary position. For example:

> X argues for stricter gun control legislation, saying that the crime rate is on the rise and that we need to restrict the circulation of guns. I agree that the crime rate is on the rise, but that's precisely why I oppose stricter gun control legislation. We need to own guns to protect ourselves against criminals.

In this example of the "twist it" move, the writer agrees with X's claim that the crime rate is on the rise but then argues that this increasing crime rate is in fact a valid reason for *opposing* gun control legislation.

At times you might be reluctant to express disagreement, for any number of reasons—not wanting to be unpleasant, to hurt someone's feelings, or to make yourself vulnerable to being disagreed with in return. One of these reasons may in fact explain why the conference speaker we described at the start of Chapter 1 avoided mentioning the disagreement he had with other scholars until he was provoked to do so in the discussion that followed his talk.

As much as we understand such fears of conflict and have experienced them ourselves, we nevertheless believe it is better to state our disagreements in frank yet considerate ways than to deny them. After all, suppressing disagreements doesn't make them go away; it only pushes them underground, where they can fester in private unchecked. Nevertheless, disagreements do not need to take the form of personal put-downs. Furthermore, there is usually no reason to take issue with *every* aspect of someone else's views. You can single out for criticism only those aspects of what someone else has said that are troubling, and then agree with the rest—although such an approach, as we will see later in this chapter, leads to the somewhat more complicated terrain of both agreeing and disagreeing at the same time.

## AGREE—BUT WITH A DIFFERENCE

Like disagreeing, agreeing is less simple than it may appear. Just as you need to avoid simply contradicting views you disagree with, you also need to do more than simply echo views you agree with. Even as you're agreeing, it's important to bring something new and fresh to the table, adding something that makes you a valuable participant in the conversation.

There are many moves that enable you to contribute something of your own to a conversation even as you agree with what someone else has said. You may point out some unnoticed evidence or line of reasoning that supports X's claims that X herself hadn't mentioned. You may cite some corroborating personal experience, or a situation not mentioned by X that her views help readers understand. If X's views are particularly challenging or esoteric, what you bring to the table could be an accessible translation—an explanation for readers not already in the know. In other words, your text can usefully contribute to the conversation simply by pointing out unnoticed implications or explaining something that needs to be better understood.

Whatever mode of agreement you choose, the important thing is to open up some difference or contrast between your position and the one you're agreeing with rather than simply parroting what it says.

### TEMPLATES FOR AGREEING

▸ I agree that <u>diversity in the student body is educationally valuable</u> because my experience <u>at Central University</u> confirms it.

▸ X is surely right about _____ because, as she may not be aware, recent studies have shown that _____.

▸ X's theory of _____ is extremely useful because it sheds light on the difficult problem of _____.

▸ Those unfamiliar with this school of thought may be interested to know that it basically boils down to _____.

Some writers avoid the practice of agreeing almost as much as others avoid disagreeing. In a culture like America's that prizes originality, independence, and competitive individualism, writers sometimes don't like to admit that anyone else has made the same point, seemingly beating them to the punch. In our view, however, as long as you can support a view taken by someone else without merely restating what he or she has said, there is no reason to worry about being "unoriginal." Indeed, there is good reason to rejoice when you agree with others since those others can lend credibility to your argument. While you don't want to present yourself as a mere copycat of someone else's views, you also need to avoid sounding like a lone voice in the wilderness.

But do be aware that whenever you agree with one person's view, you are likely disagreeing with someone else's. It is hard to align yourself with one position without at least implicitly positioning yourself against others. The psychologist Carol Gilligan does just that in an essay in which she agrees with scientists who argue that the human brain is "hard-wired" for cooperation, but in so doing aligns herself against anyone who believes that the brain is wired for selfishness and competition.

These findings join a growing convergence of evidence across the human sciences leading to a revolutionary shift in consciousness. . . . If cooperation, typically associated with altruism and self-sacrifice, sets off the same signals of delight as pleasures commonly associated with hedonism and self-indulgence; if the opposition between selfish and selfless, self vs. relationship biologically makes no sense, then a new paradigm is necessary to reframe the very terms of the conversation.

CAROL GILLIGAN, "Sisterhood Is Pleasurable:<br>A Quiet Revolution in Psychology"

In agreeing with some scientists that "the opposition between selfish and selfless . . . makes no sense," Gilligan implicitly disagrees with anyone who thinks the opposition *does* make sense. Basically, what Gilligan says could be boiled down to a template.

▸ I agree that _____, a point that needs emphasizing since so many people still believe _____.

▸ If group X is right that _____, as I think they are, then we need to reassess the popular assumption that _____.

What such templates allow you to do, then, is to agree with one view while challenging another—a move that leads into the domain of agreeing and disagreeing simultaneously.

### AGREE AND DISAGREE SIMULTANEOUSLY

This last option is often our favorite way of responding. One thing we particularly like about agreeing and disagreeing simultaneously is that it helps us get beyond the kind of "is too" / "is not" exchanges that often characterize the disputes of young children and the more polarized shouting matches of talk radio and TV.

Sanford J. Ungar makes precisely this move in his essay "The New Liberal Arts" when, in critiquing seven common "misperceptions" of liberal arts education, he concedes that several contain a grain of truth. For example, after summarizing "Misperception No. 2," that "college graduates are finding it harder to get good jobs with liberal-arts degrees," that few employers want to hire those with an "irrelevant major like philosophy or French," Ungar writes: "Yes, recent graduates have had difficulty in the job market. . . ." But then, after making this concession, Ungar insists that this difficulty affects graduates in all fields, not just those from the liberal arts. In this way, we think, Ungar paradoxically strengthens his case. By admitting that the opposing argument has a point, Ungar bolsters his credibility, presenting himself as a writer willing to acknowledge facts as they present themselves rather than one determined only to cheerlead for his own side.

## TEMPLATES FOR AGREEING AND DISAGREEING SIMULTANEOUSLY

"Yes and no." "Yes, but . . ." "Although I agree up to a point, I still insist . . ." These are just some of the ways you can make your argument complicated and nuanced while maintaining a clear, reader-friendly framework. The parallel structure—"yes and no"; "on the one hand I agree, on the other I disagree"— enables readers to place your argument on that map of positions we spoke of earlier in this chapter while still keeping your argument sufficiently complex.

Charles Murray's essay "Are Too Many People Going to College?" contains a good example of the "yes and no" move when, at the outset of his essay, Murray responds to what he sees as the prevailing wisdom about the liberal arts and college:

> We should not restrict the availability of a liberal education to a rarefied intellectual elite. More people should be going to college, not fewer.
>
> Yes and no. More people should be getting the basics of a liberal education. But for most students, the places to provide those basics are elementary and middle school.
>
> CHARLES MURRAY, "Are Too Many People Going to College?"

In other words, Murray is saying yes to more liberal arts, but not to more college.

Another aspect we like about this "yes and no," "agree and disagree" option is that it can be tipped subtly toward agreement or disagreement, depending on where you lay your stress. If you want to stress the disagreement end of the spectrum, you would use a template like the one below.

▶ **Although I agree with X up to a point, I cannot accept his overriding assumption that <u>religion is no longer a major force today</u>.**

Conversely, if you want to stress your agreement more than your disagreement, you would use a template like this one.

▶ **Although I disagree with much that X says, I fully endorse his final conclusion that _____ .**

The first template above might be called a "yes, but . . ." move, the second a "no, but . . ." move. Other versions include the following.

▶ **Though I concede that _____ , I still insist that _____ .**

▶ **X is right that _____ , but she seems on more dubious ground when she claims that _____ .**

▶ **While X is probably wrong when she claims that _____ , she is right that _____ .**

▶ **Whereas X provides ample evidence that _____ , Y and Z's research on _____ and _____ convinces me that _____ instead.**

Another classic way to agree and disagree at the same time is to make what we call an "I'm of two minds" or a "mixed feelings" move.

▸ **I'm of two minds about X's claim that _____ . On the one hand, I agree that _____ . On the other hand, I'm not sure if _____ .**

▸ **My feelings on the issue are mixed. I do support X's position that _____ , but I find Y's argument about _____ and Z's research on _____ to be equally persuasive.**

This move can be especially useful if you are responding to new or particularly challenging work and are as yet unsure where you stand. It also lends itself well to the kind of speculative investigation in which you weigh a position's pros and cons rather than come out decisively either for or against. But again, as we suggest earlier, whether you are agreeing, disagreeing, or both agreeing and disagreeing, you need to be as clear as possible, and making a frank statement that you are ambivalent is one way to be clear.

## IS BEING UNDECIDED OKAY?

Nevertheless, writers often have as many concerns about expressing ambivalence as they do about expressing disagreement or agreement. Some worry that by expressing ambivalence they will come across as evasive, wishy-washy, or unsure of themselves. Others worry that their ambivalence will end up confusing readers who require decisive, clear-cut conclusions.

The truth is that in some cases these worries are legitimate. At times ambivalence can frustrate readers, leaving them with the feeling that you failed in your obligation to offer the guidance they expect from writers. At other times, however, acknowledging that a clear-cut resolution of an issue is impossible can demonstrate your sophistication as a writer. In an academic culture that values complex thought, forthrightly declaring that you have mixed feelings can be impressive, especially after having ruled out the one-dimensional positions on your issue taken by others in the conversation. Ultimately, then, how ambivalent you end up being comes down to a judgment call based on different readers' responses to your drafts, on your knowledge of your audience, and on the challenges of your particular argument and situation.

## Exercises

1. Read one of the essays in the back of this book or on **theysayiblog.com**, identifying those places where the author agrees with others, disagrees, or both.

2. Write an essay responding in some way to the essay that you worked with in the preceding exercise. You'll want to summarize and/or quote some of the author's ideas and make clear whether you're agreeing, disagreeing, or both agreeing and disagreeing with what he or she says. Remember that there are templates in this book that can help you get started; see Chapters 1–3 for templates that will help you represent other people's ideas and Chapter 4 for templates that will get you started with your response.

# FIVE

# "AND YET"

## *Distinguishing What* You *Say from What* They *Say*

─────□─────

IF GOOD ACADEMIC WRITING involves putting yourself into dialogue with others, it is extremely important that readers be able to tell at every point when you are expressing your own view and when you are stating someone else's. This chapter takes up the problem of moving from what *they* say to what *you* say without confusing readers about who is saying what.

### DETERMINE WHO IS SAYING WHAT IN THE TEXTS YOU READ

Before examining how to signal who is saying what in your own writing, let's look at how to recognize such signals when they appear in the texts you read—an especially important skill when it comes to the challenging works assigned in school. Frequently, when students have trouble understanding difficult texts, it is not just because the texts contain unfamiliar ideas or words, but because the texts rely on subtle clues to let readers know when a particular view should be attributed to the writer or to someone else. Especially with texts that present a true dialogue of perspectives, readers need to be alert to the often subtle markers that indicate whose voice the writer is speaking in.

Consider how the social critic and educator Gregory Mantsios uses these "voice markers," as they might be called, to distinguish the different perspectives in his essay on America's class inequalities.

> "We are all middle-class," or so it would seem. Our national consciousness, as shaped in large part by the media and our political leadership, provides us with a picture of ourselves as a nation of prosperity and opportunity with an ever expanding middle-class life-style. As a result, our class differences are muted and our collective character is homogenized.
>
> Yet class divisions are real and arguably the most significant factor in determining both our very being in the world and the nature of the society we live in.
>
> GREGORY MANTSIOS, "Rewards and Opportunities:
> The Politics and Economics of Class in the U.S."

Although Mantsios makes it look easy, he is actually making several sophisticated rhetorical moves here that help him distinguish the common view he opposes from his own position.

In the opening sentence, for instance, the phrase "or so it would seem" shows that Mantsios does not necessarily agree with the view he is describing, since writers normally don't present views they themselves hold as ones that only "seem" to be true. Mantsios also places this opening view in quotation marks to signal that it is not his own. He then further distances himself from the belief being summarized in the opening paragraph by attributing it to "our national consciousness, as shaped in large part by the media and our political leadership," and then further attributing to this "consciousness" a negative, undesirable "result": one in which "our class differences" get "muted" and "our collective character" gets "homogenized," stripped of its diversity and distinctness. Hence, even before Mantsios has declared his own position in the second paragraph, readers can get a pretty solid sense of where he probably stands.

Furthermore, the second paragraph opens with the word "yet," indicating that Mantsios is now shifting to his own view (as opposed to the common view he has thus far been describing). Even the parallelism he sets up between the first and second paragraphs—between the first paragraph's claim that class differences do not exist and the second paragraph's claim that they do—helps throw into sharp relief the differences between the two voices. Finally, Mantsios's use of a direct, authoritative, declarative tone in the second paragraph also suggests a switch in voice. Although he does not use the words "I say" or "I argue," he clearly identifies the view he holds by presenting it not as one that merely *seems* to be true or that *others tell us* is true, but as a view that *is* true or, as Mantsios puts it, "real."

Paying attention to these voice markers is an important aspect of reading comprehension. Readers who fail to notice these markers often take an author's summaries of what someone else believes to be an expression of what the author himself or herself believes. Thus when we teach Mantsios's essay, some students invariably come away thinking that the statement "we are all middle-class" is Mantsios's own position rather than the perspective he is opposing, failing to see that in writing these words Mantsios acts as a kind of ventriloquist, mimicking what others say rather than directly expressing what he himself is thinking.

To see how important such voice markers are, consider what the Mantsios passage looks like if we remove them.

> We are all middle-class. . . . We are a nation of prosperity and opportunity with an ever expanding middle-class life-style. . . .
>
> Class divisions are real and arguably the most significant factor in determining both our very being in the world and the nature of the society we live in.

In contrast to the careful delineation between voices in Mantsios's original text, this unmarked version leaves it hard to tell where his voice begins and the voices of others end. With the markers removed, readers cannot tell that "We are all middle-class" represents a view the author opposes, and that "Class divisions are real" represents what the author himself believes. Indeed, without the markers, especially the "yet," readers might well miss the fact that the second paragraph's claim that "Class divisions are real" contradicts the first paragraph's claim that "We are all middle-class."

## TEMPLATES FOR SIGNALING WHO IS SAYING WHAT IN YOUR OWN WRITING

To avoid confusion in your own writing, make sure that at every point your readers can clearly tell who is saying what. To do so, you can use as voice-identifying devices many of the templates presented in previous chapters.

- Although X makes the best possible case for <u>universal, government-funded health care</u>, I <u>am not persuaded</u>.

- My view, however, contrary to what X has argued, is that _____ .

- Adding to X's argument, I would point out that _____ .

- According to both X and Y, _____ .

- Politicians, X argues, should _____ .

- Most athletes will tell you that _____ .

## BUT I'VE BEEN TOLD NOT TO USE "I"

Notice that the first three templates above use the first-person "I" or "we," as do many of the templates in this book, thereby contradicting the common advice about avoiding the first person in academic writing. Although you may have been told that the "I" word encourages subjective, self-indulgent opinions rather than well-grounded arguments, we believe that texts using "I" can be just as well supported—or just as self-indulgent—as those that don't. For us, well-supported arguments are grounded in persuasive reasons and evidence, not in the use or nonuse of any particular pronouns.

Furthermore, if you consistently avoid the first person in your writing, you will probably have trouble making the key move addressed in this chapter: differentiating your views from those of others, or even offering your own views in the first place. But don't just take our word for it. See for yourself how freely the first person is used by the writers quoted in this book, and by the writers assigned in your courses.

Nevertheless, certain occasions may warrant avoiding the first person and writing, for example, that "she is correct" instead of "I think that she is correct." Since it can be monotonous to read an unvarying series of "I" statements ("I believe . . . I think . . . I argue"), it is a good idea to mix first-person assertions with ones like the following.

▸ **X is right that <u>certain common patterns can be found in the communities</u>.**

▸ **The evidence shows that _____ .**

▸ **X's assertion that _____ does not fit the facts.**

▸ **Anyone familiar with _____ should agree that _____ .**

One might even follow Mantsios's lead, as in the following template.

▸ **But _____ are real, and are arguably the most significant factor in _____ .**

On the whole, however, academic writing today, even in the sciences and social sciences, makes use of the first person fairly liberally.

## ANOTHER TRICK FOR IDENTIFYING WHO IS SPEAKING

To alert readers about whose perspective you are describing at any given moment, you don't always have to use overt voice markers like "X argues" followed by a summary of the argument. Instead, you can alert readers about whose voice you're speaking in by *embedding* a reference to X's argument in your own sentences. Hence, instead of writing:

> Liberals believe that cultural differences need to be respected. I have a problem with this view, however.

you might write:

> I have a problem with *what liberals call cultural differences.*

> There is a major problem with the liberal doctrine of *so-called cultural differences.*

You can also embed references to something you yourself have previously said. So instead of writing two cumbersome sentences like:

> Earlier in this chapter we coined the term "voice markers." We would argue that such markers are extremely important for reading comprehension.

you might write:

> We would argue that "voice markers," as we identified them earlier, are extremely important for reading comprehension.

Embedded references like these allow you to economize your train of thought and refer to other perspectives without any major interruption.

## TEMPLATES FOR EMBEDDING VOICE MARKERS

▸ X overlooks what I consider an important point about <u>cultural differences</u>.

▸ My own view is that what X insists is a _____ is in fact a _____ .

▸ I wholeheartedly endorse what X calls _____ .

▸ These conclusions, which X discusses in _____ , add weight to the argument that _____ .

When writers fail to use voice-marking devices like the ones discussed in this chapter, their summaries of others' views tend to become confused with their own ideas—and vice versa. When readers cannot tell if you are summarizing your own views or endorsing a certain phrase or label, they have to stop and think: "Wait. I thought the author disagreed with this claim. Has she actually been asserting this view all along?" or "Hmmm, I thought she would have objected to this kind of phrase. Is she actually endorsing it?" Getting in the habit of using voice markers will keep you from confusing your readers and help alert you to similar markers in the challenging texts you read.

*Exercises*

1. To see how one writer signals when she is asserting her own views and when she is summarizing those of someone else, read the following passage by the social historian Julie Charlip. As you do so, identify those spots where Charlip refers to the views of others and the signal phrases she uses to distinguish her views from theirs.

Marx and Engels wrote: "Society as a whole is more and more splitting up into two great hostile camps, into two great classes directly facing each other—the bourgeoisie and the proletariat" (10). If only that were true, things might be more simple. But in late twentieth-century America, it seems that society is splitting more and more into a plethora of class factions—the working class, the working poor, lower-middle class, upper-middle class, lower uppers, and upper uppers. I find myself not knowing what class I'm from.

In my days as a newspaper reporter, I once asked a sociology professor what he thought about the reported shrinking of the middle class. Oh, it's not the middle class that's disappearing, he said, but the working class. His definition: if you earn thirty thousand dollars a year working in an assembly plant, come home from work, open a beer and watch the game, you are working class; if you earn twenty thousand dollars a year as a school teacher, come home from work to a glass of white wine and PBS, you are middle class.

How do we define class? Is it an issue of values, lifestyle, taste? Is it the kind of work you do, your relationship to the means of production? Is it a matter of how much money you earn? Are we allowed to choose? In this land of supposed classlessness, where we don't have the tradition of English society to keep us in our places, how do we know where we really belong? The average American will tell you he or she is "middle class." I'm sure that's what my father would tell you. But I always felt that we were in some no man's land, suspended between classes, sharing similarities with some and recognizing sharp, exclusionary differences from others. What class do I come from? What class am I in now? As an historian, I seek the answers to these questions in the specificity of my past.

> Julie Charlip, "A Real Class Act: Searching for Identity in the 'Classless' Society"

2. Study a piece of your own writing to see how many perspectives you account for and how well you distinguish your own voice from those you are summarizing. Consider the following questions:

    a. How many perspectives do you engage?
    b. What other perspectives might you include?
    c. How do you distinguish your views from the other views you summarize?
    d. Do you use clear voice-signaling phrases?
    e. What options are available to you for clarifying who is saying what?
    f. Which of these options are best suited for this particular text?

    If you find that you do *not* include multiple views or clearly distinguish between others' views and your own, revise your text to do so.

# SIX

# "SKEPTICS MAY OBJECT"

## *Planting a Naysayer in Your Text*

THE WRITER Jane Tompkins describes a pattern that repeats itself whenever she writes a book or an article. For the first couple of weeks when she sits down to write, things go relatively well. But then in the middle of the night, several weeks into the writing process, she'll wake up in a cold sweat, suddenly realizing that she has overlooked some major criticism that readers will surely make against her ideas. Her first thought, invariably, is that she will have to give up on the project, or that she will have to throw out what she's written thus far and start over. Then she realizes that "this moment of doubt and panic is where my text really begins." She then revises what she's written in a way that incorporates the criticisms she's anticipated, and her text becomes stronger and more interesting as a result.

This little story contains an important lesson for all writers, experienced and inexperienced alike. It suggests that even though most of us are upset at the idea of someone criticizing our work, such criticisms can actually work to our advantage. Although it's naturally tempting to ignore criticism of our ideas, doing so may in fact be a big mistake, since our writing improves when we not only listen to these objections but give them an explicit hearing in our writing. Indeed, no single device more quickly improves a piece of writing than planting a naysayer in the text—saying, for example, that "although some readers may object" to something in your argument, you "would reply that _____."

## ANTICIPATE OBJECTIONS

But wait, you say. Isn't the advice to incorporate critical views a recipe for destroying your credibility and undermining your argument? Here you are, trying to say something that will hold up, and we want you to tell readers all the negative things someone might say against you?

Exactly. We *are* urging you to tell readers what others might say against you, but our point is that doing so will actually *enhance* your credibility, not undermine it. As we argue throughout this book, writing well does not mean piling up uncontroversial truths in a vacuum; it means engaging others in a dialogue or debate—not only by opening your text with a summary of what others *have* said, as we suggest in Chapter 1, but also by imagining what others *might* say against your argument as it unfolds. Once you see writing as an act of entering a conversation, you should also see how opposing arguments can work for you rather than against you.

Paradoxically, the more you give voice to your critics' objections, the more you tend to disarm those critics, especially if you go on to answer their objections in convincing ways. When you entertain a counterargument, you make a kind of preemptive strike, identifying problems with your argument before others can point them out for you. Furthermore, by entertaining counterarguments, you show respect for your readers, treating them not as gullible dupes who will believe anything you say but as independent, critical thinkers who are aware that your view is not the only one in town. In addition, by imagining what others might say against your claims, you come across as a generous, broad-minded person who is confident enough to open himself or herself to debate—like the writer in the figure on the following page.

Conversely, if you don't entertain counterarguments, you may very likely come across as closed-minded, as if you think your beliefs are beyond dispute. You might also leave important questions hanging and concerns about your arguments unaddressed. Finally, if you fail to plant a naysayer in your text, you may find that you have very little to say. Our own students often say that entertaining counterarguments makes it easier to generate enough text to meet their assignment's page-length requirements.

Planting a naysayer in your text is a relatively simple move, as you can see by looking at the following passage from a book by the writer Kim Chernin. Having spent some thirty pages complaining about the pressure on American women to be thin, Chernin inserts a whole chapter entitled "The Skeptic," opening it as follows.

> At this point I would like to raise certain objections that have been inspired by the skeptic in me. She feels that I have been ignoring some of the most common assumptions we all make about our bodies and these she wishes to see addressed. For example: "You know perfectly well," she says to me, "that you feel better when you lose weight. You buy new clothes. You look at yourself more eagerly in the mirror. When someone invites you to a party you don't stop and ask yourself whether you want to go. You feel sexier. Admit it. You like yourself better."
>
> KIM CHERNIN, *The Obsession:*
> *Reflections on the Tyranny of Slenderness*

The remainder of Chernin's chapter consists of her answers to this inner skeptic. In the face of the skeptic's challenge to her book's central premise (that the pressure to diet seriously harms women's lives), Chernin responds neither by repressing the skeptic's critical voice nor by giving in to it and relinquishing her own position. Instead, she embraces that voice and writes it into her text. Note too that instead of dispatching this naysaying voice quickly, as many of us would be tempted to do, Chernin stays with it and devotes a full paragraph to it. By borrowing some of Chernin's language, we can come up with templates for entertaining virtually any objection.

## TEMPLATES FOR ENTERTAINING OBJECTIONS

▸ **At this point I would like to raise some objections that have been inspired by the skeptic in me. She feels that I have been ignoring <u>the complexities of the situation</u>.**

▸ **Yet some readers may challenge my view by insisting that**
_____.

▸ **Of course, many will probably disagree on the grounds that**
_____.

Note that the objections in the above templates are attributed not to any specific person or group, but to "skeptics," "readers," or "many." This kind of nameless, faceless naysayer is perfectly appropriate in many cases. But the ideas that motivate arguments and objections often can—and, where possible, should—be ascribed to a specific ideology or school of thought (for example, liberals, Christian fundamentalists, neopragmatists) rather than to anonymous anybodies. In other words, naysayers can be labeled, and you can add precision and impact to your writing by identifying what those labels are.

## TEMPLATES FOR NAMING YOUR NAYSAYERS

▸ Here many *feminists* would probably object that <u>gender does influence language</u>.

▸ But *social Darwinists* would certainly take issue with the argument that _____ .

▸ *Biologists*, of course, may want to question whether _____ .

▸ Nevertheless, both *followers and critics of Malcolm X* will probably suggest otherwise and argue that _____ .

To be sure, some people dislike such labels and may even resent having labels applied to themselves. Some feel that labels put individuals in boxes, stereotyping them and glossing over what makes each of us unique. And it's true that labels can be used inappropriately, in ways that ignore individuality and promote stereotypes. But since the life of ideas, including many of our most private thoughts, is conducted through groups and types rather than solitary individuals, intellectual exchange requires labels to give definition and serve as a convenient shorthand. If you categorically reject all labels, you give up an important resource and even mislead readers by presenting yourself and others as having no connection to anyone else. You also miss an opportunity to generalize the importance and relevance of your work to some larger conversation. When you attribute a position you are summarizing to liberalism, say, or historical materialism, your argument is no longer just about your own solitary views but about the intersection of broad ideas and habits of mind that many readers may already have a stake in.

The way to minimize the problem of stereotyping, then, is not to categorically reject labels but to refine and qualify their use, as the following templates demonstrate.

▸ Although not all *Christians* think alike, some of them will probably dispute my claim that _____ .

▸ *Non-native English speakers* are so diverse in their views that it's hard to generalize about them, but some are likely to object on the grounds that _____ .

Another way to avoid needless stereotyping is to qualify labels carefully, substituting "pro bono lawyers" for "lawyers" in general, for example, or "quantitative sociologists" for all "social scientists," and so on.

## TEMPLATES FOR INTRODUCING OBJECTIONS INFORMALLY

Objections can also be introduced in more informal ways. For instance, you can frame objections in the form of questions.

▸ But is my proposal realistic? What are the chances of its actually being adopted?

▸ Yet is it necessarily true that _____ ? Is it always the case, as I have been suggesting, that _____ ?

▸ However, does the evidence I've cited prove conclusively that _____ ?

You can also let your naysayer speak directly.

▸ **"Impossible," some will say. "You must be reading the research selectively."**

Moves like this allow you to cut directly to the skeptical voice itself, as the singer-songwriter Joe Jackson does in the following excerpt from a *New York Times* article complaining about the restrictions on public smoking in New York City bars and restaurants.

> I like a couple of cigarettes or a cigar with a drink, and like many other people, I only smoke in bars or nightclubs. Now I can't go to any of my old haunts. Bartenders who were friends have turned into cops, forcing me outside to shiver in the cold and curse under my breath. . . . It's no fun. Smokers are being demonized and victimized all out of proportion.
>
> "Get over it," say the anti-smokers. "You're the minority." I thought a great city was a place where all kinds of minorities could thrive. . . . "Smoking kills," they say. As an occasional smoker with otherwise healthy habits, I'll take my chances. Health consciousness is important, but so are pleasure and freedom of choice.
>
> JOE JACKSON, "Want to Smoke? Go to Hamburg"

Jackson could have begun his second paragraph, in which he shifts from his own voice to that of his imagined naysayer, more formally, as follows: "Of course anti-smokers will object that since we smokers are in the minority, we should simply stop complaining and quietly make the sacrifices we are being called on to make for the larger social good." Or "Anti-smokers might insist, however, that the smoking minority should submit to the nonsmoking majority." We think, though, that Jackson gets the job done in a far more lively way with the more colloquial form he chooses. Borrowing a standard move of playwrights and novelists, Jackson cuts directly to the objectors' view and then to his own retort, then back to the objectors' view and then to his own retort again, thereby creating a kind of dialogue or miniature play within his own text. This move works well for Jackson, but only because he uses quotation marks and other voice markers to make clear at every point whose voice he is in.

See Chapter 5 for more advice on using voice markers.

## REPRESENT OBJECTIONS FAIRLY

Once you've decided to introduce a differing or opposing view into your writing, your work has only just begun, since you still need to represent and explain that view with fairness and generosity. Although it is tempting to give opposing views short shrift, to hurry past them, or even to mock them, doing so is usually counterproductive. When writers make the best case they can for their critics (playing Peter Elbow's "believing game"), they actually bolster their credibility with readers rather than undermine it. They make readers think, "This is a writer I can trust."

See pp. 31–32 for more on the believing game.

We recommend, then, that whenever you entertain objections in your writing, you stay with them for several sentences or even paragraphs and take them as seriously as possible. We also recommend that you read your summary of opposing views with an outsider's eye: put yourself in the shoes of someone who disagrees with you and ask if such a reader would recognize himself in your summary. Would that reader think you have taken his views seriously, as beliefs that reasonable people might hold? Or would he detect a mocking tone or an oversimplification of his views?

There will always be certain objections, to be sure, that you believe do not deserve to be represented, just as there will be objections that seem so unworthy of respect that they inspire ridicule. Remember, however, that if you do choose to mock a view that you oppose, you are likely to alienate those readers who don't already agree with you—likely the very readers you want to reach. Also be aware that in mocking another's view you may contribute to a hostile argument culture in which someone may ridicule you in return.

## ANSWER OBJECTIONS

Do be aware that when you represent objections successfully, you still need to be able to answer those objections persuasively. After all, when you write objections into a text, you take the risk that readers will find those objections more convincing than the argument you yourself are advancing. In the editorial quoted above, for example, Joe Jackson takes the risk that readers will identify more with the anti-smoking view he summarizes than with the pro-smoking position he endorses.

This is precisely what Benjamin Franklin describes happening to himself in *The Autobiography of Benjamin Franklin* (1793), when he recalls being converted to Deism (a religion that exalts reason over spirituality) by reading *anti*-Deist books. When he encountered the views of Deists being negatively summarized by authors who opposed them, Franklin explains, he ended up finding the Deist position more persuasive. To avoid having this kind of unintentional reverse effect on readers, you need to do your best to make sure that any counter-arguments you address are not more convincing than your own claims. It is good to address objections in your writing, but only if you are able to overcome them.

One surefire way to *fail* to overcome an objection is to dismiss it out of hand—saying, for example, "That's just wrong." The difference between such a response (which offers no supporting reasons whatsoever) and the types of nuanced responses we're promoting in this book is the difference between bullying your readers and genuinely persuading them.

Often the best way to overcome an objection is not to try to refute it completely but to agree with part of it while challenging only the part you dispute. In other words, in answering counterarguments, it is often best to say "yes, but" or "yes and no," treating the counterview as an opportunity to revise and refine your own position. Rather than build your argument into an impenetrable fortress, it is often best to make concessions while still standing your ground, as Kim Chernin does in the following response to the counterargument quoted above. While in the voice of the "skeptic," Chernin writes: "Admit it. You like yourself better when you've lost weight." In response, Chernin replies as follows.

See pp. 59–62 for more on agreeing, with a difference.

Can I deny these things? No woman who has managed to lose weight would wish to argue with this. Most people feel better about themselves when they become slender. And yet, upon reflection, it seems to me that there is something precarious about this well-being. After all, 98 percent of people who lose weight gain it back. Indeed, 90 percent of those who have dieted "successfully" gain back more than they ever lost. Then, of course, we can no longer bear to look at ourselves in the mirror.

In this way, Chernin shows how you can use a counterview to improve and refine your overall argument by making a concession. Even as she concedes that losing weight feels good in the short run, she argues that in the long run the weight always returns, making the dieter far more miserable.

## TEMPLATES FOR MAKING CONCESSIONS
## WHILE STILL STANDING YOUR GROUND

▶ **Although I grant that <u>the book is poorly organized</u>, I still maintain that <u>it raises an important issue</u>.**

▶ **Proponents of X are right to argue that _____. But they exaggerate when they claim that _____ .**

▶ **While it is true that _____ , it does not necessarily follow that _____ .**

▶ **On the one hand, I agree with X that _____ . But on the other hand, I still insist that _____ .**

Templates like these show that answering naysayers' objections does not have to be an all-or-nothing affair in which you either definitively refute your critics or they definitively refute you. Often the most productive engagements among differing views end with a combined vision that incorporates elements of each one.

But what if you've tried out all the possible answers you can think of to an objection you've anticipated and you *still* have a nagging feeling that the objection is more convincing than your argument itself? In that case, the best remedy is to go back and make some fundamental revisions to your argument, even reversing your position completely if need be. Although finding out late in the game that you aren't fully convinced by your own argument can be painful, it can actually make your final text more intellectually honest, challenging, and serious. After all, the goal of writing is not to keep proving that whatever you initially said is right, but to stretch the limits of your thinking. So if planting a strong naysayer in your text forces you to change your mind, that's not a bad thing. Some would argue that that is what the academic world is all about.

## Exercises

1. Read the following passage by the cultural critic Eric Schlosser. As you'll see, he hasn't planted any naysayers in this text. Do it for him. Insert a brief paragraph stating an objection to his argument and then responding to the objection as he might.

   The United States must declare an end to the war on drugs. This war has filled the nation's prisons with poor drug addicts and small-time drug dealers. It has created a multibillion-dollar black market, enriched organized crime groups and promoted the corruption of government officials throughout the world. And it has not stemmed the widespread use of illegal drugs. By any rational measure, this war has been a total failure.

   We must develop public policies on substance abuse that are guided not by moral righteousness or political expediency but by common sense. The United States should immediately decriminalize the cultivation and possession of small amounts of marijuana for personal use. Marijuana should no longer be classified as a Schedule I narcotic, and those who seek to use marijuana as medicine should no longer face criminal sanctions. We must shift our entire approach to drug abuse from the criminal justice system to the public health system. Congress should appoint an independent commission to study the harm-reduction policies that have been adopted in Switzerland, Spain, Portugal, and the Netherlands. The commission should recommend policies for the United States based on one important criterion: what works.

In a nation where pharmaceutical companies advertise powerful antidepressants on billboards and where alcohol companies run amusing beer ads during the Super Bowl, the idea of a "drug-free society" is absurd. Like the rest of American society, our drug policy would greatly benefit from less punishment and more compassion.

ERIC SCHLOSSER, "A People's Democratic Platform"

2. Look over something you've written that makes an argument. Check to see if you've anticipated and responded to any objections. If not, revise your text to do so. If so, have you anticipated all the likely objections? Who if anyone have you attributed the objections to? Have you represented the objections fairly? Have you answered them well enough, or do you think you now need to qualify your own argument? Could you use any of the language suggested in this chapter? Does the introduction of a naysayer strengthen your argument? Why, or why not?

# SEVEN

# "SO WHAT? WHO CARES?"
## *Saying Why It Matters*

———◁□▷———

BASEBALL IS THE NATIONAL PASTIME. Bernini was the best sculptor of the baroque period. All writing is conversational. So what? Who cares? Why does any of this matter?

How many times have you had reason to ask these questions? Regardless of how interesting a topic may be to you as a writer, readers always need to know what is at stake in a text and why they should care. All too often, however, these questions are left unanswered—mainly because writers and speakers assume that audiences will know the answers already or will figure them out on their own. As a result, students come away from lectures feeling like outsiders to what they've just heard, just as many of us feel left hanging after talks we've attended. The problem is not necessarily that the speakers lack a clear, well-focused thesis or that the thesis is inadequately supported with evidence. Instead, the problem is that the speakers don't address the crucial question of why their arguments matter.

That this question is so often left unaddressed is unfortunate since the speakers generally *could* offer interesting, engaging answers. When pressed, for instance, most academics will tell you that their lectures and articles matter because they address some belief that needs to be corrected or updated—and because their arguments have important, real-world consequences. Yet many academics fail to identify these reasons and consequences explicitly in what they say and write. Rather than assume that audiences will know why their claims matter, all writers need to answer the "so what?" and "who cares?" questions up front. Not everyone can claim to have a cure for cancer or a solution to end poverty. But writers who fail to show that others *should* care or already *do* care about their claims will ultimately lose their audiences' interest.

This chapter focuses on various moves that you can make to answer the "who cares?" and "so what?" questions in your own writing. In one sense, the two questions get at the same thing: the relevance or importance of what you are saying. Yet they get at this significance in different ways. Whereas "who cares?" literally asks you to identify a person or group who cares about your claims, "so what?" asks about the real-world applications and consequences of those claims—what difference it would make if they were accepted. We'll look first at ways of making clear who cares.

## "WHO CARES?"

To see how one writer answers the "who cares?" question, consider the following passage from the science writer Denise Grady. Writing in the *New York Times*, she explains some of the latest research into fat cells.

> Scientists used to think body fat and the cells it was made of were pretty much inert, just an oily storage compartment. But within the past decade research has shown that fat cells act like chemical factories and that body fat is potent stuff: a highly active

tissue that secretes hormones and other substances with profound and sometimes harmful effects. . . .

In recent years, biologists have begun calling fat an "endocrine organ," comparing it to glands like the thyroid and pituitary, which also release hormones straight into the bloodstream.

Denise Grady, "The Secret Life of a Potent Cell"

Notice how Grady's writing reflects the central advice we give in this book, offering a clear claim and also framing that claim as a response to what someone else has said. In so doing, Grady immediately identifies at least one group with a stake in the new research that sees fat as "active," "potent stuff": namely, the scientific community, which formerly believed that body fat is inert. By referring to these scientists, Grady implicitly acknowledges that her text is part of a larger conversation and shows who besides herself has an interest in what she says.

Consider, however, how the passage would read had Grady left out what "scientists used to think" and simply explained the new findings in isolation.

Within the past few decades research has shown that fat cells act like chemical factories and that body fat is potent stuff: a highly active tissue that secretes hormones and other substances. In recent years, biologists have begun calling fat an "endocrine organ," comparing it to glands like the thyroid and pituitary, which also release hormones straight into the bloodstream.

Though this statement is clear and easy to follow, it lacks any indication that anyone needs to hear it. Okay, one nods while reading this passage, fat is an active, potent thing. Sounds plausible enough; no reason to think it's not true. But does anyone really care? Who, if anyone, is interested?

## TEMPLATES FOR INDICATING WHO CARES

To address "who cares?" questions in your own writing, we suggest using templates like the following, which echo Grady in refuting earlier thinking.

▸ <u>Parents</u> used to think <u>spanking was necessary</u>. But recently [or within the past few decades] <u>experts</u> suggest that <u>it can be counterproductive</u>.

▸ This interpretation challenges the work of those critics who have long assumed that _____ .

▸ These findings challenge the work of earlier researchers, who tended to assume that _____ .

▸ Recent studies like these shed new light on _____ , which previous studies had not addressed.

Grady might have been more explicit by writing the "who cares?" question directly into her text, as in the following template.

▸ But who really cares? Who besides me and a handful of recent researchers has a stake in these claims? At the very least, the researchers who formerly believed _____ should care.

To gain greater authority as a writer, it can help to name specific people or groups who have a stake in your claims and to go into some detail about their views.

▸ Researchers have long assumed that _____ . For instance, one eminent scholar of cell biology, _____ , assumed in _____ , her seminal work on cell structures and functions, that fat cells _____ . As _____ herself put it, "_____" (2012). Another leading scientist, _____ , argued that fat cells "_____" (2011). Ultimately, when it came to the nature of fat, the basic assumption was that _____.

But a new body of research shows that fat cells are far more complex and that _____.

In other cases, you might refer to certain people or groups who *should* care about your claims.

▸ If sports enthusiasts stopped to think about it, many of them might simply assume that the most successful athletes _____. However, new research shows _____.

▸ These findings challenge neoliberals' common assumption that _____.

▸ At first glance, teenagers might say _____. But on closer inspection _____.

As these templates suggest, answering the "who cares?" question involves establishing the type of contrast between what others say and what you say that is central to this book. Ultimately, such templates help you create a dramatic tension or clash of views in your writing that readers will feel invested in and want to see resolved.

## "SO WHAT?"

Although answering the "who cares?" question is crucial, in many cases it is not enough, especially if you are writing for general readers who don't necessarily have a strong investment in the particular clash of views you are setting up. In the case of Grady's argument about fat cells, such readers may still wonder why it matters that some researchers think fat cells are active, while others think they're inert. Or, to move to a different field of study, American literature, *so what* if some scholars disagree about Huck Finn's relationship with the runaway slave Jim in Mark Twain's *Adventures of Huckleberry Finn*? Why should anyone besides a few specialists in the field care about such disputes? What, if anything, hinges on them?

The best way to answer such questions about the larger consequences of your claims is to appeal to something that your audience already figures to care about. Whereas the "who cares?" question asks you to identify an interested person or group, the "so what?" question asks you to link your argument to some larger matter that readers already deem important. Thus in analyzing *Huckleberry Finn*, a writer could argue that seemingly narrow disputes about the hero's relationship with Jim actually shed light on whether Twain's canonical, widely read novel is a critique of racism in America or is itself marred by it.

Let's see how Grady invokes such broad, general concerns in her article on fat cells. Her first move is to link researchers' interest in fat cells to a general concern with obesity and health.

> Researchers trying to decipher the biology of fat cells hope to find new ways to help people get rid of excess fat or, at least, prevent obesity from destroying their health. In an increasingly obese world, their efforts have taken on added importance.

Further showing why readers should care, Grady's next move is to demonstrate the even broader relevance and urgency of her subject matter.

> Internationally, more than a billion people are overweight. Obesity and two illnesses linked to it, heart disease and high blood pressure, are on the World Health Organization's list of the top 10 global health risks. In the United States, 65 percent of adults weigh too much,

compared with about 56 percent a decade ago, and government researchers blame obesity for at least 300,000 deaths a year.

What Grady implicitly says here is "Look, dear reader, you may think that these questions about the nature of fat cells I've been pursuing have little to do with everyday life. In fact, however, these questions are extremely important—particularly in our 'increasingly obese world' in which we need to prevent obesity from destroying our health."

Notice that Grady's phrase "in an increasingly _____ world" can be adapted as a strategic move to address the "so what?" question in other fields as well. For example, a sociologist analyzing back-to-nature movements of the past thirty years might make the following statement.

> In a world increasingly dominated by cell phones and sophisticated computer technologies, these attempts to return to nature appear futile.

This type of move can be readily applied to other disciplines because no matter how much disciplines may differ from one another, the need to justify the importance of one's concerns is common to them all.

## TEMPLATES FOR ESTABLISHING WHY YOUR CLAIMS MATTER

▸ *Huckleberry Finn* matters/is important because <u>it is one of the most widely taught novels in the American school system.</u>

▸ Although X may seem trivial, it is in fact crucial in terms of today's concern over _____ .

▶ Ultimately, what is at stake here is _____.

▶ These findings have important implications for the broader domain of _____.

▶ If we are right about _____, then major consequences follow for _____.

▶ These conclusions/This discovery will have significant applications in _____ as well as in _____.

Finally, you can also treat the "so what?" question as a related aspect of the "who cares?" question.

▶ Although X may seem of concern to only a small group of _____, it should in fact concern anyone who cares about _____.

All these templates help you hook your readers. By suggesting the real-world applications of your claims, the templates not only demonstrate that others care about your claims but also tell your readers why *they* should care. Again, it bears repeating that simply stating and proving your thesis isn't enough. You also need to frame it in a way that helps readers care about it.

## WHAT ABOUT READERS WHO ALREADY KNOW WHY IT MATTERS?

At this point, you might wonder if you need to answer the "who cares?" and "so what?" questions in *everything* you write. Is it really necessary to address these questions if you're proposing something so obviously consequential as, say, a treatment for autism or a program to eliminate illiteracy? Isn't it obvious that everyone cares about such problems? Does it really need to be spelled out? And what about when you're writing for audiences who you know are already interested in your claims and who understand perfectly well why they're important? In other words, do you always need to address the "so what?" and "who cares?" questions?

As a rule, yes—although it's true that you can't keep answering them forever and at a certain point must say enough is enough. Although a determined skeptic can infinitely ask why something matters—"Why should I care about earning a salary? And why should I care about supporting a family?"—you have to stop answering at some point in your text. Nevertheless, we urge you to go as far as possible in answering such questions. If you take it for granted that readers will somehow intuit the answers to "so what?" and "who cares?" on their own, you may make your work seem less interesting than it actually is, and you run the risk that readers will dismiss your text as irrelevant and unimportant. By contrast, when you are careful to explain who cares and why, it's a little like bringing a cheerleading squad into your text. And though some expert readers might already know why your claims matter, even they need to be reminded. Thus the safest move is to be as explicit as possible in answering the "so what?" question, even for those already in the know. When you step back from the text and explain why it matters, you are urging your audience to keep reading, pay attention, and care.

*Exercises*

1. Find several texts (scholarly essays, newspaper articles, emails, memos, blogs, etc.) and see whether they answer

the "so what?" and "who cares?" questions. Probably some do, some don't. What difference does it make whether they do or do not? How do the authors who answer these questions do so? Do they use any strategies or techniques that you could borrow for your own writing? Are there any strategies or techniques recommended in this chapter, or that you've found or developed on your own, that you'd recommend to these authors?

2. Look over something you've written yourself. Do you indicate "so what?" and "who cares"? If not, revise your text to do so. You might use the following template to get started.

My point here (that _____) should interest those who _____. Beyond this limited audience, however, my point should speak to anyone who cares about the larger issue of _____.

## EIGHT

# "AS A RESULT"
## *Connecting the Parts*

—⌐囗⌐—

WE ONCE HAD A STUDENT named Bill, whose characteristic sentence pattern went something like this.

Spot is a good dog. He has fleas.

"Connect your sentences," we urged in the margins of Bill's papers. "What does Spot being good have to do with his fleas?" "These two statements seem unrelated. Can you connect them in some logical way?" When comments like these yielded no results, we tried inking in suggested connections for him.

Spot is a good dog, *but* he has fleas.
Spot is a good dog, *even though* he has fleas.

But our message failed to get across, and Bill's disconnected sentence pattern persisted to the end of the semester.

And yet Bill did focus well on his subjects. When he mentioned Spot the dog (or Plato, or any other topic) in one sentence, we could count on Spot (or Plato) being the topic of the following sentence as well. This was not the case with some of Bill's classmates, who sometimes changed topic from sentence to sentence or even from clause to clause within a single sentence. But because Bill neglected to mark his connections, his writing was as frustrating to read as theirs. In all these cases, we had to struggle to figure out on our own how the sentences and paragraphs connected or failed to connect with one another.

What makes such writers so hard to read, in other words, is that they never gesture back to what they have just said or forward to what they plan to say. "Never look back" might be their motto, almost as if they see writing as a process of thinking of something to say about a topic and writing it down, then thinking of something else to say about the topic and writing that down, too, and on and on until they've filled the assigned number of pages and can hand the paper in. Each sentence basically starts a new thought, rather than growing out of or extending the thought of the previous sentence.

When Bill talked about his writing habits, he acknowledged that he never went back and read what he had written. Indeed, he told us that, other than using his computer software to check for spelling errors and make sure that his tenses were all aligned, he never actually reread what he wrote before turning it in. As Bill seemed to picture it, writing was something one did while sitting at a computer, whereas reading was a separate activity generally reserved for an easy chair, book in hand. It had never occurred to Bill that to write a good sentence he had to think about how it connected to those that came before and after; that he had to think hard about how that sentence fit into the sentences that surrounded it. Each sentence for Bill existed in a sort of tunnel isolated from every other sentence on the page. He never bothered to fit all the parts of his essay together because he apparently thought of writing as a matter of piling up information or observations rather than building a sustained argument. What we suggest in this chapter, then, is that you converse not only with others in your writing but with yourself: that you establish clear relations between one statement and the next by connecting those statements.

This chapter addresses the issue of how to connect all the parts of your writing. The best compositions establish a sense of momentum and direction by making explicit connections among their different parts, so that what is said in one sentence (or paragraph) both sets up what is to come and is clearly informed by what has already been said. When you write a sentence, you create an expectation in the reader's mind that the next sentence will in some way echo and extend it, even if—*especially if*—that next sentence takes your argument in a new direction.

It may help to think of each sentence you write as having arms that reach backward and forward, as the figure below suggests. When your sentences reach outward like this, they establish connections that help your writing flow smoothly in a way readers appreciate. Conversely, when writing lacks such connections and moves in fits and starts, readers repeatedly have to go back over the sentences and guess at the connections on their own. To prevent such disconnection and make your writing flow, we advise

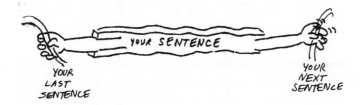

YOUR LAST SENTENCE     YOUR SENTENCE     YOUR NEXT SENTENCE

following a "do-it-yourself" principle, which means that it is your job as a writer to do the hard work of making the connections rather than, as Bill did, leaving this work to your readers.

This chapter offers several strategies you can use to put this principle into action: (1) using transition terms (like "therefore" and "as a result"); (2) adding pointing words (like "this" or "such"); (3) developing a set of key terms and phrases for each text you write; and (4) repeating yourself, but with a difference—a move that involves repeating what you've said, but with enough variation to avoid being redundant. All these moves require that you always look back and, in crafting any one sentence, think hard about those that precede it.

Notice how we ourselves have used such connecting devices thus far in this chapter. The second paragraph of this chapter, for example, opens with the transitional "And yet," signaling a change in direction, while the opening sentence of the third includes the phrase "in other words," telling you to expect a restatement of a point we've just made. If you look through this book, you should be able to find many sentences that contain some word or phrase that explicitly hooks them back to something said earlier, to something about to be said, or both. And many sentences in *this* chapter repeat key terms related to the idea of connection: "connect," "disconnect," "link," "relate," "forward," and "backward."

## USE TRANSITIONS

For readers to follow your train of thought, you need not only to connect your sentences and paragraphs to each other, but also to mark the kind of connection you are making. One of the easiest ways to make this move is to use *transitions* (from the Latin root *trans*, "across"), which help you cross from one point to another in your text. Transitions are usually placed at or near the start of sentences so they can signal to readers where your text is going: in the same direction it has been moving, or in a new direction. More specifically, transitions tell readers whether your text is echoing a previous sentence or paragraph ("in other words"), adding something to it ("in addition"), offering an example of it ("for example"), generalizing from it ("as a result"), or modifying it ("and yet").

The following is a list of commonly used transitions, categorized according to their different functions.

**ADDITION**

| | |
|---|---|
| also | in fact |
| and | indeed |
| besides | moreover |
| furthermore | so too |
| in addition | |

**ELABORATION**

| | |
|---|---|
| actually | to put it another way |
| by extension | to put it bluntly |
| in other words | to put it succinctly |
| in short | ultimately |
| that is | |

**EXAMPLE**

| | |
|---|---|
| after all | for instance |
| as an illustration | specifically |
| consider | to take a case in point |
| for example | |

**CAUSE AND EFFECT**

| | |
|---|---|
| accordingly | so |
| as a result | then |
| consequently | therefore |
| hence | thus |
| since | |

**COMPARISON**

| | |
|---|---|
| along the same lines | likewise |
| in the same way | similarly |

**CONTRAST**

| | |
|---|---|
| although | nevertheless |
| but | nonetheless |
| by contrast | on the contrary |
| conversely | on the other hand |
| despite | regardless |
| even though | whereas |
| however | while yet |
| in contrast | |

**CONCESSION**

| | |
|---|---|
| admittedly | naturally |
| although it is true | of course |
| granted | to be sure |

**CONCLUSION**

| | |
|---|---|
| as a result | in sum |
| consequently | therefore |
| hence | thus |
| in conclusion | to sum up |
| in short | to summarize |

Ideally, transitions should operate so unobtrusively in a piece of writing that they recede into the background and readers do not even notice that they are there. It's a bit like what happens when drivers use their turn signals before turning right or left: just as other drivers recognize such signals almost unconsciously, readers should process transition terms with a minimum of thought. But even though such terms should function unobtrusively in your writing, they can be among the most powerful tools in your vocabulary. Think how your heart sinks when someone, immediately after praising you, begins a sentence with "but" or "however." No matter what follows, you know it won't be good.

Notice that some transitions can help you not only to move from one sentence to another, but to combine two or more sentences into one. Combining sentences in this way helps prevent the choppy, staccato effect that arises when too many short sentences are strung together, one after the other. For instance, to combine Bill's two choppy sentences ("Spot is a good dog. He has fleas.") into one, better-flowing sentence, we suggested that he rewrite them as "Spot is a good dog, *even though* he has fleas."

Transitions like these not only guide readers through the twists and turns of your argument but also help ensure that you *have* an argument in the first place. In fact, we think of words like "but," "yet," "nevertheless," "besides," and others as argument words, since it's hard to use them without making some kind of argument. The word "therefore," for instance, commits you to making sure that the claims preceding it lead logically to the conclusion that it introduces. "For example" also assumes an argument, since it requires the material you are introducing to stand as an instance or proof of some preceding generalization. As a result, the more you use transitions, the more you'll be able not only to connect the parts of your text but also to construct a strong argument in the first place. And if you draw on them frequently enough, using them should eventually become second nature.

To be sure, it is possible to overuse transitions, so take time to read over your drafts carefully and eliminate any transitions that are unnecessary. But following the maxim that you need to learn the basic moves of argument before you can deliberately depart from them, we advise you not to forgo explicit transition terms until you've first mastered their use. In all our years of teaching, we've read countless essays that suffered from having few or no transitions, but cannot recall one in which the transitions were overused. Seasoned writers sometimes omit explicit transitions, but only because they rely heavily on the other types of connecting devices that we turn to in the rest of this chapter.

Before doing so, however, let us warn you about inserting transitions without really thinking through their meanings—using "therefore," say, when your text's logic actually requires "nevertheless" or "however." So beware. Choosing transition terms should involve a bit of mental sweat, since the whole point of using them is to make your writing *more* reader-friendly, not less. The only thing more frustrating than reading Bill-style passages like "Spot is a good dog. He has fleas" is reading misconnected sentences like "Spot is a good dog. For example, he has fleas."

## USE POINTING WORDS

Another way to connect the parts of your argument is by using pointing words—which, as their name implies, point or refer backward to some concept in the previous sentence. The most common of these pointing words include "this," "these," "that," "those," "their," and "such" (as in "these pointing words" near the start of this sentence) and simple pronouns like "his," "he," "her," "she," "it," and "their." Such terms help you create the flow we spoke of earlier that enables readers to move effortlessly through your text. In a sense, these terms are like an invisible hand reaching out of your sentence, grabbing what's needed in the previous sentences and pulling it along.

Like transitions, however, pointing words need to be used carefully. It's dangerously easy to insert pointing words into your text that don't refer to a clearly defined object, assuming that because the object you have in mind is clear to you it will also be clear to your readers. For example, consider the use of "this" in the following passage.

> Alexis de Tocqueville was highly critical of democratic societies, which he saw as tending toward mob rule. At the same time, he accorded democratic societies grudging respect. *This* is seen in Tocqueville's statement that . . .

When "this" is used in such a way it becomes an ambiguous or free-floating pointer, since readers can't tell if it refers to Tocqueville's critical attitude toward democratic societies, his grudging respect for them, or some combination of both. "This what?" readers mutter as they go back over such passages and try to figure them out. It's also tempting to try to cheat with pointing words, hoping that they will conceal or make up for conceptual confusions that may lurk in your argument. By referring to a fuzzy idea as "this" or "that," you might hope the fuzziness will somehow come across as clearer than it is.

You can fix problems caused by a free-floating pointer by making sure there is one and only one possible object in the vicinity that the pointer could be referring to. It also often helps to name the object the pointer is referring to at the same time that you point to it, replacing the bald "this" in the example above with a more precise phrase like "this ambivalence toward democratic societies" or "this grudging respect."

## REPEAT KEY TERMS AND PHRASES

A third strategy for connecting the parts of your argument is to develop a constellation of key terms and phrases, including their synonyms and antonyms, that you repeat throughout your text. When used effectively, your key terms should be items that readers could extract from your text in order to get a solid sense of your topic. Playing with key terms also can be a good way to come up with a title and appropriate section headings for your text.

Notice how often Martin Luther King Jr. uses the key words "criticism," "statement," "answer," and "correspondence" in the opening paragraph of his famous "Letter from Birmingham Jail."

> Dear Fellow Clergymen:
>
>   While confined here in the Birmingham city jail, I came across your recent *statement* calling my present activities "unwise and untimely." Seldom do I pause to *answer criticism* of my work and ideas. If I sought to *answer* all the *criticisms* that cross my desk, my secretaries would have little time for anything other than *such correspondence* in the course of the day, and I would have no time for constructive work. But since I feel that you are men of genuine good will and that your *criticisms* are sincerely set forth, I want to try to *answer* your *statement* in what I hope will be patient and reasonable terms.
>
>   Martin Luther King Jr., "Letter from Birmingham Jail"

Even though King uses the terms "criticism" and "answer" three times each and "statement" twice, the effect is not overly repetitive. In fact, these key terms help build a sense of momentum in the paragraph and bind it together.

For another example of the effective use of key terms, consider the following passage, in which the historian Susan Douglas develops a constellation of sharply contrasting key terms around the concept of "cultural schizophrenics": women like herself who, Douglas claims, have mixed feelings about the images of ideal femininity with which they are constantly bombarded by the media.

In a variety of ways, the mass media helped make us the cultural schizophrenics we are today, women who rebel against yet submit to prevailing images about what a desirable, worthwhile woman should be. . . . [T]he mass media has engendered in many women a kind of cultural identity crisis. We are ambivalent toward femininity on the one hand and feminism on the other. Pulled in opposite directions—told we were equal, yet told we were subordinate; told we could change history but told we were trapped by history—we got the bends at an early age, and we've never gotten rid of them.

When I open *Vogue*, for example, I am simultaneously infuriated and seduced. . . . I adore the materialism; I despise the materialism. . . . I want to look beautiful; I think wanting to look beautiful is about the most dumb-ass goal you could have. The magazine stokes my desire; the magazine triggers my bile. And this doesn't only happen when I'm reading *Vogue*; it happens all the time. . . . On the one hand, on the other hand—that's not just me—that's what it means to be a woman in America.

To explain this schizophrenia . . .

Susan Douglas, *Where the Girls Are:*
*Growing Up Female with the Mass Media*

In this passage, Douglas establishes "schizophrenia" as a key concept and then echoes it through synonyms like "identity crisis," "ambivalent," "the bends"—and even demonstrates it through a series of contrasting words and phrases:

rebel against / submit
told we were equal / told we were subordinate
told we could change history / told we were trapped by history
infuriated / seduced
I adore / I despise
I want / I think wanting . . . is about the most dumb-ass goal
stokes my desire / triggers my bile
on the one hand / on the other hand

These contrasting phrases help flesh out Douglas's claim that women are being pulled in two directions at once. In so doing, they bind the passage together into a unified whole that, despite its complexity and sophistication, stays focused over its entire length.

## REPEAT YOURSELF—BUT WITH A DIFFERENCE

The last technique we offer for connecting the parts of your text involves repeating yourself, but with a difference—which basically means saying the same thing you've just said, but in a slightly different way that avoids sounding monotonous. To effectively connect the parts of your argument and keep it moving forward, be careful not to leap from one idea to a different idea or introduce new ideas cold. Instead, try to build bridges between your ideas by echoing what you've just said while simultaneously moving your text into new territory.

Several of the connecting devices discussed in this chapter are ways of repeating yourself in this special way. Key terms, pointing terms, and even many transitions can be used in a way that not only brings something forward from the previous sentence but in some way alters it. When Douglas, for instance, uses the key term "ambivalent" to echo her earlier reference to schizophrenics, she is repeating herself with a difference— repeating the same concept, but with a different word that adds new associations.

In addition, when you use transition phrases like "in other words" and "to put it another way," you repeat yourself with a difference, since these phrases help you restate earlier claims but in a different register. When you open a sentence with "in other words," you are basically telling your readers that in case they didn't fully understand what you meant in the last sentence, you are now coming at it again from a slightly different angle, or that since you're presenting a very important idea, you're not going to skip over it quickly but will explore it further to make sure your readers grasp all its aspects.

We would even go so far as to suggest that after your first sentence, almost every sentence you write should refer back to previous statements in some way. Whether you are writing a "furthermore" comment that adds to what you have just said or a "for example" statement that illustrates it, each sentence should echo at least one element of the previous sentence in some discernible way. Even when your text changes direction and requires transitions like "in contrast," "however," or "but," you still need to mark that shift by linking the sentence to the one just before it, as in the following example.

Cheyenne loved basketball. Nevertheless, she feared her height would put her at a disadvantage.

These sentences work because even though the second sentence changes course and qualifies the first, it still echoes key concepts from the first. Not only does "she" echo "Cheyenne," since both refer to the same person, but "feared" echoes "loved" by establishing the contrast mandated by the term "nevertheless." "Nevertheless," then, is not an excuse for changing subjects radically. It too requires repetition to help readers shift gears with you and follow your train of thought.

Repetition, in short, is the central means by which you can move from point A to point B in a text. To introduce one last analogy, think of the way experienced rock climbers move up a steep slope. Instead of jumping or lurching from one handhold to the next, good climbers get a secure handhold on the position they have established before reaching for the next ledge. The same thing applies to writing. To move smoothly from point to point in your argument, you need to firmly ground what you say in what you've already said. In this way, your writing remains focused while simultaneously moving forward.

"But hold on," you may be thinking. "Isn't repetition precisely what sophisticated writers should avoid, on the grounds that it will make their writing sound simplistic—as if they are belaboring the obvious?" Yes and no. On the one hand, writers certainly can run into trouble if they merely repeat themselves and nothing more. On the other hand, repetition is key to creating continuity in writing. It is impossible to stay on track in a piece of writing if you don't repeat your points throughout the length of the text. Furthermore, writers would never make an impact on readers if they didn't repeat their main points often enough to reinforce those points and make them stand out above subordinate points. The trick therefore is not to avoid repeating yourself but to repeat yourself in varied and interesting enough ways that you advance your argument without sounding tedious.

*Exercises*

1. Read the following opening to Chapter 2 of *The Road to Wigan Pier*, by George Orwell. Annotate the connecting devices by underlining the transitions, circling the key terms, and putting boxes around the pointing terms.

Our civilisation . . . is founded on coal, more completely than one realises until one stops to think about it. The machines that keep us alive, and the machines that make the machines, are all directly or indirectly dependent upon coal. In the metabolism of the Western world the coal-miner is second in importance only to the man who ploughs the soil. He is a sort of grimy caryatid upon whose shoulders nearly everything that is not grimy is supported. For this reason the actual process by which coal is extracted is well worth watching, if you get the chance and are willing to take the trouble.

When you go down a coal-mine it is important to try and get to the coal face when the "fillers" are at work. This is not easy, because when the mine is working visitors are a nuisance and are not encouraged, but if you go at any other time, it is possible to come away with a totally wrong impression. On a Sunday, for instance, a mine seems almost peaceful. The time to go there is when the machines are roaring and the air is black with coal dust, and when you can actually see what the miners have to do. At those times the place is like hell, or at any rate like my own mental picture of hell. Most of the things one imagines in hell are there—heat, noise, confusion, darkness, foul air, and, above all, unbearably cramped space. Everything except the fire, for there is no fire down there except the feeble beams of Davy lamps and electric torches which scarcely penetrate the clouds of coal dust.

When you have finally got there—and getting there is a job in itself: I will explain that in a moment—you crawl through the last line of pit props and see opposite you a shiny black wall three or four feet high. This is the coal face. Overhead is the smooth ceiling made by the rock from which the coal has been cut; underneath is the rock again, so that the gallery you are in is only as high as the ledge of coal itself, probably not much more than a yard. The first impression of all, overmastering everything else for a while, is the frightful, deafening din from the conveyor belt which carries the coal away. You cannot see very far, because the fog of coal dust throws back the beam of your lamp, but you can see on either side of you the line of half-naked kneeling men, one to every four or five yards, driving their shovels under the fallen coal and flinging it swiftly over their left shoulders. . . .

GEORGE ORWELL, *The Road to Wigan Pier*

2. Read over something you've written with an eye for the devices you've used to connect the parts. Underline all the transitions, pointing terms, key terms, and repetition. Do you see any patterns? Do you rely on certain devices more than others? Are there any passages that are hard to follow—and if so, can you make them easier to read by trying any of the other devices discussed in this chapter?

# NINE

# "YOU MEAN I CAN JUST SAY IT THAT WAY?"

## *Academic Writing Doesn't Mean Setting Aside Your Own Voice*

———

WE WISH WE HAD A DOLLAR for each time a student has asked us a version of the above question. It usually comes when the student is visiting us during our office hours, seeking advice about how to improve a draft of an essay he or she is working on. When we ask the student to tell us in simple words the point he or she is trying to make in the essay, the student will almost invariably produce a statement that is far clearer and more incisive than anything in the draft.

"Write that down," we will urge. "What you just said is sooo much better than anything you wrote in your draft. We suggest going home and revising your paper in a way that makes that claim the focal point of your essay."

"Really?" our student will ask, looking surprised. "You mean I can just say it that way?"

"Sure. Why not?"

"Well, saying it that way seems just so elementary—so obvious. I mean, I don't want to sound stupid."

NINE    "YOU MEAN I CAN JUST SAY IT THAT WAY?"

The goal of this chapter is to counteract this common misconception: that relying in college on the straightforward, down-to-earth language you use every day will make you sound stupid; that to impress your teachers you need to set aside your everyday voice and write in a way that nobody can understand.

It's easy to see how this misconception took hold, since academic writing is notoriously obscure. Students can't be blamed for such obscurity when so much of the writing they're assigned to read is so hard to understand—as we can see in the following sentence from a science paper that linguist Steven Pinker quotes in his essay "Why Academics Stink at Writing":

> Participants read assertions whose veracity was either affirmed or denied by the subsequent presentation of an assessment word.

After struggling to determine what the writer of this sentence was trying to say, Pinker finally decided it was probably something as simple as this:

> Participants read sentences, each followed by the word *true* or *false*.

Had the author revised the original statement by tapping into his or her more relaxed, everyday language, as Pinker did in revising it, much of this struggle could have been avoided. In our view, then, mastering academic writing does not mean completely abandoning your normal voice for one that's stiff, convoluted, or pompous, as students often assume. Instead, it means creating a new voice that draws on the voice you already have.

This is not to suggest that any language you use among friends has a place in academic writing. Nor is it to suggest that you may fall back on your everyday voice as an excuse to remain in your comfort zone and avoid learning the rigorous forms and habits that characterize academic culture. After all, learning new words and forms—moves or templates, as we call them in this book—is a major part of getting an education. We do, however, wish to suggest that everyday language can often enliven such moves and even enhance your precision in using academic terminology. In our view, then, it is a mistake to assume that the academic and everyday are completely separate languages that can never be used together. Ultimately, we suggest, academic writing is often at its best when it combines what we call "everydayspeak" and "academicspeak."

## BLEND ACADEMIC AND COLLOQUIAL STYLES

In fact, we would argue that, despite their bad reputation, many academics are highly successful writers who provide models of how to blend everyday and academic styles. Note, for example, how Judith Fetterley, a prominent scholar in the field of literary studies, blends academic and everyday ways of talking in the following passage on the novelist Willa Cather:

> As Merrill Skaggs has put it, "[Cather] is neurotically controlling and self-conscious about her work, but she knows at all points what she is doing. Above all else, she is self-conscious."
>
> Without question, Cather was a control freak.
>
> JUDITH FETTERLEY, "Willa Cather and the<br>Question of Sympathy: An Unofficial Story"

In this passage, Fetterley makes use of what is probably the most common technique for blending academic and everyday language: she puts them side by side, juxtaposing "neurotically controlling" and "self-conscious" from

See pp. 248–55 for an essay that mixes colloquial and academic styles.

a quoted source with her own colloquial term, "control freak." In this way, Fetterley lightens a potentially dry subject and makes it more accessible and even entertaining.

## A TRANSLATION RECIPE

But Fetterley does more than simply put academicspeak and everydayspeak side by side. She takes a step further by translating the one into the other. By translating Skaggs's polysyllabic description of Cather as "neurotically controlling and self-conscious" into the succinct, if blunt, "control freak," Fetterley shows how rarefied, academic ways of talking and more familiar language can not only coexist but actually enhance one another—her informal "control freak" serving to explain the formal language that precedes it.

To be sure, slangy, colloquial expressions like "control freak" may be far more common in the humanities than in the sciences, and even in the humanities such casual usages are a recent development. Fifty years ago academic writing in all disciplines was the linguistic equivalent of a black-tie affair. But as times have changed, so has the range of options open to academic writers—so much so that it is not surprising to find writers in all fields using colloquial expressions and referring to movies, music, and other forms of popular culture.

Indeed, Fetterley's passage offers a simple recipe for mixing styles that we encourage you to try out in your own writing: first state the point in academic language, then translate the point into everyday language. Everyone knows that academic terms like "neurotically controlling" and "self-conscious"—and others you might encounter like "subject position" or "bifurcate"—can be hard to understand. But this translation recipe, we think, eases such difficulties by making the academic familiar. Here is one way you might translate academicspeak into everydayspeak:

▸ **Scholar X argues, "_____." In other words, _____.**

Instead of "In other words," you might try variations like the following:

▸ **Essentially, X argues _____.**

▸ **X's point, succinctly put, is that _____.**

▸ **Plainly put, _____.**

Following Fetterley's lead and making moves like these can help you not only demystify challenging academic material, but also reinterpret it, showing you understand it (and helping readers understand it) by putting it into your own terms.

## SELF-TRANSLATION

But this translation recipe need not be limited to clarifying the ideas of others. It can also be used to clarify your own complex ideas, as the following passage by the philosopher Rebecca Goldstein illustrates:

> We can hardly get through our lives—in fact, it's hard to get through a week—without considering what makes specific actions right and others wrong and debating with ourselves whether that is a difference that must compel the actions we choose. (Okay, it's wrong! I get it! But why should I care?)
>
> REBECCA GOLDSTEIN, *Plato at the Googleplex:*
> *Why Philosophy Won't Go Away*

Though Goldstein's first sentence may require several rereadings, it is one that most of us, with varying degrees of effort, can come to understand: that we all wrestle regularly with the challenging philosophical questions of what the ethics of a given situation are and whether those ethics should alter our behavior. But instead of leaving us entirely on our own to figure out what she is saying, Goldstein helps us out in her closing parenthenthetical remarks, which translate the abstractions of her first sentence into the kind of concrete everydayspeak that runs through our heads.

Yet another example of self-translation—one that actually uses the word "translation"—can be found on the opening page of a book by scholar Helen Sword:

> There is a massive gap between what most readers consider to be good writing and what academics typically produce and publish. I'm not talking about the kinds of formal strictures necessarily imposed

by journal editors—article length, citation style, and the like—but about a deeper, duller kind of disciplinary monotony, a compulsive proclivity for discursive obscurantism and circumambulatory diction (translation: an addiction to big words and soggy syntax).

HELEN SWORD, Stylish Academic Writing

In this passage, Sword gives her own unique twist to the translation technique we've been discussing. After a stream of difficult polysyllabic words—"a compulsive proclivity for discursive obscurantism and circumambulatory diction"—she then concludes by translating these words into everydayspeak: "an addiction to big words and soggy syntax." The effect is to dramatize her larger point: the "massive gap between what most readers consider to be good writing and what academics typically produce and publish."

## FAMOUS EXAMPLES

Even notoriously difficult thinkers could be said to use the translation practice we have been advocating in this chapter, as the following famous and widely quoted claims illustrate:

I think, therefore I am.
—RENÉ DESCARTES

The master's tools will never dismantle the master's house.
—AUDRE LORDE

The medium is the message.
—MARSHALL MCLUHAN

Form follows function.
—LOUIS SULLIVAN

These sentences can be read almost as sound bites, short, catchy statements that express a more complex idea. Though the term "sound bite" is usually used to refer to mindless media simplifications, the succinct statements above show what valuable work they can do. These distillations are admittedly reductive in that they do not capture all the nuances of the more complex ideas they represent. But consider their power to stick in the minds of readers. Without these memorable translations, we wonder if these authors' ideas would have achieved such widespread circulation.

Consider Descartes' "I think, therefore I am," for example, which comes embedded in the following passage, in which Descartes is struggling to find a philosophical foundation for absolute truth in the face of skeptical doctrines that doubt that anything can be known for certain. After putting himself in the shoes of a radical skeptic and imagining what it would be like to believe all apparent truths to be false, Descartes "immediately ... observed," he writes,

> whilst I thus wished to think that all was false, it was absolutely necessary that I, who thus thought, should be somewhat; and as I observed that this truth, I think, therefore I am (*cogito ergo sum*), was so certain and of such evidence that no ground of doubt, however extravagant, could be alleged by the sceptics capable of shaking it, I concluded that I might, without scruple, accept it as the first principle of the philosophy of which I was in search.
>
> René Descartes, "Discourse on the Method, Part IV"

Had Descartes been less probing and scrupulous, we speculate, he would have stopped writing and ended the passage after the statement "it was absolutely necessary that I, who thus thought, should be somewhat." After all, the passage up to this point contains all the basic ingredients that the rest of it goes on to explain, the simpler, more accessible formulation

"I think, therefore I am" being merely a reformulation of this earlier material. But just imagine if Descartes had decided that his job as a writer was finished after his initial claim and had failed to add the more accessible phrase "I think, therefore I am." We suspect this idea of his would not have become one of the most famous touchstones of Western philosophy.

## EVERYDAY LANGUAGE AS A THINKING TOOL

As the examples in this chapter suggest, then, translating academic language into everydayspeak can be an indispensable tool for clarifying and underscoring ideas for readers. But at an even more basic level, such translation can be an indispensable means for you as a writer to clarify your ideas to yourself. In other words, translating academicspeak into everydayspeak can function as a thinking tool that enables you to discover what you are trying to say to begin with.

For as writing theorists often note, writing is generally not a process in which we start with a fully formed idea in our heads that we then simply transcribe in an unchanged state onto the page. On the contrary, writing is more often a means of discovery in which we use the writing process to figure out what our idea is. This is why writers are often surprised to find that what they end up with on the page is quite different from what they thought it would be when they started. What we are trying to say here is that everydayspeak is often crucial for this discovery process, that translating your ideas into more common, simpler terms can help you figure out what your ideas really are, as opposed to what you initially imagined they were. Even Descartes, for example, may not have had the formulation "I think, therefore I am" in mind before he wrote the passage above; instead, he may have arrived at it as he worked through the writing process.

We ourselves have been reminded of this point when engaged in our own writing. One major benefit of writing collaboratively, as the two of us do, is that it repeatedly forces us to explain in simpler terms our less-than-clear ideas when one of us doesn't already know what the other means. In the process of writing and revising this book, for instance, we were always turning to each other after reading something the other had written and asking a version of the "Can-you-explain-that-more-simply?" question that we described asking our students in our office in this chapter's opening anecdote: "What do you mean?" "I don't get it—can you explain?" "Huh!?" Sometimes, when the idea is finally stated in plain, everyday terms, we realize that it doesn't make sense or that it amounts to nothing more than a cliché—or that we have something worth pursuing. It's as if using everyday language to talk through a draft—as any writer can do by asking others to critique his or her drafts—shines a bright light on our writing to expose its strengths and weaknesses.

## STILL NOT CONVINCED?

To be sure, not everyone will be as enthusiastic as we are about the benefits of everydayspeak. Many will insist that, while some fields in the humanities may be open to everyday language, colloquial expressions, and slang, most fields in the sciences are not. And some people in both the humanities and the sciences will argue that some ideas simply can't be done justice to in everyday language. "Theory X," they will say, "is just too complex to be explained in simple terms," or "You have to be in the field to understand it." Perhaps so. But at least one distinguished scientist, the celebrated atomic physicist Enrico Fermi, thought otherwise. Fermi, it is said, believed that all faculty in his field should teach basic physics to undergraduates, because having to explain the science in relatively plain English helped to clarify their thinking. This last point can be stated as a rule of thumb: if you can't explain it to your Aunt Franny, chances are you don't understand it yourself.

Furthermore, when writers tell themselves that their ideas are just too complex to be explained to nonspecialists, they risk fooling themselves into thinking that they are making more sense than they actually are. Translating academicspeak into everydayspeak functions as a kind of baloney detector, a way of keeping us honest when we're in danger of getting carried away by our own verbosity.

## CODE-MESHING

"But come on," some may say. "Get real! Academic writing must, in many cases, mean setting aside our own voices." Sure, it may be fine to translate challenging academic ideas into plain everyday language, as Goldstein, Sword, and Descartes do above, when it's a language that your audience will understand and find acceptable. But what if your everyday language—the one you use when you're most relaxed, with family and friends—is filled with slang and questionable grammar? And what if your everyday language is an ethnic or regional dialect—or a different language altogether? Is there really a place for such language in academic, professional, or public writing?

Yes and no. On the one hand, there are many situations—like when you're applying for a job or submitting a proposal to be read by an official screening body—in which it's probably safest to write in "standard" English. On the other hand, the line between language that might confuse audiences and language that engages or challenges them is not always obvious. Nor is the line between foreign words that readers don't already know and those that readers might happily learn. After all, "standard" written English is more open and inclusive than it may at first appear. And readers often appreciate writers who take risks and mix things up.

Many prominent writers mix standard written English with other dialects or languages, employing a practice that cultural and linguistic theorists Vershawn Ashanti Young and Suresh Canagarajah call "code-meshing." For instance, in the titles of two of her books, *Talkin and Testifyin: The Language of Black America* and *Black Talk: Words and Phrases From the Hood to the Amen Corner*, the language scholar Geneva Smitherman mixes African American vernacular phrases with more scholarly language in order to suggest, as she explicitly argues in these books, that black vernacular English is as legitimate a variety of language as "standard" English. Here are three typical passages:

> In Black America, the oral tradition has served as a fundamental vehicle for gittin ovah. That tradition preserves the Afro-American heritage and reflects the collective spirit of the race.

> Blacks are quick to ridicule "educated fools," people who done gone to school and read all dem books and still don't know nothin!

> It is a socially approved verbal strategy for black rappers to talk about how bad they is.

> GENEVA SMITHERMAN, *Talkin and Testifyin:*
> *The Language of Black America*

In these examples, Smitherman blends the types of terms we expect in scholarly writing like "oral tradition" and "fundamental vehicle" with black vernacular phrases like "gittin ovah." She even blends the standard English spelling of words with African American English variants like "dem" and "ovah" in a way that evokes how some speakers of African American English sound. Some might object to these unconventional practices, but this is precisely Smitherman's point: that our habitual language practices need to be opened up, and that the number of participants in the academic conversation needs to be expanded.

Along similar lines, the writer and activist Gloria Anzaldúa mixes standard English with what she calls Chicano Spanish to make a political point about the suppression of the Spanish language in the United States. In one typical passage, she writes:

> From this racial, ideological, cultural, and biological cross-pollinization, an "alien" consciousness is presently in the making— a new *mestiza* consciousness, *una conciencia de mujer*.
>
> GLORIA ANZALDÚA,<br>*Borderlands / La Frontera: The New Mestiza*

Anzaldúa gets her point across not only through *what* she says but through the *way* she says it, showing that the new hybrid, or "*mestiza* consciousness," that she celebrates is, as she puts it, "presently in the making." Ultimately, such code-meshing suggests that languages, like the people who speak them, are not distinct, separate islands.

Because there are so many options in writing, then, there is no need to ever feel limited in your choice of words. You can always experiment with your language and improve it. Depending on your audience and purpose, and how much risk you're willing to take, you can dress up your language, dress it down, or some combination of both. You could even recast the title of this book, *"They Say / I Say,"* as a teenager might say it: "She Goes / I'm Like."

We hope you agree with us, then, that to succeed as a college writer, you need not always set aside your everyday voice, even when that voice may initially seem unwelcome in the academic world. It is by blending everyday language with standard written English that what counts as "standard" changes and the range of possibilities open to academic writers continues to grow.

*Exercises*

1. Take a paragraph from this book and dress it down, rewriting it in informal colloquial language. Then rewrite the same paragraph again by dressing it up, making it much more formal. Then rewrite the paragraph one more time in a way that blends the two styles. Share your paragraphs with a classmate, and discuss which versions are most effective and why.

2. Find something you've written for a course, and study it to see whether you've used any of your own everyday expressions, any words or structures that are not "academic." If by chance you don't find any, see if there's a place or two where shifting into more casual or unexpected language would help you make a point, get your reader's attention, or just add liveliness to your text. Be sure to keep your audience and purpose in mind, and use language that will be appropriate to both.

# TEN

# "BUT DON'T GET ME WRONG"
## *The Art of Metacommentary*

———※———

WHEN WE TELL PEOPLE that we are writing a chapter on the art of metacommentary, they often give us a puzzled look and tell us that they have no idea what "metacommentary" is. "We know what commentary is," they'll sometimes say, "but what does it mean when it's *meta?*" Our answer is that whether or not they know the term, they practice the art of metacommentary on a daily basis whenever they make a point of explaining something they've said or written: "What I meant to say was _____," "My point was not _____, but _____," or "You're probably not going to like what I'm about to say, but _____." In such cases, they are not offering new points but telling an audience how to interpret what they have already said or are about to say. In short, then, metacommentary is a way of commenting on your claims and telling others how—and how not—to think about them.

It may help to think of metacommentary as being like the chorus in a Greek play that stands to the side of the drama unfolding on the stage and explains its meaning to the audience—or like a voice-over narrator who comments on and explains the action in a television show or movie. Think of metacommentary as a sort of second text that stands alongside your main text and explains what it means. In the main text you say something; in the metatext you guide your readers in interpreting and processing what you've said.

What we are suggesting, then, is that you think of your text as two texts joined at the hip: a main text in which you make your argument and another in which you "work" your ideas, distinguishing your views from others they may be confused with, anticipating and answering objections, connecting one point to another, explaining why your claim might be controversial, and so forth. The figure below demonstrates what we mean.

**THE MAIN TEXT SAYS SOMETHING. THE METATEXT TELLS READERS HOW—AND HOW NOT—TO THINK ABOUT IT.**

## USE METACOMMENTARY TO CLARIFY
## AND ELABORATE

But why do you need metacommentary to tell readers what you mean and guide them through your text? Can't you just clearly say what you mean up front? The answer is that, no matter how clear and precise your writing is, readers can still fail to understand it in any number of ways. Even the best writers can provoke reactions in readers that they didn't intend, and even good readers can get lost in a complicated argument or fail to see how one point connects with another. Readers may also fail to see what follows from your argument, or they may follow your reasoning and examples yet fail to see the larger conclusion you draw from them. They may fail to see your argument's overall significance, or mistake what you are saying for a related argument that they have heard before but that you want to distance yourself from. As a result, no matter how straightforward a writer you are, readers still need you to help them grasp what you really mean. Because the written word is prone to so much mischief and can be interpreted in so many different ways, we need metacommentary to keep misinterpretations and other communication misfires at bay.

Another reason to master the art of metacommentary is that it will help you develop your ideas and generate more text. If you have ever had trouble producing the required number of pages for a writing project, metacommentary can help you add both length and depth to your writing. We've seen many students who try to produce a five-page paper sputter to a halt at two or three pages, complaining they've said everything they can think of about their topic. "I've stated my thesis and presented my reasons and evidence," students have told us. "What else is there to do?" It's almost as if such writers have generated a thesis and don't know what to do with it. When these students learn to use metacommentary, however, they get more out of their ideas and write longer, more substantial texts. In sum, metacommentary can help you extract the full potential from your ideas, drawing out important implications, explaining ideas from different perspectives, and so forth.

So even when you may think you've said everything possible in an argument, try inserting the following types of metacommentary.

▸ **In other words, <u>she doesn't realize how right she is.</u>**

▸ **What _____ really means is _____ .**

▸ **My point is not _____ but _____ .**

▸ **Ultimately, then, my goal is to demonstrate that _____ .**

Ideally, such metacommentary should help you recognize some implications of your ideas that you didn't initially realize were there.

Let's look at how the cultural critic Neil Postman uses metacommentary in the following passage describing the shift in American culture when it began to move from print and reading to television and movies.

*It is my intention in this book to show* that a great . . . shift has taken place in America, with the result that the content of much of our public discourse has become dangerous nonsense. *With this in view, my task in the chapters ahead is* straightforward. *I must, first, demonstrate* how, under the governance of the printing press, discourse in America was different from what it is now— generally coherent, serious and rational; *and then* how, under the governance of television, it has become shriveled and absurd. *But to avoid the possibility that my analysis will be interpreted as* standard-brand academic whimpering, a kind of elitist complaint against "junk" on television, *I must first explain that . . .* I appreciate junk as much as the next fellow, *and I know full well that* the printing press has generated enough of it to fill the Grand Canyon to overflowing. Television is not old enough to have matched printing's output of junk.

> NEIL POSTMAN, *Amusing Ourselves to Death:*
> *Public Discourse in the Age of Show Business*

To see what we mean by metacommentary, look at the phrases above that we have italicized. With these moves, Postman essentially stands apart from his main ideas to help readers follow and understand what he is arguing.

He previews what he will argue: *It is my intention in this book to show . . .*

He spells out how he will make his argument: *With this in view, my task in the chapters ahead is . . . I must, first, demonstrate . . . and then . . .*

He distinguishes his argument from other arguments it may easily be confused with: *But to avoid the possibility that my analysis will be interpreted as . . . I must first explain that . . .*

## TITLES AS METACOMMENTARY

Even the title of Postman's book, *Amusing Ourselves to Death: Public Discourse in the Age of Show Business*, functions as a form of metacommentary since, like all titles, it stands apart from the text itself and tells readers the book's main point: that the very pleasure provided by contemporary show business is destructive.

Titles, in fact, are one of the most important forms of metacommentary, functioning rather like carnival barkers telling passersby what they can expect if they go inside. Subtitles, too, function as metacommentary, further explaining or elaborating on the main title. The subtitle of this book, for example, not only explains that it is about "the moves that matter in academic writing," but indicates that "they say / I say" is one of these moves. Thinking of a title as metacommentary can actually help you develop sharper titles, ones that, like Postman's, give readers a hint of what your argument will be. Contrast such titles with unhelpfully open-ended ones like "Shakespeare" or "Steroids" or "English Essay" or essays with no titles at all. Essays with vague titles (or no titles) send the message that the writer has simply not bothered to reflect on what he or she is saying and is uninterested in guiding or orienting readers.

## USE OTHER MOVES AS METACOMMENTARY

Many of the other moves covered in this book function as metacommentary: entertaining objections, adding transitions, framing quotations, answering "so what?" and "who cares?" When you entertain objections, you stand outside of your text and imagine what a critic might say; when you add transitions, you essentially explain the relationship between various claims. And when you answer the "so what?" and "who cares?" questions, you look beyond your central argument and explain who should be interested in it and why.

## TEMPLATES FOR INTRODUCING
## METACOMMENTARY

### TO WARD OFF POTENTIAL MISUNDERSTANDINGS

The following moves help you differentiate certain views from ones they might be mistaken for.

▸ Essentially, I am arguing not that <u>we should give up the policy</u>, but that we should monitor effects far more closely.

▸ This is not to say _____ , but rather _____ .

▸ X is concerned less with _____ than with _____ .

### TO ELABORATE ON A PREVIOUS IDEA

The following moves elaborate on a previous point, saying to readers: "In case you didn't get it the first time, I'll try saying the same thing in a different way."

▸ In other words, _____ .

▸ To put it another way, _____ .

▸ What X is saying here is that _____ .

### TO PROVIDE A ROAD MAP TO YOUR TEXT

This move orients readers, clarifying where you have been and where you are going—and making it easier for them to process and follow your text.

▸ Chapter 2 explores _____ , while Chapter 3 examines _____ .

▸ Having just argued that _____ , I want now to complicate the point by _____ .

## TO MOVE FROM A GENERAL CLAIM TO A SPECIFIC EXAMPLE

These moves help you explain a general point by providing a concrete example that illustrates what you're saying.

▸ For example, _____.

▸ _____, for instance, demonstrates _____.

▸ Consider _____, for example.

▸ To take a case in point, _____.

## TO INDICATE THAT A CLAIM IS MORE, LESS, OR EQUALLY IMPORTANT

The following templates help you give relative emphasis to the claim that you are introducing, showing whether that claim is of more or less weight than the previous one, or equal to it.

▸ Even more important, _____.

▸ But above all, _____.

▸ Incidentally, we will briefly note, _____.

▸ Just as important, _____.

▸ Equally, _____.

▸ Finally, _____.

## TO EXPLAIN A CLAIM WHEN YOU ANTICIPATE OBJECTIONS

Here's a template to help you anticipate and respond to possible objections.

▸ Although some readers may object that _____, I would answer that _____.

**TO GUIDE READERS TO YOUR MOST GENERAL POINT**

These moves show that you are wrapping things up and tying up various subpoints previously made.

Chapter 6 has more templates for anticipating objections.

▶ In sum, then, _____.

▶ My conclusion, then, is that _____.

▶ In short, _____.

In this chapter we have tried to show that the most persuasive writing often doubles back and comments on its own claims in ways that help readers negotiate and process them. Instead of simply piling claim upon claim, effective writers are constantly "stage-managing" how their claims will be received. It's true of course that to be persuasive a text has to have strong claims to argue in the first place. But even the strongest arguments will flounder unless writers use metacommentary to prevent potential misreadings and make their arguments shine.

*Exercises*

1. Read an essay or article and annotate it to indicate the different ways the author uses metacommentary. Use the templates on pages 137–39 as your guide. For example, you may want to circle transitional phrases and write "trans" in the margins, to put brackets around sentences that elaborate on earlier sentences and mark them "elab," or underline sentences in which the author sums up what he or she has been saying, writing "sum" in the margins.

   How does the author use metacommentary? Does the author follow any of the templates provided in this book word for word? Did you find any forms of metacommentary not discussed in this chapter? If so, can you identify them, name them, and perhaps devise templates based on them for use in your own writing? And finally, how do you think the author's use of metacommentary enhances (or harms) his or her writing?

2.  Complete each of the following metacommentary templates in any way that makes sense.

    ▸ In making a case for the medical use of marijuana, I am not saying that _____.

    ▸ But my argument will do more than prove that one particular industrial chemical has certain toxic properties. In this article, I will also _____.

    ▸ My point about the national obsessions with sports reinforces the belief held by many _____ that _____.

    ▸ I believe, therefore, that the war is completely unjustified. But let me back up and explain how I arrived at this conclusion: _____. In this way, I came to believe that this war is a big mistake.

# ELEVEN

# "HE ~~SAYS~~ CONTENDS"

## *Using the Templates to Revise*

—⊡—

ONE OF THE MOST IMPORTANT stages of the writing process is revision, when you look at a draft with an eye for how well you've made your argument and what you need to do to make it better. The challenge is to figure out what needs work—and then what exactly you need to do.

Sometimes you'll have specific comments and suggestions from a teacher, noting that you need to state your position more explicitly, that your point is unclear, that you've misunderstood an author you're summarizing, and so forth. But what if you don't have any such guidance, or aren't sure what to do with it? The list of guidelines below offers help and points you back to relevant advice and templates in this book.

Do you present your argument as a response to what others say? Do you make reference to other views besides your own? Do you use voice markers to distinguish clearly for readers between your views and those of others? In order to make your argument as convincing as possible, would it help to add more concessions to opposing views, using "yes but" templates?

Asking yourself these large-scale revision questions will help you see how well you've managed the "they say / I say" framework and this in turn should help you see where further revisions are needed. The checklist below follows the order of chapters in this book.

## How Do You Represent What Others Say?

*Do you start with what others say?* If not, try revising to do so. See pages 23–28 for templates that can help.

*Do you summarize or paraphrase what they've said?* If so, have you represented their views accurately—and adequately?

*Do you quote others?* Do you frame each quotation successfully, integrating it into your text? Does the quotation support your argument? Have you introduced each quotation adequately, naming the person you're quoting (and saying who that person is if your readers won't know)? Do you explain in your own words what the quotation means? Do you then clearly indicate how the quotation bears on your own argument? See pages 45–47 for tips on creating a "quotation sandwich."

*Check the verbs* you use to introduce any summaries and quotations: do they express accurately what was said? If you've used common signal phrases such as "X said" or "Y believes," is there a verb that reflects more accurately what was said? See pages 40–41 for a list of verbs for introducing summaries and quotations.

*Have you documented all summaries and quotations,* both with parenthetical documentation in your text and a references or works-cited list?

*Do you remind readers of what others say* at various points throughout your text? If not, see pages 27–28 for help revising in order to do so.

## What Do You Say?

*Do you agree, disagree, or both* with those you're responding to? Have you said so explicitly?

*If you disagree,* do you give reasons why you disagree? If you agree, what more have you added to the conversation? If you both agree and disagree, do you do so without confusing readers or seeming evasive?

*Have you stated your position and the one it responds to as a connected unit?*

*What reasons and evidence* do you offer to support your "I say"? In other words, do your argument and the argument you are responding to—your "I say" and "they say"—address the same topic or issue, or does a switch occur that takes you on a tangent that will confuse readers? One way to ensure that your "I say" and "they say" are aligned rather than seeming like ships passing in the night is to use the same key terms in both. See Chapter 8 for tips on how to do so.

*Will readers be able to distinguish what you say from what others say?* See Chapter 5 for advice about using voice markers to make that distinction clear, especially at moments when you are moving from your view to someone else's view or back.

## Have You Introduced Any Naysayers?

*Have you acknowledged likely objections* to your argument? If so, have you represented these views fairly—and responded to them persuasively? See Chapter 6 for tips on how to do so.

*If not,* think about what other perspectives exist on your topic, and incorporate them into your draft.

## Have You Used Metacommentary to Clarify What You Do or Don't Mean?

*No matter how clearly you've explained your points,* it's a good idea to explain what you mean—or *don't* mean—with phrases like "in other words" or "don't get me wrong." See Chapter 10 for examples of how to do so.

*Do you have a title?* If so, does it tell readers what your main point or issue is, and does it do so in a lively manner? Should you add a subtitle to elaborate on the title?

## Have You Tied It All Together?

*Can readers follow your argument* from one sentence and paragraph to the next and see how each successive point supports your overall argument?

*Check your use of transitions,* words like "however" and "therefore." Such words make clear how your ideas relate to one another; if you need to add transitions, see pages 105–06 for a complete list.

*Check your use of pointing words.* Do you use common pointers like "this" and "that," which help lead readers from one sentence to the next? If so, is it always clear what "this" and "that" refer to, or do you need to add nouns in order to avoid ambiguity? See pages 108–10 for help working with pointing words.

*Have you used what we call "repetition with a difference"* to help connect parts of your argument? See pages 112–14 for examples of how to do so.

## Have You Shown Why Your Argument Matters?

*Don't assume* that readers will see why your argument is important—or why they should care. Be sure that you have told them why. See Chapter 7 if you need help.

## A REVISED STUDENT ESSAY

Here is an example of how one student, Antonia Peacocke, used this book to revise an essay. Starting with an article she'd written for her high school newspaper, Peacocke then followed the advice in our book as she turned her article into a college-level academic essay. Her original article was a brief account of why she liked *Family Guy*, and her first step in revising was to open with a "they say" and an "I say," previewing her overall argument in brief form at the essay's beginning. While her original version had acknowledged that many find the show "objectionable," she hadn't named these people or indicated why they didn't like the show. In her revised version, after doing further research, Peacocke identified those with whom she disagreed and responded to them at length, as the essay itself illustrates.

In addition, Peacocke strengthened existing transitions, added new ones, and clarified the stakes of her argument, saying more explicitly why readers should care about whether *Family Guy* is good or bad. In making these revisions she gave her own spin to several templates in this book.

We've annotated Peacocke's essay in the margins to point out particular rhetorical moves discussed in our book and the chapters in which those discussions appear. We hope studying her essay and our annotations will suggest how you might craft and revise your own writing.

Antonia Peacocke wrote this essay in the summer between high school and her first year at Harvard. She is now a PhD student in philosophy at the University of California at Berkeley.

# Family Guy *and Freud: Jokes and Their Relation to the Unconscious*

## ANTONIA PEACOCKE

WHILE SLOUCHING in front of the television after a long day, you probably don't think a lot about famous psychologists of the twentieth century. Somehow, these figures don't come up often in prime-time—or even daytime—TV programming. Whether you're watching *Living Lohan* or the *NewsHour*, the likelihood is that you are not thinking of Sigmund Freud, even if you've heard of his book *Jokes and Their Relation to the Unconscious*. I say that you should be.

What made me think of Freud in the first place, actually, was *Family Guy*, the cartoon created by Seth MacFarlane. (Seriously—stay with me here.) Any of my friends can tell you that this program holds endless fascination for me; as a matter of fact, my high school rag-sheet "perfect mate" was the baby Stewie Griffin, a character on the show (see Fig. 1). Embarrassingly enough, I have almost reached the point at which I can perform

> Starts with what others are saying (Chapter 1)

> Responds to what they say (Chapter 4)

> Metacommentary wards off potential skepticism (Chapter 10)

one-woman versions of several episodes. I know every website that streams the show for free, and I still refuse to return the five *Family Guy* DVDs a friend lent me in 2006. Before I was such a devotee, however, I was adamantly opposed to the program for its particular brand of humor.

It will come as no surprise that I was not alone in this view; many still denounce *Family Guy* as bigoted and crude. *New York Times* journalist Stuart Elliott claimed just this year that "the characters on the Fox television series *Family Guy* . . . purposely offen[d] just about every group of people

Quotes and
summarizes
what others
say (Chapters
2 and 3)

Fig 1. Peter and Stewie Griffin. (Everett Collection)

you could name." Likewise Stephen Dubner, coauthor of *Freakonomics*, called *Family Guy* "a cartoon comedy that packs more gags per minute about race, sex, incest, bestiality, etc. than any other show [he] can think of." Comparing its level of offense to that of Don Imus's infamous comments about the Rutgers women's basketball team in the same year, comments that threw the popular CBS radio talk-show host off the air, Dubner said he wondered why Imus couldn't get away with as much as *Family Guy* could.

Dubner did not know about all the trouble *Family Guy* has had. In fact, it must be one of the few television shows in history that has been canceled not just once, but twice. After its premiere in April 1999, the show ran until August 2000, but was besieged by so many complaints, some of them from MacFarlane's old high school headmaster, Rev. Richardson W. Schell, that Fox shelved it until July 2001 (Weinraub). Still afraid of causing a commotion, though, Fox had the cartoon censored and irregularly scheduled; as a result, its ratings fell so low that 2002 saw its second cancellation (Weinraub). But then it came back with a vengeance—I'll get into that later.

*Family Guy* has found trouble more recently, too. In 2007, comedian Carol Burnett sued Fox for 6 million dollars, claiming that the show's parody of the Charwoman, a character that she had created for *The Carol Burnett Show*, not only violated copyright but also besmirched the character's name in revenge for Burnett's refusal to grant permission to use her theme song ("Carol Burnett Sues"). The suit came after MacFarlane had made the Charwoman into a cleaning woman for a pornography store in one episode of *Family Guy*. Burnett lost, but U.S. district judge Dean Pregerson agreed that he could "fully appreciate how distasteful and offensive the segment [was] to Ms. Burnett" (qtd. in Grossberg).

I must admit, I can see how parts of the show might seem offensive if taken at face value. Look, for example, at the mock fifties instructional video that features in the episode "I Am Peter, Hear Me Roar."

> Represents a naysayer's objections fairly (Chapter 6)

[*The screen becomes black and white. Vapid music plays in the background. The screen reads* "WOMEN IN THE WORKPLACE CA. 1956," *then switches to a shot of an office with various women working on typewriters. A businessman speaks to the camera.*]

BUSINESSMAN: Irrational and emotionally fragile by nature, female coworkers are a peculiar animal. They are very insecure about their appearance. Be sure to tell them how good they look every day, even if they're homely and unkempt. [*He turns to an unattractive female typist.*] You're doing a great job, Muriel, and you're prettier than Mamie van Doren! [*She smiles. He grins at the camera, raising one eyebrow knowingly, and winks.*]

And remember, nothing says "Good job!" like a firm open-palm slap on the behind. [*He walks past a woman bent over a file cabinet and demonstrates enthusiastically. She smiles, looking flattered. He grins at the camera again as the music comes to an end.*]

Laughing at something so blatantly sexist could cause anyone a pang of guilt, and before I thought more about the show this seemed to be a huge problem. I agreed with Dubner, and I failed to see how anyone could laugh at such jokes without feeling at least slightly ashamed.

> Agrees, but with a difference (Chapter 4)

Soon, though, I found myself forced to give *Family Guy* a chance. It was simply everywhere: my brother and many of my friends watched it religiously, and its devoted fans relentlessly proselytized for it. In case you have any doubts about its immense popularity, consider these facts. On Facebook, the universal forum for my generation, there are currently 23 separate *Family Guy* fan groups with a combined membership of 1,669 people (compared with only 6 groups protesting against *Family Guy*, with 105 members total). Users of the well-respected Internet Movie Database rate the show 8.8 out of 10. The box-set DVDs were the best-selling television DVDs of 2003 in the United States (Moloney). Among the public and within the industry, the show receives fantastic acclaim; it has won eight awards, including three prime-time Emmys (IMDb). Most importantly, each time it was cancelled fans provided the brute force necessary to get it

> Anticipates a naysayer's skepticism (Chapter 6)

back on the air. In 2000, online campaigns did the trick; in 2002, devotees demonstrated outside Fox Studios, refused to watch the Fox network, and boycotted any companies that advertised on it (Moloney). Given the show's high profile, both with my friends and family and in the world at large, it would have been more work for me to avoid the Griffin family than to let myself sink into their animated world.

With more exposure, I found myself crafting a more positive view of *Family Guy*. Those who don't often watch the program, as Dubner admits he doesn't, could easily come to think that the cartoon takes pleasure in controversial humor just for its own sake. But those who pay more attention and think about the creators' intentions can see that *Family Guy* intelligently satirizes some aspects of American culture.

Some of this satire is actually quite obvious. Take, for instance, a quip Brian the dog makes about Stewie's literary choices in a fourth-season episode, "PTV." (Never mind that a dog and a baby can both read and hold lengthy conversations.)

> [*The Griffins are in their car. Brian turns to Stewie, who sits reading in his car seat.*]

> BRIAN: *East of Eden*? So you, you, you pretty much do whatever Oprah tells you to, huh?
> STEWIE: You know, this book's been around for fifty years. It's a classic.

---

Distinguishes between what others say and what she says (Chapter 5)

Mixes academic and colloquial styles (Chapter 9)

Uses a quotation sandwich to explicate this excerpt (Chapter 3)

BRIAN: But you just got it last week. And there's a giant Oprah sticker on the front.

STEWIE: Oh—oh—oh, is that what that is? Oh, lemme just peel that right off.

BRIAN: So, uh, what are you gonna read after that one?

STEWIE: Well, she hasn't told us yet—damn!

Brian and Stewie demonstrate insightfully and comically how Americans are willing to follow the instructions of a celebrity blindly—and less willing to admit that they are doing so.

The more off-color jokes, though, those that give *Family Guy* a bad name, attract a different kind of viewer. Such viewers are not "rats in a behaviorist's maze," as *Slate* writer Dana Stevens labels modern American television consumers in her article "Thinking Outside the Idiot Box." They are conscious and critical viewers, akin to the "screenagers" identified by Douglas Rushkoff in an essay entitled "Bart Simpson: Prince of Irreverence" (294). They are not—and this I cannot stress enough, self-serving as it may seem—immoral or easily manipulated people.

Rushkoff's piece analyzes the humor of *The Simpsons*, a show criticized for many of the same reasons as *Family Guy*. "The people I call 'screenagers,'" Rushkoff explains, "speak the media language better than their parents do and they see through clumsy attempts to program them into submission" (294). He claims that gaming technology has

> Distinguishes what others say from what she says (Chapter 5)

made my generation realize that television is programmed for us with certain intentions; since we can control characters in the virtual world, we are more aware that characters on TV are similarly controlled. "Sure, [these 'screenagers'] might sit back and watch a program now and again," Rushkoff explains, "but they do so voluntarily, and with full knowledge of their complicity. It is not an involuntary surrender" (294). In his opinion, our critical eyes and our unwillingness to be programmed by the programmers make for an entirely new relationship with the shows we watch. Thus we enjoy *The Simpsons'* parodies of mass media culture since we are skeptical of it ourselves.

Rushkoff's argument about *The Simpsons* actually applies to *Family Guy* as well, except in one dimension: Rushkoff writes that *The Simpsons'* creators do "not comment on social issues as much as they [do on] the media imagery around a particular social issue" (296). MacFarlane and company seem to do the reverse. Trusting in their viewers' ability to analyze what they are watching, the creators of *Family Guy* point out the weaknesses and defects of US society in a mocking and sometimes intolerant way.

Taken in this light, the "instructional video" quoted above becomes not only funny but also insightful. In its satire, viewers can recognize the sickly sweet and falsely sensitive sexism of the 1950s in observing just how conveniently

Uses transitions to connect the parts (Chapter 8)

self-serving the speaker of the video appears. The message of the clip denounces and ridicules sexism rather than condoning it. It is an excerpt that perfectly exemplifies the bald-faced candor of the show, from which it derives a lot of its appeal.

Making such comically outrageous remarks on the air also serves to expose certain prejudiced attitudes as outrageous themselves. Taking these comments at face value would be as foolish as taking Jonathan Swift's "Modest Proposal" seriously. Furthermore, while they put bigoted words into the mouths of their characters, the show's writers cannot be accused of portraying these characters positively. Peter Griffin, the "family guy" of the show's title, probably says and does the most offensive things of all—but as a lazy, overweight, and insensitive failure of a man, he is hardly presented as someone to admire. Nobody in his or her right mind would observe Peter's behavior and deem it worth emulation.

*Family Guy* has its own responses to accusations of crudity. In the episode "PTV," Peter sets up his own television station broadcasting from home and the Griffin family finds itself confronting the Federal Communications Commission directly (see Fig. 2 for a picture of the whole family). The episode makes many tongue-in-cheek jabs at the FCC, some of which are sung in a rousing musical number, but also sneaks in some of the creator's own

Fig 2. The Griffin family watches TV. (Everett Collection)

opinions. The plot comes to a climax when the FCC
begins to censor "real life" in the town of Quahog; officials
place black censor bars in front of newly showered Griffins
and blow foghorns whenever characters curse. MacFarlane
makes an important point: that no amount of television
censorship will ever change the harsh nature of reality—
and to censor reality is mere folly. Likewise, he puts explicit
arguments about censorship into lines spoken by his

characters, as when Brian says that "responsibility lies with the parents [and] there are plenty of things that are much worse for children than television."

It must be said too that not all of *Family Guy*'s humor could be construed as offensive. Some of its jokes are more tame and insightful, the kind you might expect from *The New Yorker*. The following light commentary on the usefulness of high school algebra from "When You Wish Upon a Weinstein" could hardly be accused of upsetting anyone—except, perhaps, a few high school math teachers.

[*Shot of Peter on the couch and his son Chris lying at his feet and doing homework.*]

CHRIS: Dad, can you help me with my math? [My teacher] says if I don't learn it, I won't be able to function in the real world.

[*Shot of Chris standing holding a map in a run-down gas station next to an attendant in overalls and a trucker cap reading "PUMP THIS." The attendant speaks with a Southern accent and gestures casually to show the different road configurations.*]

ATTENDANT: Okay, now what you gotta do is go down the road past the old Johnson place, and you're gonna find two roads, one parallel and one perpendicular. Now keep going until you come to a highway that bisects it at a 45-degree angle. [*Crosses his arms.*] Solve for *x*.

[*Shot of Chris lying on the ground next to the attendant in fetal position, sucking his thumb. His map lies abandoned near him.*]

In fact, *Family Guy* does not aim to hurt, and its creators take certain measures to keep it from hitting too hard. In an interview on *Access Hollywood*, Seth MacFarlane plainly states that there are certain jokes too upsetting to certain groups to go on the air. Similarly, to ensure that the easily misunderstood show doesn't fall into the hands of those too young to understand it, Fox will not license *Family Guy* rights to any products intended for children under the age of fourteen (Elliott).

However, this is not to say that MacFarlane's mission is corrective or noble. It is worth remembering that he wants only to amuse, a goal for which he was criticized by several of his professors at the Rhode Island School of Design (Weinraub). For this reason, his humor can be dangerous. On the one hand, I don't agree with George Will's reductive and generalized statement in his article "Reality Television: Oxymoron" that "entertainment seeking a mass audience is ratcheting up the violence, sexuality, and degradation, becoming increasingly coarse and trying to be . . . shocking in an unshockable society." I believe *Family Guy*

Uses transitions to connect the parts (Chapter 8)

Agrees and disagrees; makes concessions while standing her ground (Chapters 4 and 6) has its intelligent points, and some of its seemingly "coarse" scenes often have hidden merit. I must concede, though, that a few of the show's scenes seem to be doing just what Will claims; sometimes the creators do seem to cross—or, perhaps, eagerly race past—the line of indecency. In one such crude scene, an elderly dog slowly races a paraplegic and Peter, who has just been hit by a car, to get to a severed finger belonging to Peter himself ("Whistle While Your Wife Works"). Nor do I find it particularly funny when Stewie physically abuses Brian in a bloody fight over gambling money ("Patriot Games").

Thus, while *Family Guy* can provide a sort of relief by breaking down taboos, we must still wonder whether or not these taboos exist for a reason. An excess of offensive jokes, especially those that are often misconstrued, can seem to grant tacit permission to think offensively if it's done for comedy—and laughing at others' expense can be cruel, no matter how funny. Jokes all have their origins, and the funniest ones are those that hit home the hardest; if we listen to Freud, these are the ones that let our animalistic and aggressive impulses surface from the unconscious. The distinction between a shamelessly candid but insightful joke and a merely shameless joke is a slight but important one. While I love *Family Guy* as much as any fan, it's important not to lose sight of what's truly unfunny in real life—even as we appreciate what is hilarious in fiction.

> Concludes by showing who cares and why her argument matters (Chapter 7)

## Works Cited

"Carole Burnett Sues over *Family Guy* Parody." *CBC*, 16 Mar. 2007, www.cbc.ca/news/arts/carol-burnett-sues-over-family-guy-parody-1.693570. Accessed 14 July 2008.

Dubner, Stephen J. "Why Is *Family Guy* Okay When Imus Wasn't?" *Freakonomics Blog*, 3 Dec. 2007, freakonomics.com. Accessed 14 July 2008.

Elliott, Stuart. "Crude? So What? These Characters Still Find Work in Ads." *The New York Times*, 19 June 2008, nyti.ms/2bZWSAs. Accessed 14 July 2008.

Facebook search for *Family Guy* under "Groups." www.facebook.com. Accessed 14 July 2008.

Freud, Sigmund. *Jokes and Their Relation to the Unconscious.* 1905. Translated by James Strachey, W. W. Norton, 1989.

Grossberg, Josh. "Carole Burnett Can't Stop Stewie." *E! News*, Entertainment Television, 5 June 2007, www.eonline.com. Accessed 14 July 2008.

"I Am Peter, Hear Me Roar." *Family Guy*, season 2, episode 8, 20th Century Fox, 28 Mar. 2000. *Hulu*, www.hulu.com/watch/171050. Accessed 14 July 2008.

"Family Guy." *IMDb*, 1999–2016, www.imdb.com/title/tt0182576. Accessed 14 July 2008.

MacFarlane, Seth. Interview. *Access Hollywood,* NBC Universal, 8 May 2007. *YouTube*, www.youtube.com/watch?v=rKURWCicyQU. Accessed 14 July 2008.

Moloney, Ben Adam. "*Family Guy*." *BBC.com*, 30 Sept. 2004, www.bbc.com. Accessed 14 July 2008.

"Patriot Games." *Family Guy*, season 4, episode 20, 20th
    Century Fox, 29 Jan. 2006. *Hulu*, www.hulu.com/
    watch/171089. Accessed 22 July 2008.
"PVT." *Family Guy*, season 4, episode 14, 20th Century Fox,
    6 Nov. 2005. *Hulu*, www.hulu.com/watch/171083.
    Accessed 14 July 2008.
Rushkoff, Douglas. "Bart Simpson: Prince of Irreverence."
    *Leaving Springfield: The Simpsons and the Possibility of
    Oppositional Culture*, edited by John Alberti, Wayne
    State UP, 2004, pp. 292–301.
Stevens, Dana. "Thinking Outside the Idiot Box." *Slate*,
    25 Mar. 2005, www.slate.com/articles/news_and_
    politics/surfergirl/2005/04/thinkingoutside_the_
    idiot_box.html. Accessed 14 July 2008.
Weinraub, Bernard. "The Young Guy of 'Family Guy': A
    30-Year-Old's Cartoon Hit Makes an Unexpected
    Comeback." *The New York Times*, 7 July 2004,
    nyti.ms/1IEBiUA. Accessed 14 July 2008.
"When You Wish Upon a Weinstein." *Family Guy*, season 3,
    episode 22, 20th Century Fox, 9 Nov. 2003. *Hulu*,
    www.hulu.com/watch/171136. Accessed 22 July 2008.
"Whistle While Your Wife Works." *Family Guy*, season 5,
    episode 5, 20th Century Fox, 12 Nov. 2006. *Hulu*,
    www.hulu.com/watch/171160. Accessed 22 July 2008.
Will, George F. "Reality Television: Oxymoron." *The
    Washington Post*, 21 June 2001, p. A25.

# TWELVE

# "I TAKE YOUR POINT"

## *Entering Class Discussions*

---

HAVE YOU EVER been in a class discussion that feels less like a genuine meeting of the minds than like a series of discrete, disconnected monologues? You make a comment, say, that seems provocative to you, but the classmate who speaks after you makes no reference to what you said, instead going off in an entirely different direction. Then, the classmate who speaks next makes no reference either to you or to anyone else, making it seem as if everyone in the conversation is more interested in their own ideas than in actually conversing with anyone else.

We like to think that the principles this book advances can help improve class discussions, which increasingly include various forms of online communication. Particularly important for class discussion is the point that our own ideas become more cogent and powerful the more responsive we are to others, and the more we frame our claims not in isolation but as responses to what others before us have said. Ultimately, then, a good face-to-face classroom discussion (or online communication) doesn't just happen spontaneously. It requires the same sorts of disciplined moves and practices used in many writing situations, particularly that of identifying to what and to whom you are responding.

## FRAME YOUR COMMENTS AS A RESPONSE
## TO SOMETHING THAT HAS ALREADY BEEN SAID

The single most important thing you need to do when joining a class discussion is to link what you are about to say to something that has already been said.

▸ I really liked Aaron's point about <u>the two sides being closer than they seem</u>. I'd add that <u>both seem rather moderate</u>.

▸ I take your point, Nadia, that _____ . Still . . .

▸ Though Sheila and Ryan seem to be at odds about _____ , they may actually not be all that far apart.

In framing your comments this way, it is usually best to name both the person and the idea you're responding to. If you name the person alone ("I agree with Aaron because _____ "), it may not be clear to listeners what part of what Aaron said you are referring to. Conversely, if you only summarize what Aaron said without naming him, you'll probably leave your classmates wondering whose comments you're referring to.

But won't you sound stilted and deeply redundant in class if you try to restate the point your classmate just made? After all, in the case of the first template above, the entire class will have just heard Aaron's point about the two sides being closer than they seem. Why then would you need to restate it?

We agree that in oral situations, it does often sound artificial to restate what others just said precisely because they just said it. It would be awkward if, on being asked to pass the salt at lunch, one were to reply: "If I understand you correctly, you have asked me to pass the salt. Yes, I can, and here it is." But in oral discussions about complicated issues that are open to multiple interpretations, we usually do need to resummarize what others have said to make sure that everyone is on the same page. Since Aaron may have made several points when he spoke and may have been followed by other commentators, the class will probably need you to summarize which point of his you are referring to. And even if Aaron made only one point, restating that point is helpful, not only to remind the group what his point was (since some may have missed or forgotten it) but also to make sure that he, you, and others have interpreted his point in the same way.

## TO CHANGE THE SUBJECT,
## INDICATE EXPLICITLY THAT YOU ARE DOING SO

It is fine to try to change the conversation's direction. There's just one catch: you need to make clear to listeners that this is what you are doing. For example:

▸ So far we have been talking about <u>the characters in the film</u>. But isn't the real issue here <u>the cinematography</u>?

▸ I'd like to change the subject to one that hasn't yet been addressed.

You can try to change the subject without indicating that you are doing so. But you risk that your comment will come across as irrelevant rather than as a thoughtful contribution that moves the conversation forward.

## BE EVEN MORE EXPLICIT
## THAN YOU WOULD BE IN WRITING

Because listeners in an oral discussion can't go back and reread what you just said, they are more easily overloaded than are readers of a print text. For this reason, in a class discussion you will do well to take some extra steps to help listeners follow your train of thought. (1) When you make a comment, limit yourself to one point only, though you can elaborate on this point, fleshing it out with examples and evidence. If you feel you must make two points, either unite them under one larger umbrella point, or make one point first and save the other for later. Trying to bundle two or more claims into one comment can result in neither getting the attention it deserves. (2) Use metacommentary to highlight your key point so that listeners can readily grasp it.

▶ In other words, what I'm trying to get at here is _____.

▶ My point is this: _____.

▶ My point, though, is not _____, but _____.

▶ This distinction is important because _____.

# THIRTEEN

# DON'T MAKE THEM SCROLL UP

*Entering Online Conversations*

—◻—

THE INTERNET HAS TRANSFORMED COMMUNICATION in more
ways than we can count. With just a few taps on a keyboard, we
can be connected with what others have said not only throughout history, but right now, in the most remote places. Almost
instantaneously, communities can be created that are powerful
enough to change the world. In addition, virtually the moment
we voice an opinion online, we can get responses from supporters and critics alike, while any links we provide to sources
can connect readers to voices they might otherwise never have
known about, and to conversations they might never have been
able to join.

Because of this connectivity, the internet lends itself perfectly to the type of conversational writing at the core of this
book. Just the other day, we were on a discussion board in which
one of the participants wrote to another, let's call him X, in
a form that could have provided a template for this textbook:
"Fascinating point about _____, X. I'd never thought of it
that way before. I'd always thought that _____, but if you're
right, then that would explain why _____."

## IDENTIFY WHAT YOU'RE RESPONDING TO

Unfortunately, not all online writers make clear who or what prompted them to write. As a result, too many online exchanges end up being not true conversations but a series of statements without clear relationships to one another. All too often, it's hard to tell if the writer is building on what someone else has said, challenging it, or trying to change the discussion topic altogether. So although the digital world may connect us far more rapidly and with far more people than ever, it doesn't always encourage a genuine meeting of minds.

We've seen this type of confusion in the writing our own students submit to online discussions. Even students who use the "they say / I say" framework routinely and effectively in the essays they write often neglect to make those same moves online. While our students engage enthusiastically in online discussions, their posts are often all "I say" with little or no "they say." As a result, they end up talking past rather than to one another.

What is happening here, we suspect, is that the easy accessibility made possible by the internet makes slowing down and summarizing or even identifying what others say seem unnecessary. Why repeat the views you are responding to, writers seem to assume, when readers can easily find them by simply scrolling up or clicking on a link?

The problem with this way of thinking is that readers won't always take the time to track down the comments you're responding to, assuming they can figure out what those comments are to begin with. And even when readers do make the effort to find the comments you're responding to, they may not be sure what aspect or part of those comments you're referring to,

or how you interpret them. Ultimately, when you fail to identify your "they say," you leave readers guessing, like someone
listening to one side of a phone conversation trying to piece
together what's being said at the other end.

It is true, of course, that there are some situations online
where summarizing what you're responding to would indeed
be redundant. When, for instance, you're replying to a friend's
text asking, "Meet in front of the theater at 7?" a mere "OK"
suffices, whereas a more elaborate response—"With regard to
your suggestion that we meet in front of the theater at 7, my
answer is yes"—would be not only redundant but downright
bizarre. But in more complex academic conversations where
the ideas are challenging, many people are involved, and there
is therefore a greater chance of misunderstanding, you do need
to clarify whom or what you're responding to.

To see how hard it can be to make sense of a post that
fails to identify the "they say" it is responding to, consider the
following example from an online class discussion devoted to
Nicholas Carr's article "Is Google Making Us Stupid?"

> Blogs and social media allow us to reach many people all at
> once. The internet makes us more efficient.

When we first read this post, we could see that this writer was
making a claim about the efficiency of the internet, but we
weren't sure what the claim had to do with Carr or with any of
the other comments in the discussion. After all, the writer never
names Carr or anyone else in the conversation. Nor does she
use templates such as "Like Carr, I believe _____" or "What
X overlooks is _____" to indicate whether she's agreeing or
disagreeing with Carr or with one of her classmates. Indeed, we
couldn't tell if the writer had even read Carr or any of the other
posts, or if she was just expressing her own views on the topic.

We suspect, however, that in arguing that the internet is
making us more efficient, this writer was probably trying to
refute Carr's argument that the internet is, as Carr puts it in his
title, "making us stupid." Then again, she could also have been
criticizing someone who agreed with Carr—or, conversely, sid-
ing with someone else who disagreed with Carr.

It would have been better if she had used the "they say / I
say" framework taught in this book, opening not with her own
"I say," as she did, but with the "they say" that's motivated her
to respond, perhaps using one of the following templates:

▶ **X argues that _____ .**

▶ **Like X, Y would have us believe that _____ .**

▶ **In challenging X's argument that _____ , Y asserts
   that _____ .**

It would also have helped if, in her "I say," she had identified the "they say" she is addressing, using a template like one of these:

- But what X overlooks is that _____.

- What both X and Y fail to see is that _____.

- Z's point is well taken. Like him, I contend that _____ is not, as X insists, _____ but _____.

Here's one way this writer might have responded:

> Carr argues that Google is undermining our ability to think and read deeply. But far from making people "stupid," as Carr puts it in his title, the internet, in my view, is making people more efficient. What Carr ignores is how blogs and social media allow us to reach many people at once.

This version makes clear that the writer is not just making a claim out of the blue, but that she had a reason for making her claim: to take a position in a conversation or debate.

## TECHNOLOGY WON'T DO ALL THE WORK

But still, you might wonder, doesn't the internet enable writers to connect so directly with others that summarizing their claims is unnecessary? Granted, the internet does provide several unique ways of referring to what others are saying, like linking and embedding, that help us connect to what others are saying. But as the following examples show, these techniques don't mean that technology will do all the work for you.

## LINKING TO WHAT "THEY SAY"

One way the internet makes it especially easy to connect directly with others is by allowing us to insert a link to what others have said into our own text. Anything with a URL can be linked to—blog posts, magazine articles, *Facebook* posts, and so forth. Readers can then click on the words to which you've attached the link and be taken directly to that page, as we can see in the following comment in another online class discussion about how the internet affects our brains.

> In his essay "Is Google Making Us Stupid?" Nicholas Carr argues that the kind of skimming we do when we read online destroys deep reading and thinking. But I would argue the opposite: that all the complex information we're exposed to online actually makes us read and think more deeply.

By including a link to Carr's essay, this writer gives her readers direct access to Carr's arguments, allowing them to assess how well she has summarized and responded to what he wrote. But the reason the writer's post succeeds is that she introduces the link to Carr's essay, summarizes what she takes Carr to be saying, and gives her response to it.

Here are a few templates for framing a link:

▸ **As X mentions in this article, " _____ ."**

▸ **In making this comment, X warns that _____ .**

▸ **Economists often assume _____ ; however, new research by X suggests _____ .**

## JUXTAPOSING YOUR "THEY SAY"
## WITH YOUR "I SAY"

Another way that online forums enhance our ability to connect with others is by allowing readers to respond—not only to the original article or post but also to one another through what we might call juxtaposition. On many online forums, when you reply to someone else's comment, your response appears below the original comment and indented slightly, so that it is visually clear whom you're responding to. This means that, in many cases, your "they say" and "I say" are presented almost as a single conversational unit, as the following example from the online discussion of Carr's article illustrates:

Lee, 4/12/17, 3:02 PM

Carr argues that the internet has harmed us by making it hard for us to read without breaks to look at other things. That might be true, but overall I think it has improved our lives by giving us access to so many different viewpoints.

Cody, 4/12/17, 5:15 PM

Like Lee, I think the internet has improved our lives more than it's hurt them. I would add that it's enabled us to form and participate in political communities online that make people way more politically engaged.

*Twitter* also allows for this type of close proximity, by enabling you to embed someone else's tweet inside your own. For instance, consider the following tweet:

**Jade T. Moore** @JadeTMoore

@willwst I agree—access to books is a social justice issue.

**William West** @willwst

Every child has the right to access to a school library.

Cody's response in the discussion board and Jade's on *Twitter* are effective not only because the platforms connect Cody and Jade to their "they say" but also because they take the time to make those connections clear. Cody connects his comment to his "they say" by including the words "Like Lee" and restating Lee's view, while Jade does so by including West's *Twitter* handle, @willwst, and the words "I agree." Sure, the technology does some of the work, by making the comments being answered directly available for readers to see—no scrolling or searching involved. But it can't do it all. Imagine if Cody, for instance, had merely written, "We're able to form and participate in political communities online that make people way more politically engaged." Or if Jade hadn't included an "I agree" with her comment. As readers, we'd have been left scratching our heads, unable to tell what Cody's claim had to do with Lee's claim, or what Jade's claim had to do with William's, despite how close together these claims are on the screen.

Digital communication, then, does shrink the world, as is often said, allowing us to connect with others in ways we couldn't before. But technology doesn't relieve writers of the need to use the "they say / I say" framework. A central premise of this book is that this framework is a rhetorical move that transcends the differences between all types of writing. Whether you're writing online or off, if you want others to listen to what you say, you'd better pay attention to what they think, and start with what they say. However limited your space, whatever your format, and whatever the technology, you can always find a way to identify and summarize your "they say."

*Exercises*

1. Look back on some of your old posts on a social media site, a class discussion board, or some other website. How well did you let other readers know whom and what you were responding to and what your own position was? What kinds of moves did you make? Does that site have any conventions or special features that you used? Are there any features not available on that site that might have helped you connect your comment to other people's comments? Having read this chapter, try revising one of your posts to reflect the advice covered here.

2. Choose an online forum (*Facebook*, theysayiblog.com, etc.) and describe how you might apply the advice given here to that site. Are there any features or norms specific to that forum (e.g., embedding, linking, etc.) that would influence how you formulate your "they say"? Go to that site and evaluate how well people use these specific features to communicate their "they say." Is it easy to tell whom and what people are responding to? Why or why not? Can

you make your own contribution to the forum using the "they say / I say" format?

3. As a test case for thinking about the questions raised in this chapter, go to the blog that accompanies this book, theysayiblog.com. Examine some of the exchanges that appear there and evaluate the quality of the responses. For example, how well do the participants in these exchanges summarize one another's claims before making their own responses? How would you characterize any discussion? How well do people listen to each other? How do these online discussions compare with the face-to-face discussions you have in class? What advantages does each offer? Go to other blogs on topics that interest you and ask these same questions.

# FOURTEEN

# WHAT'S MOTIVATING THIS WRITER?

## Reading for the Conversation

—◻︎—

"WHAT IS THE AUTHOR'S ARGUMENT? What is he or she trying to say?" For many years, these were the first questions we would ask our classes in a discussion of an assigned reading. The discussion that resulted was often halting, as our students struggled to get a handle on the argument, but eventually, after some awkward silences, the class would come up with something we could all agree was an accurate summary of the author's main thesis. Even after we'd gotten over that hurdle, however, the discussion would often still seem forced, and would limp along as we all struggled with the question that naturally arose next: now that we had determined what the author was saying, what did we ourselves have to say?

For a long time we didn't worry much about these halting discussions, justifying them to ourselves as the predictable result of assigning difficult, challenging readings. Several years ago, however, as we started writing this book and began thinking about writing as the art of entering conversations, we latched on to the idea of leading with some different questions: "What other argument(s) is the writer responding to?" "Is the writer disagreeing or agreeing with something, and if so, what?" "What is motivating the writer's argument?" "Are there other ideas that you have encountered in this class or elsewhere that might be pertinent?" The results were often striking. The discussions that followed tended to be far livelier and to draw in a greater number of students. We were still asking students to look for the main argument, but we were now asking them to see that argument as a response to some other argument that provoked it, gave it a reason for being, and helped all of us see why we should care about it.

What had happened, we realized, was that by changing the opening question, we changed the way our students approached reading, and perhaps the way they thought about academic work in general. Instead of thinking of the argument of a text as an isolated entity, they now thought of that argument as one that responded to and provoked other arguments. Since they were now dealing not with *one* argument but at least *two* (the author's argument and the one[s] he or she was responding to), they now had alternative ways of seeing the topic at hand. This meant that, instead of just trying to understand the view presented by the author, they were more able to question that view intelligently and engage in the type of discussion and debate that is the hallmark of a college education. In our discussions, animated debates often arose between students who found the author's argument convincing and others who were more convinced by the view it was challenging. In the best of these debates, the binary positions would be questioned by other students, who suggested each was too simple, that both might be right or that a third alternative was possible. Still other students might object that the discussion thus far had missed the author's real point and suggest that we all go back to the text and pay closer attention to what it actually said.

We eventually realized that the move from reading for the author's argument in isolation to reading for how the author's argument is in conversation with the arguments of others helps readers become active, critical readers rather than passive recipients of knowledge. On some level, reading for the conversation is more rigorous and demanding than reading for what one author says. It asks that you determine not only what the author thinks, but how what the author thinks fits with what others think, and ultimately with what you yourself think. Yet on another level, reading this way is a lot simpler and more familiar than reading for the thesis alone, since it returns writing to the familiar, everyday act of communicating with other people about real issues.

## DECIPHERING THE CONVERSATION

We suggest, then, that when assigned a reading, you imagine the author not as sitting alone in an empty room hunched over a desk or staring at a screen, but as sitting in a crowded coffee shop talking to others who are making claims that he or she is engaging with. In other words, imagine the author as participating in an ongoing, multisided conversation in which everyone is trying to persuade others to agree or at least to take his or her position seriously.

The trick in reading for the conversation is to figure out *what views the author is responding to* and *what the author's own argument is*—or, to put it in the terms used in this book, to determine the "they say" and how the author responds to it. One of the challenges in reading for the "they say" and

"I say" can be figuring out which is which, since it may not be obvious when writers are summarizing others and when they are speaking for themselves. Readers need to be alert for any changes in voice that a writer might make, since instead of using explicit road-mapping phrases like "although many believe," authors may simply summarize the view that they want to engage with and indicate only subtly that it is not their own.

Consider again the opening to the selection by David Zinczenko on page 245.

> If ever there were a newspaper headline custom-made for Jay Leno's monologue, this was it. Kids taking on McDonald's this week, suing the company for making them fat. Isn't that like middle-aged men suing Porsche for making them get speeding tickets? Whatever happened to personal responsibility?
>
> I tend to sympathize with these portly fast-food patrons, though. Maybe that's because I used to be one of them.
>
> DAVID ZINCZENKO, "Don't Blame the Eater"

Whenever we teach this passage, some students inevitably assume that Zinczenko must be espousing the view expressed in his first paragraph: that suing McDonald's is ridiculous. When their reading is challenged by their classmates, these students point to the page and reply, "Look. It's right here on the page. This is what Zinczenko wrote. These are his exact words." The assumption these students are making is that if something appears on the page, the author must endorse it. In fact, however, we ventriloquize views that we don't believe in, and may in fact passionately disagree with, all the time. The central clues that Zinczenko disagrees with the view expressed in his opening paragraph come in the second

See Chapter 6 for more discussion of naysayers.

paragraph, when he finally offers a first-person declaration and uses a contrastive transition, "though," thereby resolving any questions about where he stands.

## WHEN THE "THEY SAY" IS UNSTATED

Another challenge can be identifying the "they say" when it is not explicitly identified. Whereas Zinczenko offers an up-front summary of the view he is responding to, other writers assume that their readers are so familiar with these views that they need not name or summarize them. In such cases, you the reader have to reconstruct the unstated "they say" that is motivating the text through a process of inference.

See, for instance, if you can reconstruct the position that Tamara Draut is challenging in the opening paragraph of her essay "The Growing College Gap."

> "The first in her family to graduate from college." How many times have we heard that phrase, or one like it, used to describe a successful American with a modest background? In today's United States, a four-year degree has become the all-but-official ticket to middle-class security. But if your parents don't have much money or higher education in their own right, the road to college—and beyond—looks increasingly treacherous. Despite a sharp increase in the proportion of high school graduates going on to some form of postsecondary education, socio-economic status continues to exert a powerful influence on college admission and completion; in fact, gaps in enrollment by class and race, after declining in the 1960s and 1970s, are once again as wide as they were thirty years ago, and getting wider, even as college has become far more crucial to lifetime fortunes.
>
> TAMARA DRAUT, "The Growing College Gap"

You might think that the "they say" here is embedded in the third sentence: they say (or we all think) that a four-year degree is "the all-but-official ticket to middle-class security," and you might assume that Draut will go on to disagree.

If you read the passage this way, however, you would be mistaken. Draut is not questioning whether a college degree has become the "ticket to middle-class security," but whether most Americans can obtain that ticket, whether college is within the financial reach of most American families. You may have been thrown off by the "but" following the statement that college has become a prerequisite for middle-class security. However, unlike the "though" in Zinczenko's opening, this "but" does not signal that Draut will be disagreeing with the view she has just summarized, a view that in fact she takes as a given. What Draut disagrees with is that this ticket to middle-class security is still readily available to the middle and working classes.

Were one to imagine Draut in a room talking with others with strong views on this topic, one would need to picture her challenging not those who think college is a ticket to financial security (something she agrees with and takes for granted), but those who think the doors of college are open to anyone willing to put forth the effort to walk through them. The view that Draut is challenging, then, is not summarized in her opening. Instead, she assumes that readers are already so familiar with this view that it need not be stated.

Draut's example suggests that in texts where the central "they say" is not immediately identified, you have to construct it yourself based on the clues the text provides. You have to start by locating the writer's thesis and then imagine some of the arguments that might be made against it. What would it look like to disagree with this view? In Draut's case, it is relatively easy to construct a counterargument: it is the familiar faith in the

American Dream of equal opportunity when it comes to access to college. Figuring out the counterargument not only reveals what motivated Draut as a writer but helps you respond to her essay as an active, critical reader. Constructing this counterargument can also help you recognize how Draut challenges your own views, questioning opinions that you previously took for granted.

## WHEN THE "THEY SAY" IS ABOUT SOMETHING "NOBODY HAS TALKED ABOUT"

Another challenge in reading for the conversation is that writers sometimes build their arguments by responding to a *lack* of discussion. These writers build their case not by playing off views that can be identified (like faith in the American Dream or the idea that we are responsible for our body weight), but by pointing to something others have overlooked. As the writing theorists John M. Swales and Christine B. Feak point out, one effective way to "create a research space" and "establish a niche" in the academic world is "by indicating a gap in . . . previous research." Much research in the sciences and humanities takes this "Nobody has noticed X" form.

In such cases, the writer may be responding to scientists, for example, who have overlooked an obscure plant that offers insights into global warming, or to literary critics who have been so busy focusing on the lead character in a play that they have overlooked something important about the minor characters.

## READING PARTICULARLY CHALLENGING TEXTS

Sometimes it is difficult to figure out the views that writers are responding to not because these writers do not identify those views but because their language and the concepts they are dealing with are particularly challenging. Consider, for instance, the first two sentences of *Gender Trouble: Feminism and the Subversion of Identity*, a book by the feminist philosopher and literary theorist Judith Butler, thought by many to be a particularly difficult academic writer.

> Contemporary feminist debates over the meaning of gender lead time and again to a certain sense of trouble, as if the indeterminacy of gender might eventually culminate in the failure of feminism. Perhaps trouble need not carry such a negative valence.
>
> JUDITH BUTLER, *Gender Trouble:*
> *Feminism and the Subversion of Identity*

There are many reasons readers may stumble over this relatively short passage, not the least of which is that Butler does not explicitly indicate where her own view begins and the view she is responding to ends. Unlike Zinczenko, Butler does not use the first-person "I" or a phrase such as "in my own view" to show that the position in the second sentence is her own. Nor does Butler offer a clear transition such as "but" or "however" at the start of the second sentence to indicate, as Zinczenko does with "though," that in the second sentence she is questioning the argument she has summarized in the first. And finally, like many academic writers, Butler uses abstract, challenging words that many readers may need to look up, like "contemporary" (occurring in the present), "indeterminacy" (the quality of being impossible to define or pin down), "culminate" (finally result in), and "negative valence" (a term borrowed from chemistry, roughly denoting "negative significance" or "meaning"). For all these reasons, we can imagine many readers feeling intimidated before they reach the third sentence of Butler's book.

But readers who break down this passage into its essential parts will find that it is actually a lucid piece of writing that conforms to the classic "they say / I say" pattern. Though it can be difficult to spot the clashing arguments in the two sentences, close analysis reveals that the first sentence offers a way of looking at a certain type of "trouble" in the realm of feminist politics that is being challenged in the second.

For more on translating, see Chapter 9. To understand difficult passages of this kind, you need to translate them into your own words—to build a bridge, in effect, between the passage's unfamiliar terms and ones more familiar to you. Building such a bridge should help you connect what you already know to what the author is saying—and will then help you move from reading to writing, providing you with some of the language you will need to summarize the text. One major challenge in translating the author's words into your own, however, is to stay true to what the author is actually saying, avoiding what we call "the closest cliché syndrome," in which one mistakes a commonplace idea for an author's more complex one (mistaking Butler's critique of the concept of "woman," for instance, for the common idea that women must have equal rights). The work of complex writ-For more on the closest cliché syndrome, see Chapter 2.ers like Butler, who frequently challenge conventional thinking, cannot always be collapsed into the types of ideas most of us are already familiar with. Therefore, when you translate, do not try to fit the ideas of such writers into your preexisting beliefs, but instead allow your own views to be challenged. In building a bridge to the writers you read, it is often necessary to meet those writers more than halfway.

So what, then, does Butler's opening say? Translating But-ler's words into terms that are easier to understand, we can see that the first sentence says that for many feminists today, "the indeterminacy of gender"—the inability to define the essence of sexual identity—spells the end of feminism; that for many feminists the inability to define "gender," presumably the building block of the feminist movement, means serious "trouble" for feminist politics. In contrast, the second sentence suggests that this same "trouble" need not be thought of in such "negative" terms, that the inability to define femininity, or "gender trouble" as Butler calls it in her book's title, may not be such a bad thing—and, as she goes on to argue in the pages that follow, may even be something that feminist activists can profit from. In other words, Butler suggests, highlighting uncertainties about masculinity and femininity can be a powerful feminist tool.

Pulling all these inferences together, then, the opening sentences can be translated as follows: "While many contemporary feminists believe that uncertainty about what it means to be a woman will undermine feminist politics, I, Judith Butler, believe that this uncertainty can actually help strengthen feminist politics." Translating Butler's point into our own book's basic move: "They say that if we cannot define 'woman,' feminism is in big trouble. But I say that this type of trouble is precisely what feminism needs." Despite its difficulty, then, we hope you agree that this initially intimidating passage does make sense if you stay with it.

We hope it is clear that critical reading is a two-way street. It is just as much about being open to the way that writers can challenge you, maybe even transform you, as it is about questioning those writers. And if you translate a writer's argument into your own words as you read, you should allow the text to take you outside the ideas that you already hold and to introduce you to new terms and concepts. Even if you end up disagreeing with an author, you first have to show that you have really listened to what he or she is saying, have fully grasped his or her arguments, and can accurately summarize those arguments. Without such deep, attentive listening, any critique you make will be superficial and decidedly *uncritical*. It will be a critique that says more about you than about the writer or idea you're supposedly responding to.

In this chapter we have tried to show that reading for the conversation means looking not just for the thesis of a text in isolation but for the view or views that motivate that thesis— the "they say." We have also tried to show that reading for the conversation means being alert for the different strategies writers use to engage the view(s) that are motivating them, since not all writers engage other perspectives in the same way. Some writers explicitly identify and summarize a view they are responding to at the outset of their text and then return to it frequently as their text unfolds. Some refer only obliquely to a view that is motivating them, assuming that readers will be able to reconstruct that view on their own. Other writers may not explicitly distinguish their own view from the views they are questioning in ways that all of us find clear, leaving some readers to wonder whether a given view is the writer's own or one that he or she is challenging. And some writers push off against the "they say" that is motivating them in a challenging academic language that requires readers to translate what they are saying into more accessible, everyday terms. In sum, then, though most persuasive writers do follow a conversational "they say / I say" pattern, they do so in a great variety of ways. What this means for readers is that they need to be armed with various strategies for detecting the conversations in what they read, even when those conversations are not self-evident.

# FIFTEEN

# "ON CLOSER EXAMINATION"

## *Entering Conversations about Literature*

———◻———

IN CHINUA ACHEBE'S NOVEL *Things Fall Apart*, Okonkwo, the main character, is a tragic hero.

So what? Who cares?

Why does this typical way of opening an essay on a literary work leave readers wondering, "Why are you telling me this?" Because, in our view, such statements leave it unclear who would say otherwise. Would anyone deny that the main character of Achebe's novel is a tragic hero? Is there some other view of the subject that this writer is responding to? Since no such alternative interpretation is indicated, the reader thinks, "OK, Okonkwo is a tragic hero—as opposed to what?"

Now compare this opening with another possible one:

> Several members of our class have argued that Okonkwo, the main character of *Things Fall Apart*, is a hateful villain. My own view, however, is that, while it is true that Okonkwo commits villainous acts, he is ultimately a tragic hero—a flawed but ultimately sympathetic figure.

We hope you agree that the second version, which responds to what someone else says about Okonkwo, makes for more engaging writing than the first. Since the first version fails to present itself as a response to any alternative view of its subject, it comes at readers out of the blue, leaving them wondering why it needs to be said at all.

As we stress in this book, it is the views of others and our desire to respond to these views that gives our writing its underlying motivation and helps readers see why what we say matters, why others should care, and why we need to say it in the first place. In this chapter we suggest that this same principle applies to writing about literature. Literary critics, after all, don't make assertions about literary works out of the blue. Rather, they contribute to discussions and debates about the meaning and significance of literary works, some of which may continue for years and even centuries.

Indeed, this commitment to discussion animates most literature courses, in which students discuss and debate assigned works in class before writing papers about them. The premise is that engaging with classmates and teachers enables us to make discoveries about the work that we might not arrive at in simply reading the work alone.

We suggest that you think of writing about literature as a natural extension of such in-class discussions, listening carefully to others and using what they say to set up and motivate what you have to say.

## START WITH WHAT OTHERS ARE SAYING

But in writing about literature, where do views to respond to— "they say"s—come from? Many sources. Published literary criticism is perhaps the most obvious:

- Critic X complains that Author Y's story is compromised by his _____ perspective. While there's some truth to this critique, I argue that Critic X overlooks _____ .

- According to Critic A, novel X suggests _____ . I agree, but would add that _____ .

But the view that you respond to in writing about literature can be far closer to home than published literary criticism. As our opening example illustrates, it can be something said about the literary work by a classmate or teacher:

- Several members of our class have suggested that the final message of play X is _____ . I agree up to a point, but I still think that _____ .

Another tactic is to start with something you yourself thought about the work that on second thought you now want to revise:

- On first reading play Z, I thought it was an uncritical celebration of _____ . After rereading the play and discussing it in class, however, I see that it is more critical of _____ than I originally thought.

You can even respond to something that hasn't actually been said about the work, but might hypothetically be said:

- It might be said that poem Y is chiefly about _____ . But the problem with this reading, in my view, is _____ .

- Though religious readers might be tempted to analyze poem X as a parable about _____ , a closer examination suggests that the poem is in fact _____ .

Sometimes, the "they say" that you respond to in writing about a literary work can be found in the work itself, as distinct from what some critic or other reader has said *about* the work. Much great literary criticism responds directly to the literary work, summarizing some aspect of the work's form or content and then assessing it, in much the same way you can do in response to a persuasive essay:

> ▸ Ultimately, as I read it, *The Scarlet Letter* seems to say _____. I have trouble accepting this proposition, however, on the grounds that _____.

One of the more powerful ways of responding to a literary work is to address any contradictions or inconsistencies:

> ▸ At the beginning of the poem, we encounter the generalization, seemingly introducing the poem's message, that "_____." But this statement is then contradicted by the suggestion made later in the poem that "_____." This opens up a significant inconsistency in the text: is it suggesting _____ or, on the contrary, _____?

> ▸ At several places in novel X, Author Y leads us to understand that the story's central point is that _____. Yet elsewhere the text suggests _____, indicating that Y may be ambivalent on this issue.

If you review the above templates, you'll notice that each does what a good discussion, lecture, or essay does: it makes an argument about some aspect of a work that can be interpreted in various ways. Instead of just making a claim about the work in isolation—character X is a tragic hero; sonnet Y is about the loss of a loved one—these templates put one claim as a response to another, making clear what motivated the argument to begin with. They thus act as conversation starters that can invite or even provoke other readers to respond with their own interpretations and judgments.

## FIGURING OUT
## WHAT A LITERARY WORK "MEANS"

In order to enter conversations and debates about literature, you need to meet the time-honored challenge of being able to read and make sense of literary works, understanding and analyzing what the text says. On the one hand, like the types of persuasive essays we focus on throughout this book, literary works make arguments their authors want to convey, things they are for and against, ideas they want to endorse or condemn. On the other hand, discovering "the argument" of a literary work—what it's "saying"—can be a special challenge because, unlike persuasive essays, literary works usually do not spell out their arguments explicitly. Though poets, novelists, and playwrights may have the same level of conviction as persuasive writers, rarely do they step out from behind the pages of their texts and say, "Okay, folks, this is what it all means. What I'm trying to say in a nutshell is _____." That is, since literary texts do not include an explicit thesis statement identifying their main point, it's left up to us as readers to figure it out.

Because literary works tend to avoid such explicitness, their meanings often need to be teased out from the clues they provide: from the dialogue between characters, the plot, the imagery and symbolism, and the kind of language the author uses. In fact, it is this absence of overt argument that makes literature so endlessly debatable—and explains why scholars and critics argue so much about what literary works mean in ways similar to the classroom discussions that you have likely participated in as a student.

## The Elusive Literary Author

Indeed, not even the use of the first person "I" in a literary work is an indication that you have located the author's own position or stance, as it usually is in an essay. When David Zinczenko, for example, in his essay "Don't Blame the Eater" (pp. 245–47) writes, "I tend to sympathize with these portly fast-food patrons" who file lawsuits against the fast food industry, we can be confident that the "I" is Zinczenko himself, and that the position he expresses is his own and informs everything else in his essay. But we cannot assume that the "I" who addresses us in a work of fiction or poetry is necessarily the author, for he or she is a fictional character—and one who may be unreliable and untrustworthy.

Take, for example, the first sentence of Edgar Allan Poe's short story "The Cask of Amontillado":

> The thousand injuries of Fortunato I had borne as I best could, but when he ventured upon insult I vowed revenge.

As soon becomes clear in the story, the "I" who speaks as the narrator here is not Poe himself but an insanely vengeful murderer whose words must be seen through to get at the point of Poe's story.

Instead of a readily identifiable position, literary works often present the perspectives of a number of different characters and leave it to readers to determine which if any speaks for the author. Thus when we encounter the seemingly eloquent lines in *Hamlet* "To thine own self be true, . . . / And canst thou not be false to any man," we can't assume, as we might if we encountered this statement in an essay, that it represents the author's own view. For these words are uttered by Polonius, a character whom Shakespeare presents as a tedious, cliché-spouting bore—not someone he leads us to trust. After all, part of Hamlet's problem is that it's not clear to him what being "true" to his own self would require him to do.

This elusive quality of literary texts helps explain why some of our students complain about the challenge of finding the "hidden meaning," as they sometimes call it, let alone summarizing that meaning in the way assignments often require. Sure, some students say, they enjoy reading literature for pleasure. But analyzing literature in school for its "meaning" or "symbolism"—that's another matter. Some even say that the requirement that they hunt for meanings and symbols robs literature of its fun.

In fact, as most students come to recognize, analyzing meanings, symbols, and other elements should enhance rather than stifle the pleasure we get from reading literature. But it can indeed be hard to figure out what literary works mean. How do we determine the point of a story or poem when the author, unlike an essayist like Zinczenko, does not tell us explicitly what he or she is trying to say? How do you go from a fictional event or poetic image (an insane man committing murder, two roads that diverge in the woods) or from a dialogue between fictional characters ("Frankly, my dear, I don't give a damn.") to what these events, images, or lines of dialogue mean?

## Look for Conflict *in* the Work

There is no simple recipe for figuring out what a literary work means, but one tactic that seems to help our own students is to look for the conflict or debate in the literary work itself and then ask what the text is leading us to think about that conflict. Asking these questions—what is the conflict in the work and which side, if any, should we favor?—will help you think about and formulate a position on what the work means. And since such claims are often ones that literary scholars argue about, thinking about the conflict *in* a literary work will often lead you to discussions and debates *about* the work that you can then respond to in your writing. Because literary authors don't tell us explicitly what the text means, it's always going to be *arguable*—and your task in writing about a literary work is to argue for what *you* think it means. Here are two templates to help get you started responding to other interpretations:

▸ **It might be argued that in the clash between characters X and Y in play Z, the author wants us to favor character Y, since she is presented as the play's heroine. I contend, however, that _____.**

▸ **Several critics seem to assume that poem X endorses the values of discipline and rationality represented by the image of _____ over those of play and emotion represented by the image of _____. I agree, but with the following caveat: that the poem ultimately sees both values as equally important and even suggests that ideally they should complement one another.**

This tactic of looking for the conflicts in literary works is part of a long tradition of critical thought that sees conflict as central to literature. In ancient Greece, Aristotle argued that conflict between characters or forces underlies the plots of tragic dramas such as *Oedipus*. Indeed, the ancient Greek word *agon*, which means antagonism, conflict, or debate, leaves its traces in the term "protagonist," the hero or leading character of a narrative work who comes into conflict with other characters or with the fates. And Plato noted the pervasiveness of conflict in literature when he banished poets from his ideal community on the grounds that their works depict endless conflict and division.

This emphasis on the centrality of conflict in literature has been echoed by modern theorists like the New Critics of the 1940s and 50s, who focused on such tensions and paradoxes as good and evil or innocence and experience—and more recently by poststructuralists and political theorists who see literature, like society, as saturated by such polarities as male/female, gay/straight, white/black, and so on. Writers today continue to recognize conflict as the engine of good storytelling. As the Hollywood screenwriter Robert McKee puts it, "Nothing moves forward in a story except through conflict."

Building on this idea that conflict is central to literature, we suggest the following four questions to help you understand and formulate your own position on any literary work:

1. What is the central conflict?
2. Which side—if any—does the text seem to favor?
3. What's your evidence? How might others interpret the evidence differently?
4. What's your opinion of the text?

## WHAT IS THE CENTRAL CONFLICT?

Conflicts tend to manifest themselves in different ways in different literary genres. In works that take a narrative or story form (novels, short stories, and plays), the central conflict will often be represented in an actual debate between characters. These debates between characters will often reflect larger questions and debates in the society or historical era in which they were written, over such issues as the responsibility of rulers, the consequences of capitalism and consumerism, or the struggle for gender equality. Sometimes these debates will be located within an individual character, appearing as a struggle in someone caught between conflicting or incompatible choices. Whatever form they may take, these debates can provide you with points of entry into the issues raised by the work, its historical context, and its author's vision of the world.

One narrative work that lends itself to such an approach is Flannery O'Connor's 1961 short story "Everything That Rises Must Converge," which is reprinted on pages 275–94. The story presents a running debate between a mother and her son Julian about the civil rights movement for racial equality that had erupted in the American South at the time the story was written, with Julian defending the outlook of this movement and his mother defending the South's traditional racial hierarchy. The story raises the debatable question of which character we should side with: Julian, his mother, both, or neither?

## WHICH SIDE—IF ANY—DOES THE TEXT SEEM TO FAVOR?

When we teach this story, most of our students first assume the story sides with Julian's outlook, which to them as Northern, urban college students in the twenty-first century seems the obviously enlightened position. Who, after all, could fail to see that the mother's views are backward and racist? As our class discussions unfold, however, most students come to reject this view as a misreading, one based more on their own views than on what's in the text. Sooner or later, someone points out that at several points Julian is presented in highly critical ways—and that his apparently progressive sympathy for racial integration rests on arid intellectual abstractions and a hypocritical lack of self-knowledge, in contrast with his mother's heartfelt loyalty to her roots. Eventually another possible interpretation surfaces, that both characters suffer from a common malady: that they're living in a mental bubble that keeps them from being able to see themselves as they really are.

The writing assignment we often give builds on this class discussion by offering students the following template for thinking about which character, if any, the text leads them to favor:

▸ **Some might argue that when it comes to the conflict between Julian and his mother over _____, our sympathies should lie with _____. My own view is that _____.**


## WHAT'S YOUR EVIDENCE?

In entering the types of discussions and debates modeled by the above template, how do you determine where your "sympathies should lie"? More generally, how do you arrive at and justify an interpretation of what a literary text says?

The answer lies in the *evidence* provided by the work: its images, dialogue, plot, historical references, tone, stylistic details, and so forth.

It is important to remember, however, that evidence is not set in stone. Students sometimes assume that there exists some fixed code that unlocks the meaning of literary works, symbols, images, and other evidence. A character dies? This must mean that he or she is being condemned. A stairway appears? A symbol for upward mobility. A garden? Must be something sexual.

But evidence itself is open to interpretation and thus to debate. The mother's death in O'Connor's story, for instance, *could* be seen as evidence that we are supposed to disapprove of her as someone whose racial views are regressive and on the way out. On the other hand, her death may instead be evidence that she is to be seen as a heroic martyr too good for this cruel, harsh world. What a character's death means, then, depends—on how he or she is treated in the work, positively or negatively, which in turn may be subject to debate.

As we've repeatedly emphasized in this book, others will often disagree with you and may even use the same evidence you do to support interpretations that are contrary to your own. Like other objects of study, literary works are like the famous ambiguous drawing that can be seen as either a duck or a rabbit, depending how one views it.

Since the same piece of evidence in a literary work will often support differing, even opposing interpretations, you need to argue for what you think the evidence shows—and to acknowledge that others may read that evidence differently.

In writing about literature, then, you need to show that the evidence you are citing supports your interpretation and to anticipate other alternative ones:

> ▸ **Although some might read the metaphor of _____ in this poem as evidence that, for Author X, modern technology undermines community traditions and values, I see it as _____.**

To present evidence in such a "they say / I say" way, you need to be alert for how others may read the work differently than you—and even use this very same evidence in support of an opposing interpretation:

> ▸ **Some might claim that evidence X suggests _____, but I argue that, on the contrary, it suggests _____.**

> ▸ **I agree with my classmate _____ that the image of _____ in novel Y is evidence of childhood innocence that has been lost. Unlike _____, however, I think this loss of innocence is to be read not as a tragic event but as a necessary, even helpful, stage in human development.**

### Are Some Interpretations Simply Wrong?

No matter how flexible and open to debate evidence might be, not all interpretations we arrive at using that evidence are equally valid. And some interpretations are simply unsupported by that evidence. Let us illustrate.

As we noted earlier, some of our students first favored Julian over his mother. One student, let us call her Nancy, cited as evidence a passage early in the story in which Julian is compared to Saint Sebastian, a Christian martyr who is said to have exhibited exceptional faith under extreme suffering and persecution. As the mother stood preparing for Julian to take her to her weekly swimming class, Julian is described as standing "pinned to the door frame, waiting like Saint Sebastian for the arrows to begin piercing him."

Thinking this passage proves that Julian is the more sympathetic character, Nancy pointed to other evidence as well, including the following passage:

> [Julian] was free of prejudice and unafraid to face facts. Most miraculous of all, instead of being blinded by love for [his mother] as she was for him, he had cut himself emotionally free of her and could see her with complete objectivity. He was not dominated by his mother. (412)

Citing passages like this in her essay, Nancy concluded: "Julian represents the future of society, a nonracist and an educated thinker."

After rereading the story, however, and hearing other students' views, Nancy came to realize that the passages she had cited—comparing Julian to a saint, suggesting that he is racially progressive, and that he is "free of" his mother and "objective" about her—were all intended ironically. Julian congratulates *himself* for being saintlike, free of prejudice, and objective, but the story ultimately implies that he deludes himself.

How did the supporters of the ironic reading convince Nancy to revise her initial reading—to see it as wrong, unsupported by the evidence? First, they pointed to the glaring discrepancy between the situations and kinds of suffering endured by Julian and Saint Sebastian. Could anyone be serious, they asked, in comparing something as mundane as being forced to wait a few minutes to go to the YMCA to a martyr dying for his faith? No, they answered, and the jarring incongruity of the events being compared, they argued, suggests that Julian, far from saintlike, is presented in this passage as an impatient, ungrateful, undutiful son. In addition, students pointed out that the gap between Julian's self-image as a progressive man of "complete objectivity" and "facts," "free of [his mother]" and the blubbering young man crying "Mama, Mama!" with "guilt and sorrow" at the end of the story suggests that Julian's righteous, high-minded image of himself is not to be taken at face value.

At this point you may be wondering, how can we say that some interpretations of literature must be ruled out as *wrong*? Isn't the great thing about interpreting literary works—in contrast to scientific and historical texts—that there are no wrong answers? Are we saying that there is one "correct" way to read a literary work—the one way the work itself tells us we "should" read it?

No, we aren't saying that there is only one way to read a literary work. If we believed there were, we would not be offering a method of literary analysis based on multiple interpretations and debate. But yes, acknowledging that literary interpretations are open to debate is not to say that a work can mean anything we want it to mean, as if all interpretations are equally good. In our view, and that of most literature teachers, some interpretations are better than others—more persuasively reasoned and better grounded in the evidence of the text.

If we maintain that all interpretations are equally valid, we risk confusing the perspective of the work's author with our own, as did the students who confused their own views on the civil rights movement of the 1960s with Flannery O'Connor's. Such misreadings are reminiscent of what we call "the closest cliché syndrome," where what's summarized is not the view the author actually expresses but a familiar cliché—or, in O'Connor's case,

See p. 33 for more on the closest cliché syndrome.

a certain social belief—that the writer believes and mistakenly assumes the author must too. The view that there are no wrong answers in literary interpretation encourages a kind of solipsism that erases the difference between us and others and transforms everything we encounter into a version of ourselves.

As the literary theorist Robert Scholes puts it, reading, conceived "as a submission to the intentions of another is the first step" to understanding what a literary work is saying. For "if we do not postulate the existence of [an author] behind the verbal text," we will "simply project our own subjective modes of thought and desire upon the text." In other words, unless we do the best we can to get at what the author is saying, we will never truly recognize his or her ideas except as some version of our own. Scholes acknowledges that good reading often involves going beyond the author's intention, pointing out contradictions and ideological blind spots, but he argues that we must recognize the author's intention *before* we can try to see beyond it in these ways.

## WHAT'S YOUR OPINION OF THE TEXT?

In accord with the principle that we must try to understand the text on its own terms before responding to it, we have thus far in this chapter focused on how to understand and unpack what literary texts say and do. Our approach to get at what they say involves looking for the central conflict in the work and then asking yourself how the author uses various types of evidence (characters, dialogue, imagery, events, plot, etc.) to guide you in thinking about that conflict. Ultimately, your job as a reader of literature is to be open to a work as its author presents it, or else your reading will fail to see what makes that work worth reading and thinking about.

But once you have reached a good understanding of the work, it is time to allow your own opinion to come into play. Offering your own interpretation of a work and opening that interpretation to response are crucial steps in any act of literary analysis, but they are not the end of the process. The final step involves offering your own insight into or critique of the work and its vision, assessing whether, as you see it, it is morally justified or questionable, unified or contradictory, historically regressive or progressive, and so forth. For example:

> Though she is one of the most respected Southern authors of the American literary canon, Flannery O'Connor continually deni-grates the one character in her 1961 story who represents the civil rights movement, and in so doing disparages progressive ideas that I believe deserve a far more sympathetic hearing.

Offering a critique, however, doesn't necessarily mean finding fault:

> Some criticize O'Connor's story by suggesting that it has a politi-cally regressive agenda. But I see the story as a laudable critique of politics as such. In my view, O'Connor's story rightly criticizes the polarization of political conflicts—North vs. South, liberal vs. conservative, and the like—and suggests that they need to come together: to "converge," as O'Connor's title implies, through reli-gious love, understanding, and forgiveness.

We realize that the prospect of critiquing a literary work can be daunting. Indeed, simply stating what you think an author is saying can be intimidating, since it means going out on a limb, asserting something about highly respected figures—works that are often complex, contradictory, and connected to larger historical movements. Nevertheless, if you can master these challenges, you may find that figuring out what a literary work is saying, offering an opinion about it, and entering into conversation and debate with others about such questions is what makes literature matter. And if you do it well, what *you* say will invite its own response: your "I say" will become someone else's "they say," and the conversation will go on and on.

# SIXTEEN

# "THE DATA SUGGEST"
## Writing in the Sciences

### CHRISTOPHER GILLEN

————▢————

CHARLES DARWIN DESCRIBED *On the Origin of Species* as "one long argument." In *Dialogue Concerning the Two Chief World Systems*, Galileo Galilei cast his argument for a sun-centered solar system as a series of conversations. As these historical examples show, scientific writing is fundamentally argumentative. Like all academic writers, scientists make and defend claims. They address disagreements and explore unanswered questions. They propose novel mechanisms and new theories. And they advance certain explanations and reject others. Though their vocabulary may be more technical and their emphasis more numerical, science writers use the same

————

CHRISTOPHER GILLEN is a professor of biology at Kenyon College and the faculty director of the Kenyon Institute in Biomedical and Scientific Writing. He teaches courses in animal physiology, biology of exercise, and introductory biology, all stressing the critical reading of primary research articles.

rhetorical moves as other academic writers. Consider the following example from a book about the laws of physics.

> The common refrain that is heard in elementary discussions of quantum mechanics is that a physical object is in some sense both a wave and a particle, with its wave nature apparent when you measure a wave property such as wavelength, and its particle nature apparent when you measure a particle property such as position. But this is, at best, misleading and, at worst, wrong.
>
> <div align="right">V. J. Stenger, <i>The Comprehensible Cosmos</i></div>

The "they say / I say" structure of this passage is unmistakable: they say that objects have properties of both waves and particles; I say they are wrong. This example is not a lonely argumentative passage cherry-picked from an otherwise non-argumentative text. Rather, Stenger's entire book makes the argument that is foreshadowed by its title, *The Comprehensible Cosmos*: that although some might see the universe as hopelessly complex, it is essentially understandable.

Here's another argumentative passage, this one from a research article about the role of lactic acid in muscle fatigue:

> In contrast to the often suggested role for acidosis as a cause of muscle fatigue, it is shown that in muscles where force was depressed by high $[K^+]_o$, acidification by lactic acid produced a pronounced recovery of force.
>
> <div align="right">O. B. Nielsen, F. de Paoli, and K. Overgaard,<br>"Protective Effects of Lactic Acid on Force Production in<br>Rat Skeletal Muscle," <i>The Journal of Physiology</i></div>

In other words: many scientists think that lactic acid causes muscle fatigue, but our evidence shows that it actually promotes recovery. Notice that the authors frame their claim with a version of the "they say / I say" formula: although previous work suggests _____, our data argue _____. This basic move and its many variations are widespread in scientific writing. The essential argumentative moves taught in this book transcend disciplines, and the sciences are no exception. The examples in this chapter were written by professional scientists, but they show moves that are appropriate in any writing that addresses scientific issues.

Despite the importance of argument in scientific writing, newcomers to the genre often see it solely as a means for communicating uncontroversial, objective facts. It's easy to see how this view arises. The objective tone of scientific writing can obscure its argumentative nature, and many textbooks reinforce a nonargumentative vision of science when they focus on accepted conclusions and ignore ongoing controversies. And because science writers base their arguments on empirical data, a good portion of many scientific texts *does* serve the purpose of delivering uncontested facts.

However, scientific writing often does more than just report facts. Data are crucial to scientific argumentation, but they are by no means the end of the story. Given important new data, scientists assess their quality, draw conclusions from them, and ponder their implications. They synthesize the new data with existing information, propose novel theories, and design the next experiments. In short, scientific progress depends on the insight and creativity that scientists bring to their data. The thrill of doing science, and writing about it, comes from the ongoing struggle to use data to better understand our world.

## START WITH THE DATA

Data are the fundamental currency of scientific argument. Scientists develop hypotheses from existing data and then test those by comparing their predictions to new experimental data. Summarizing data is therefore a basic move in science writing. Because data can often be interpreted in different ways, describing the data opens the door to critical analysis, creating opportunities to critique previous interpretations and develop new ones.

Describing data requires more than simply reporting numbers and conclusions. Rather than jumping straight to the punch line—to what X concluded—it is important first to describe the hypotheses, methods, and results that led to the conclusion: "To test the hypothesis that _____, X measured _____ and found that _____. Therefore, X concluded _____." In the following sections, we explore the three key rhetorical moves for describing the data that underpin a scientific argument: presenting the prevailing theories, explaining methodologies, and summarizing findings.

## Present the Prevailing Theories

Readers must understand the prevailing theories that a study responds to before they can fully appreciate the details. So before diving into specifics, place the work in context by describing the prevailing theories and hypotheses. In the following passage from a journal article about insect respiration, the authors discuss an explanation for discontinuous gas exchange (DGC), a phenomenon where insects periodically close valves on their breathing tubes.

See how a computer scientist describes a prevailing theory on p. 258.

Lighton (1996, 1998; see also Lighton and Berrigan, 1995) noted the prevalence of DGC in fossorial insects, which inhabit microclimates where $CO_2$ levels may be relatively high. Consequently, Lighton proposed the chthonic hypothesis, which suggests that

DGC originated as a mechanism to improve gas exchange while at the same time minimizing respiratory water loss.

> A. G. GIBBS AND R. A. JOHNSON, "The Role of Discontinuous Gas Exchange in Insects: The Chthonic Hypothesis Does Not Hold Water," *The Journal of Experimental Biology*

Notice that Gibbs and Johnson not only describe Lighton's hypothesis but also recap the evidence that supports it. By presenting this evidence, Gibbs and Johnson set the stage for engaging with Lighton's ideas. For example, they might question the chthonic hypothesis by pointing out shortcomings of the data or flaws in its interpretation. Or they might suggest new approaches that could verify the hypothesis. The point is that by incorporating a discussion of experimental findings into their summary of Lighton's hypothesis, Gibbs and Johnson open the door to a conversation with Lighton.

Here are some templates for presenting the data that underpin prevailing explanations:

▸ **Experiments showing _____ and _____ have led scientists to propose _____ .**

▸ **Although most scientists attribute _____ to _____ , X's result _____ leads to the possibility that _____ .**

## Explain the Methods

Even as we've argued that scientific arguments hinge on data, it's important to note that the quality of data varies depending on how they were collected. Data obtained with sloppy techniques or poorly designed experiments could lead to faulty conclusions. Therefore, it's crucial to explain the methods used to collect data. In order for readers to evaluate a method, you'll need to indicate its purpose, as the following passage from a journal article about the evolution of bird digestive systems demonstrates:

> To test the hypothesis that flowerpiercers have converged with hummingbirds in digestive traits, we compared the activity of intestinal enzymes and the gut nominal area of cinnamon-bellied flowerpiercers (*Diglossa baritula*) with those of eleven hummingbird species.
>
> J. E. SCHONDUBE AND C. MARTINEZ DEL RIO,
> "Sugar and Protein Digestion in Flowerpiercers and
> Hummingbirds: A Comparative Test of Adaptive Convergence,"
> *Journal of Comparative Physiology*

You need to indicate purpose whether describing your own work or that of others. Here are a couple of templates for doing so:

▸ **Smith and colleagues evaluated _____ to determine whether _____.**

▸ **Because _____ does not account for _____, we instead used _____.**

## Summarize the Findings

Scientific data often come in the form of numbers. Your task when presenting numerical data is to provide the context readers need to understand the numbers—by giving supporting information and making comparisons. In the following passage from a book about the interaction between organisms and their environments, Turner uses numerical data to support an argument about the role of the sun's energy on Earth.

> The potential rate of energy transfer from the Sun to Earth is prodigious—about 600 W m$^{-2}$, averaged throughout the year. Of this, only a relatively small fraction, on the order of 1–2 percent,

is captured by green plants. The rest, if it is not reflected back into space, is available to do other things. The excess can be considerable: although some natural surfaces reflect as much as 95% of the incoming solar beam, many natural surfaces reflect much less (Table 3.2), on average about 15–20 percent. The remaining absorbed energy is then capable of doing work, like heating up surfaces, moving water and air masses around to drive weather and climate, evaporating water, and so forth.

J. S. TURNER, *The Extended Organism*

Turner supports his point that a huge amount of the sun's energy is directly converted to work on Earth by quoting an actual value (600) with units of measurement (W m$^{-2}$, watts per square meter). Readers need the units to evaluate the value; 600 watts per square inch is very different from 600 W m$^{-2}$. Turner then makes comparisons using percent values, saying that only 1 to 2 percent of the total energy that reaches Earth is trapped by plants. Finally, Turner describes the data's variability by reporting comparisons as ranges—1 to 2 percent and 15 to 20 percent—rather than single values.

Supporting information—such as units of measurement, sample size ($n$), and amount of variability—helps readers assess the data. In general, the reliability of data improves as its sample size increases and its variability decreases. Supporting information can be concisely presented as:

▸ _____ ± _____ *(mean ± variability)* _____ *(units)*, *n* = _____ *(sample size)*.

For example: before training, resting heart rate of the subjects was 56 ± 7 beats per minute, $n = 12$. Here's another way to give supporting information:

▸ We measured _____ (*sample size*) subjects, and the average response was _____ (*mean with units*) with a range of _____ (*lower value*) to _____ (*upper value*).

To help readers understand the data, make comparisons with values from the same study or from other similar work.

Here are some templates for making comparisons:

▸ Before training, average running speed was _____ ± _____ kilometers per hour, _____ kilometers per hour slower than running speed after training.

▸ We found athletes' heart rates to be _____ ± _____ % lower than nonathletes'.

▸ The subjects in X's study completed the maze in _____ ± _____ seconds, _____ seconds slower than those in Y's study.

You will sometimes need to present qualitative data, such as that found in some images and photographs, that cannot be reduced to numbers. Qualitative data must be described precisely with words. In the passage below from a review article about connections between cellular protein localization and cell growth, the author describes the exact locations of three proteins: Scrib, Dlg, and Lgl.

> Epithelial cells accumulate different proteins on their apical (top) and basolateral (bottom) surfaces. . . . Scrib and Dlg are localized at the septate junctions along the lateral cell surface, whereas Lgl coats vesicles that are found both in the cytoplasm and "docked" at the lateral surface of the cell.
>
> M. Peifer, "Travel Bulletin—Traffic Jams
> Cause Tumors," *Science*

## EXPLAIN WHAT THE DATA MEAN

Once you summarize experiments and results, you need to say what the data mean. Consider the following passage from a study in which scientists fertilized plots of tropical rainforest with nitrogen (N) and / or phosphorus (P).

> Although our data suggest that the mechanisms driving the observed respiratory responses to increased N and P may be different, the large $CO_2$ losses stimulated by N and P fertilization suggest that knowledge of such patterns and their effects on soil $CO_2$ efflux is critical for understanding the role of tropical forests in a rapidly changing global C [carbon] cycle.
>
> C. C. CLEVELAND AND A. R. TOWNSEND, "Nutrient Additions to a Tropical Rain Forest Drive Substantial Soil Carbon Dioxide Losses to the Atmosphere," *Proceedings of the National Academy of Sciences*

Notice that in discussing the implications of their data, Cleveland and Townsend use language—including the verbs "suggest" and "may be"—that denotes their level of confidence in what they say about the data.

Whether you are summarizing what others say about their data or offering your own interpretation, pay attention to the verbs that connect data to interpretations.

To signify a moderate level of confidence:

▶ **The data *suggest / hint / imply* _____ .**

To express a greater degree of certainty:

▶ **Our results *show / demonstrate* _____ .**

Almost never will you use the verb "prove" in reference to a single study, because even very powerful evidence generally falls short of proof unless other studies support the same conclusion.

Scientific consensus arises when multiple studies point toward the same conclusion; conversely, contradictions among studies often signal research questions that need further work. For these reasons, you may need to compare one study's findings to those of another study. Here, too, you'll need to choose your verbs carefully.

▸ Our data *support / confirm / verify* the work of X by showing that _____ .

▸ By demonstrating _____ , X's work *extends* the findings of Y.

▸ The results of X *contradict / refute* Y's conclusion that _____ .

▸ X's findings *call into question* the widely accepted theory that _____ .

▸ Our data *are consistent with* X's hypothesis that _____ .

## MAKE YOUR OWN ARGUMENTS

Now we turn toward the part of scientific writing where you express your own opinions. One challenge is that the statements of other scientists about their methods and results usually must be accepted. You probably can't argue, for example, that "X and Y claim to have studied six elephants, but I think they actually only studied four." However, it might be fair to say, "X and Y studied only six elephants, and this small sample size casts doubts on their conclusions." The second statement doesn't question what the scientists did or found but instead examines how the findings are interpreted.

When developing your own arguments—the "I say"—you will often start by assessing the interpretations of other scientists. Consider the following example from a review article about the beneficial acclimation hypothesis (BAH), the idea that organisms exposed to a particular environment become better suited to that environment than unexposed animals.

> To the surprise of most physiologists, all empirical examinations of the BAH have rejected its generality. However, we suggest that these examinations are neither direct nor complete tests of the functional benefit of acclimation.
>
> R. S. WILSON AND C. E. FRANKLIN, "Testing the Beneficial Acclimation Hypothesis," *Trends in Ecology & Evolution*

Wilson and Franklin use a version of the "twist it" move: they acknowledge the data collected by other physiologists but question how those data have been interpreted, creating an opportunity to offer their own interpretation.

For more on the "twist it" move, see p. 58.

You might ask whether we should question how other scientists interpret their own work. Having conducted a study, aren't they in the best position to evaluate it? Perhaps, but as the above example demonstrates, other scientists might see the work from a different perspective or through more objective eyes. And in fact the culture of science depends on vigorous debate in which scientists defend their own findings and challenge those of others—a give and take that helps improve science's reliability. So expressing a critical view about someone else's work is an integral part of the scientific process. Let's examine some of the basic moves for entering scientific conversations: agreeing, with a difference; disagreeing and explaining why; simultaneously agreeing and disagreeing; anticipating objections; and saying why it matters.

## Agree, But with a Difference

Scientific research passes through several levels of critical analysis before being published. Scientists get feedback when they discuss work with colleagues, present findings at conferences, and receive reviews of their manuscripts. So the juiciest debates may have been resolved before publication, and you may find little to disagree with in the published literature of a research field. Yet even if you agree with what you've read, there are still ways to join the conversation—and reasons to do so.

One approach is to suggest that further work should be done:

▸ **Now that _____ has been established, scientists will likely turn their attention toward _____ .**

▸ **X's work leads to the question of _____ . Therefore, we investigated _____ .**

▸ **To see whether these findings apply to _____ , we propose to _____ .**

Another way to agree and at the same time jump into the conversation is to concur with a finding and then propose a mechanism that explains it. In the following sentence from a review article about dietary deficiencies, the author agrees with a previous finding and offers a probable explanation.

> Inadequate dietary intakes of vitamins and minerals are widespread, most likely due to excessive consumption of energy-rich, micronutrient-poor, refined food.
>
> B. AMES, "Low Micronutrient Intake
> May Accelerate the Degenerative Diseases of Aging through
> Allocation of Scarce Micronutrients by Triage,"
> *Proceedings of the National Academy of Sciences*

Here are some templates for explaining an experimental result.

▸ **One explanation for X's finding of _____ is that _____ . An alternative explanation is _____ .**

▸ **The difference between _____ and _____ is probably due to _____ .**

## Disagree—and Explain Why

Although scientific consensus is common, healthy disagreement is not unusual. While measurements conducted by different teams of scientists under the same conditions should produce the same result, scientists often disagree about which techniques are most appropriate, how well an experimental design tests a hypothesis, and how results should be interpreted. To illustrate such disagreement, let's return to the debate about whether or not lactic acid is beneficial during exercise. In the following passage, Lamb and Stephenson are responding to work by Kristensen and colleagues, which argues that lactic acid might be beneficial to resting muscle but not to active muscle.

The argument put forward by Kristensen and colleagues (12) . . . is not valid because it is based on observations made with isolated whole soleus muscles that were stimulated at such a high rate that >60% of the preparation would have rapidly become completely anoxic (4). . . . Furthermore, there is no reason to expect that adding more H+ to that already being generated by the muscle activity should in any way be advantageous. It is a bit like opening up the carburetor on a car to let in too much air or throwing gasoline over the engine and then concluding that air and gasoline are deleterious to engine performance.

G. D. LAMB AND D. G. STEPHENSON,
"Point: Lactic Acid Accumulation Is an Advantage during
Muscle Activity," *Journal of Applied Physiology*

Lamb and Stephenson bring experimental detail to bear on their disagreement with Kristensen and colleagues. First, they criticize methodology, arguing that the high muscle stimulation rate used by Kristensen and colleagues created very low oxygen levels (anoxia). They also criticize the logic of the experimental design, arguing that adding more acid (H+) to a muscle that is already producing it isn't informative. It's also worth noting how they drive home their point, likening Kristensen and colleagues' methodology to flooding an engine with air or gasoline. Even in technical scientific writing, you don't need to set aside your own voice completely.

In considering the work of others, look for instances where the experimental design and methodology fail to adequately test a hypothesis.

▸ **The work of Y and Z appears to show that _____ , but their experimental design does not control for _____ .**

Also, consider the possibility that results do not lead to the stated conclusions.

▸ **While X and Y claim that _____ , their finding of _____ actually shows that _____ .**

## Okay, But . . .

Science tends to progress incrementally. New work may refine or extend previous work but doesn't often completely overturn it. For this reason, science writers frequently agree up to a point and then express some disagreement. In the following example from a commentary about methods for assessing how proteins interact, the authors acknowledge the value of the two-hybrid studies, but they also point out their shortcomings.

> The two-hybrid studies that produced the protein interaction map for *D. melanogaster* (12) provide a valuable genome-wide view of protein interactions but have a number of shortcomings (13). Even if the protein-protein interactions were determined with high accuracy, the resulting network would still require careful interpretation to extract its underlying biological meaning. Specifically, the map is a representation of all possible interactions, but one would only expect some fraction to be operating at any given time.
>
> J. J. Rice, A. Kershenbaum, and G. Stolovitzky,
> "Lasting Impressions: Motifs in Protein-Protein Maps
> May Provide Footprints of Evolutionary Events."
> *Proceedings of the National Academy of Sciences*

Delineating the boundaries or limitations of a study is a good way to agree up to a point. Here are templates for doing so.

- ▸ **While X's work clearly demonstrates _____, _____ will be required before we can determine whether _____.**

- ▸ **Although Y and Z present firm evidence for _____, their data cannot be used to argue that _____.**

- ▸ **In summary, our studies show that _____, but the issue of _____ remains unresolved.**

## Anticipate Objections

Skepticism is a key ingredient in the scientific process. Before an explanation is accepted, scientists demand convincing evidence and assess whether alternative explanations have been thoroughly explored, so it's essential that scientists consider possible objections to their ideas before presenting them. In the following example from a book about the origin of the universe, Tyson and Goldsmith first admit that some might doubt the existence of the poorly understood "dark matter" that physicists have proposed, and then they go on to respond to the skeptics.

> Unrelenting skeptics might compare the dark matter of today with the hypothetical, now defunct "ether," proposed centuries ago as the weightless, transparent medium through which light moved. . . . But dark matter ignorance differs fundamentally from ether ignorance. While ether amounted to a placeholder for our incomplete understanding, the existence of dark matter derives not from mere presumption but from the observed effects of its gravity on visible matter.
>
> N. D. Tyson and D. Goldsmith,
> *Origins: Fourteen Billion Years of Cosmic Evolution*

Anticipating objections in your own writing will help you clarify and address potential criticisms. Consider objections to your overall approach, as well as to specific aspects of your interpretations. Here are some templates for doing so.

▸ **Scientists who take a _____ (*reductionist / integrative / biochemical / computational / statistical*) approach might view our results differently.**

▸ This interpretation of the data might be criticized by X, who has argued that _____.

▸ Some may argue that this experimental design fails to account for _____.

## Say Why It Matters

Though individual studies can be narrowly focused, science ultimately seeks to answer big questions and produce useful technologies. So it's essential when you enter a scientific conversation to say why the work—and your arguments about it—matter. The following passage from a commentary on a research article notes two implications of work that evaluated the shape of electron orbitals.

> The classic textbook shape of electron orbitals has now been directly observed. As well as confirming the established theory, this work may be a first step to understanding high-temperature superconductivity.
>
> C. J. HUMPHREYS, "Electrons Seen in Orbit," *Nature*

Humphreys argues that the study confirms an established theory and that it may lead to better understanding in another area. When thinking about the broad significance of a study, consider both the practical applications and the impact on future scientific work.

▸ These results open the door to studies that _____.

▸ The methodologies developed by X will be useful for _____.

▸ Our findings are the first step toward _____.

▸ Further work in this area may lead to the development of
_____ .

## READING AS A WAY OF ENTERING SCIENTIFIC CONVERSATIONS

In science, as in other disciplines, you'll often start with work done by others, and therefore you will need to critically evaluate their work. To that end, you'll need to probe how well their data support their interpretations. Doing so will lead you toward your own interpretations—your ticket into an ongoing scientific conversation. Here are some questions that will help you read and respond to scientific research.

How well do the methods test the hypothesis?

- Is the sample size adequate?

- Is the experimental design valid? Were the proper controls performed?

- What are the limitations of the methodology?

- Are other techniques available?

How fairly have the results been interpreted?

- How well do the results support the stated conclusion?

- Has the data's variability been adequately considered?

- Do other findings verify (or contradict) the conclusion?

- What other experiments could test the conclusion?

What are the broader implications of the work, and why does it matter?

- Can the results be generalized beyond the system that was studied?

- What are the work's practical implications?

- What questions arise from the work?

- Which experiments should be done next?

The examples in this chapter show that scientists do more than simply collect facts; they also interpret those facts and make arguments about their meaning. On the frontiers of science, where we are probing questions that are just beyond our capacity to answer, the data are inevitably incomplete and controversy is to be expected. Writing about science presents the opportunity to add your own arguments to the ongoing discussion.

# SEVENTEEN

# "ANALYZE THIS"

## Writing in the Social Sciences

### ERIN ACKERMAN

SOCIAL SCIENCE is the study of people—how they behave and relate to one another, and the organizations and institutions that facilitate these interactions. People are complicated, so any study of human behavior is at best partial, taking into account some elements of what people do and why, but not always explaining those actions definitively. As a result, it is the subject of constant conversation and argument.

Consider some of the topics studied in the social sciences: minimum wage laws, immigration policy, health care, what causes aggressive behavior, employment discrimination. Got an opinion on any of these topics? You aren't alone. But in the writing you do as a student of the social sciences, you need to write about more

ERIN ACKERMAN is the Social Sciences Librarian at The College of New Jersey and formerly taught political science at John Jay College, City University of New York. Her research and teaching interests include American law and politics, women and law, and information literacy in the social sciences.

than just your opinions. Good writing in the social sciences, as in other academic disciplines, requires that you demonstrate that you have examined what you think and why. The best way to do that is to bring your views into conversation with those expressed by others and to test what you and others think against a review of evidence. In other words, you'll need to start with what others say and then present what you say as a response.

Consider the following example from an op-ed in the *New York Times* by two psychology professors:

> Is video game addiction a real thing?
>
> It's certainly common to hear parents complain that their children are "addicted" to video games. Some researchers even claim that these games are comparable to illegal drugs in terms of their influence on the brain—that they are "digital heroin" (the neuroscientist Peter C. Whybrow) or "digital pharmakeia" (the neuroscientist Andrew Doan). The American Psychiatric Association has identified internet gaming disorder as a possible psychiatric illness, and the World Health Organization has proposed including "gaming disorder" in its catalog of mental diseases, along with drug and alcohol addiction.
>
> This is all terribly misguided. Playing video games is not addictive in any meaningful sense. It is normal behavior that, while perhaps in many cases a waste of time, is not damaging or disruptive of lives in the way drug or alcohol use can be.
>
> CHRISTOPHER J. FERGUSON AND PATRICK MARKEY,
> "Video Games Aren't Addictive"

In other words, "they" (parents, other researchers, health organizations) say that the video games are addictive, whereas Ferguson and Markey disagree. In the rest of the op-ed, they argue that video game critics have misinterpreted the evidence and are not being very precise with what counts as "addiction."

This chapter explores some of the basic moves social science writers make. Writing in the social sciences often takes the form of a research paper that generally includes several core components: a strong introduction and thesis, a literature review, and the writer's own analysis, including presentation of evidence/data and consideration of implications. The introduction sets out the thesis, or point, of the paper, briefly explaining the topic or question you are investigating and previewing what you will say in your paper and how it fits into the preexisting conversation. The literature review summarizes what has already been said on your topic. Your analysis allows you to present evidence (the information, or data, about human behavior that you are measuring or testing against what other people have said), to explain the conclusions you have drawn based on your investigation, and to discuss the implications of your research. Do you agree, disagree, or some combination of both with what has been said by others? What reasons can you give for why you feel that way? And so what? Who should be interested in what you have to say, and why?

You may get other types of writing assignments in the social sciences, such as preparing a policy memo, writing a legal brief, or designing a grant or research proposal. While there may be differences from the research papers in terms of the format and audience for these assignments, the purposes of sections of the research paper and the moves discussed here will help you with those assignments as well.

## THE INTRODUCTION AND THESIS: "THIS PAPER CHALLENGES . . ."

Your introduction sets forth what you plan to say in your essay. You might evaluate the work of earlier scholars or certain widely held assumptions and find them incorrect when measured against new events or data. Alternatively, you might point out that an author's work is largely correct, but that it could use some qualifications or be extended in some way. Or you might identify a gap in our knowledge—we know a great deal about topic X but almost nothing about some other closely related topic. In each of these instances, your introduction needs to cover both "they say" and "I say" perspectives. If you stop after the "they say," your readers won't know what you are bringing to the conversation. Similarly, if you were to jump right to the "I say" portion of your argument, readers might wonder why you need to say anything at all.

Sometimes you join the conversation at a point where the discussion seems settled. One or more views about a topic have become so widely accepted among a group of scholars or society at large that these views are essentially the conventional way of thinking about the topic. You may wish to offer new reasons to support this interpretation, or you may wish to call these standard views into question. To do so, you must first introduce and identify these widely held beliefs and then present your own view. In fact, much of the writing in the social sciences takes the form of calling into question that which we think we already know. Consider the following example from an article in *The Journal of Economic Perspectives*:

> Fifteen years ago, Milton Friedman's 1957 treatise *A Theory of the Consumption Function* seemed badly dated. Dynamic optimization theory had not been employed much in economics when Friedman wrote, and utility theory was still comparatively primitive, so his statement of the "permanent income hypothesis" never actually specified a formal mathematical model of behavior derived explicitly from utility maximization . . . [W]hen other economists subsequently

found multiperiod maximizing models that could be solved explicitly, the implications of those models differed sharply from Friedman's intuitive description of his "model." Furthermore, empirical tests in the 1970s and 1980s often rejected these rigorous versions of the permanent income hypothesis in favor of an alternative hypothesis that many households simply spent all of their current income.

Today, with the benefit of a further round of mathematical (and computational) advances, Friedman's (1957) original analysis looks more prescient than primitive . . .

> CHRISTOPHER D. CARROLL, "A Theory of Consumption
> Function, With and Without Liquidity Constraints,"
> *The Journal of Economic Perspectives*

This introduction makes clear that Carroll will defend Milton Friedman against some major criticisms of his work. Carroll mentions what has been said about Friedman's work and then goes on to say that the critiques turn out to be wrong and to suggest that Friedman's work reemerges as persuasive. A template of Carroll's introduction might look something like this: Economics research in the last fifteen years suggested Friedman's 1957 treatise was _____ because _____. In other words, they say that Friedman's work is not accurate because of _____, _____, and _____. Recent research convinces me, however, that Friedman's work makes sense.

In some cases, however, there may not be a strong consensus among experts on a topic. You might enter the ongoing debate by casting your vote with one side or another or by offering an alternative view. In the following example, Sheri Berman identifies two competing accounts of how to explain world events in the twentieth century and then puts forth a third view.

Conventional wisdom about twentieth-century ideologies rests on two simple narratives. One focuses on the struggle for dominance between democracy and its alternatives. . . . The other narrative focuses on the competition between free-market capitalism and its rivals. . . . Both of these narratives obviously contain some truth. . . . Yet both only tell part of the story, which is why their common conclusion—neoliberalism as the "end of History"—is unsatisfying and misleading.

What the two conventional narratives fail to mention is that a third struggle was also going on: between those ideologies that believed in the primacy of economics and those that believed in the primacy of politics.

SHERI BERMAN, "The Primacy of Economics versus the Primacy of Politics: Understanding the Ideological Dynamics of the Twentieth Century," *Perspectives on Politics*

After identifying the two competing narratives, Berman suggests a third view—and later goes on to argue that this third view explains current debates over globalization. A template for this type of introduction might look something like this: In recent discussions of _____, a controversial aspect has been _____. On the one hand, some argue that _____. On the other hand, others argue that _____. Neither of these arguments, however, considers the alternative view that _____.

Given the complexity of many of the issues studied in the social sciences, however, you may sometimes agree *and* disagree with existing views—pointing out things that you believe are correct or have merit, while disagreeing with or refining other points. In the example below, anthropologist Sally Engle Merry agrees with another scholar about something that is a key trait of modern society but argues that this trait has a different origin than the other author identifies.

For more on different ways of responding, see Chapter 4.

Although I agree with Rose that an increasing emphasis on governing the soul is characteristic of modern society, I see the transformation not as evolutionary but as the product of social mobilization and political struggle.

> SALLY ENGLE MERRY, "Rights, Religion, and Community: Approaches to Violence against Women in the Context of Globalization," *Law and Society Review*

Here are some templates for agreeing and disagreeing:

▸ **Although I agree with X up to a point, I cannot accept his overall conclusion that _____.**

▸ **Although I disagree with X on _____ and _____, I agree with her conclusion that _____.**

▸ **Political scientists studying _____ have argued that it is caused by _____. While _____ contributes to the problem, _____ is also an important factor.**

▸ **While noting _____, I contend _____.**

In the process of examining people from different angles, social scientists sometimes identify gaps—areas that have not been explored in previous research.

In the following example, several sociologists identify such a gap.

Family scholars have long argued that the study of dating deserves more attention (Klemer, 1971), as dating is an important part of the life course at any age and often a precursor to marriage (Levesque & Caron, 2004). . . .

The central research questions we seek to answer with this study are whether and how the significance of particular dating rituals are patterned by gender and race simultaneously. We use a racially diverse data set of traditional-aged college students from a variety of college contexts. Understanding gender and racial differences in the assessment of dating rituals helps us explore the extent to which relationship activities are given similar importance across institutional and cultural lines. Most of the studies that inform our knowledge of dating and relationships are unable to draw conclusions regarding racial differences because the sample is Caucasian (e.g., Bogle, 2008), or primarily so (e.g., Manning & Smock, 2005). Race has been recently argued to be an often-overlooked variable in studies examining social psychological processes because of the prevalence of sample limitations as well as habitual oversight in the literature (Hunt, Jackson, Powell, & Steelman, 2000). Additionally, a failure to examine both gender and race prevents assessment of whether gendered beliefs are shared across groups. Gauging the extent of differences in beliefs among different population subgroups is critical to advancing the study of relationship dynamics (see Weaver & Ganong, 2004).

PAMELA BRABOY JACKSON, SIBYL KLEINER, CLAUDIA GEIST, AND KARA CEBULKO, "Conventions of Courtship: Gender and Race Differences in the Significance of Dating Rituals," *Journal of Family Issues*

Jackson and her coauthors note that, while other scholars have said that studying dating is important and have examined some aspects of dating, we have little information about whether attitudes about dating activities (such as sexual intimacy, gift exchange, and meeting the family) vary across groups by gender and race. Their study aims to fill this gap in our understanding of relationships.

Here are some templates for introducing gaps in the existing research:

▸ **Studies of X have indicated _____. It is not clear, however, that this conclusion applies to _____.**

▸ **_____ often take for granted that _____. Few have investigated this assumption, however.**

▸ **X's work tells us a great deal about _____. Can this work be generalized to _____?**

▸ **Our understanding of _____ remains incomplete because previous work has not examined _____.**

Again, a good introduction indicates what you have to say in the larger context of what others have said. Throughout the rest of your paper, you will move back and forth between the "they say" and the "I say," adding more details.

## THE LITERATURE REVIEW:
## "PRIOR RESEARCH INDICATES . . ."

The point of a literature review is to establish the state of knowledge on your topic. Before you (and your reader) can properly consider an issue, you need to understand the conversation about your topic that has already taken place (and is likely still in progress). In the literature review, you explain what "they say" in more detail, summarizing, paraphrasing, or quoting the viewpoints to which you are responding. But you need to balance what they are saying with your own focus. You need to characterize someone else's work fairly and accurately but set up the points you yourself want to make by selecting the details that are relevant to your own perspective and observations.

It is common in the social sciences to summarize several arguments in a single paragraph or even a single sentence, grouping several sources together by their important ideas or other attributes. The example below cites some key findings and conclusions of psychological research that should be of interest to motivated college students looking to improve their academic performance.

> Some people may associate sacrificing hours of sleep with being studious, but the reality is that sleep deprivation can hurt your cognitive functioning without your being aware of it (e.g., becoming worse at paying attention and remembering things; Goel, Rao, Durmer, & Dinges, 2009; Pilcher & Walters, 1997).... Sleep affects learning and memory by organizing and consolidating memories from the day (Diekelmann & Born, 2010; Rasch & Born, 2013), which can lead to better problem-solving ability and creativity (Verleger, Rose, Wagner, Yordanova, & Kolev, 2013).
>
> ADAM L. PUTNAM, VICTOR W. SUNGKHASETTEE, AND
> HENRY L. ROEDIGER, III, "Optimizing Learning in College:
> Tips from Cognitive Psychology," *Perspectives on
> Psychological Science*

A template for this paragraph might look like this: Students believe _____, but researchers disagree because _____. According to researchers, negative consequences of sleep deprivation include _____. The research shows that a positive effect of sleep is _____, which improves _____.

Such summaries are brief, bringing together relevant arguments by several scholars to provide an overview of

scholarly work on a particular topic. In writing such a summary, you need to ask yourself how the authors themselves
might describe their positions and also consider what in their
work is relevant for the point you wish to make. This kind
of summary is especially appropriate when you have a large
amount of research material on a topic and want to identify
the major strands of a debate or to show how the work of one
author builds on that of another. Here are some templates for
overview summaries:

▸ In addressing the question of _____, researchers have
   considered several explanations for _____. X argues
   that _____. According to Y and Z, another plausible explanation is _____.

▸ What is the effect of _____ on _____? Previous work
   on _____ by X and by Y and Z supports _____.

▸ Scholars point to the role of _____ in _____.

▸ Existing research on _____ presents convincing evidence of
   _____.

Sometimes you may need to say more about the works you cite.
On a midterm or final exam, for example, you may need to
demonstrate that you have a deep familiarity with a particular
work. And in some disciplines of the social sciences, longer,
more detailed literature reviews are the standard. Your instructor and the articles he or she has assigned are your best guides
for the length and level of detail of your literature review. Other
times, the work of certain authors is especially important for
your argument, and therefore you need to provide more details
to explain what these authors have said. See how political scientists Hahrie Han and Lisa Argyle, in a report for the Ford

Foundation, summarize an argument that is central to their investigation of improving democratic participation.

> [A]t the root of declining rates of participation is the sense that people do not feel like their participation matters. People do not feel like they have any real reason or opportunity to exercise voice in the political process. People's sense of agency is in decline, especially given negative or incomplete experiences of government in their lives.
>
> This lack of caring comes as no surprise when we examine research showing that most people have negative or, at best, incomplete experiences of the role of government in their lives. Suzanne Mettler, for instance, finds that many middle-class people who benefit from different government programs—ranging from education savings accounts to welfare to tax credits—believe that they "have not used a government social program." In addition, other scholars find a trend towards increasing privatization of public goods and political processes in the twenty-first century. As a result, government is what Mettler calls a "submerged state," since the role of government in people's lives is effectively submerged from view.
>
> HAHRIE HAN AND LISA ARGYLE, "A Program Review of the Promoting Electoral Reform and Democratic Participation (PERDP) Initiative," *Ford Foundation*

Note that Han and Argyle start by identifying the broad problem of lack of participation and then explain how Mettler's work describes how middle-class people may be unaware of the role of government in their lives, leading Mettler to argue for the idea of the "submerged state."

You may want to include direct quotations of what others have said, as Han and Argyle do. Using an author's exact words helps you demonstrate that you are representing him or her fairly. But you cannot simply insert a quotation; you need to explain to your readers what it means for your point. Consider the following example drawn from a political science book on the debate over tort reform.

> The essence of *agenda setting* was well enunciated by E. E. Schattschneider: "In politics as in everything else, it makes a great difference whose game we play" (1960, 47). In short, the ability to define or control the rules, terms, or perceived options in a contest over policy greatly affects the prospects for winning.
>
> WILLIAM HALTOM AND MICHAEL MCCANN,
> *Distorting the Law: Politics, Media, and the Litigation Crisis*

Notice how Haltom and McCann first quote Schattschneider and then explain in their own words how political agenda setting can be thought of as a game, with winners and losers.

Remember that whenever you summarize, quote, or paraphrase the work of others, credit must be given in the form of a citation to the original work. The words may be your own, but if the idea comes from someone else you must give credit to the original work. There are several formats for documenting sources. Consult your instructor for help choosing which citation style to use.

## THE ANALYSIS

The literature review covers what others have said on your topic. The analysis allows you to present and support your own response. In the introduction you indicate whether you agree, disagree, or some combination of both with what others have said. You will want to expand on how you have formed your opinion and why others should care about your topic.

## "The Data Indicate . . ."

The social sciences use evidence to develop and test explanations. This evidence is often referred to as data. Data can be quantitative or qualitative and can come from a number of sources. You might use statistics related to GDP growth, unemployment, voting rates, or demographics. You might report results from an experiment or simulation. Or you could use surveys, interviews, or other first-person accounts.

Regardless of the type of data used, it is important to do three things: define your data, indicate where you got the data, and then say what you have done with your data. For a chapter in their book assessing media coverage of female candidates, political scientists Danny Hayes and Jennifer Lawless explain how they assembled a data set.

> From the perspective of campaign professionals and voters, local newspaper coverage remains the most important news source during House campaigns....
>
> We began by selecting the appropriate newspaper for each House race in 2010 and 2014.... [W]e identified every news story during the thirty days leading up to the election that mentioned at least one of the two major-party candidates....
>
> Our data collection efforts produced 10,375 stories about 1,550 candidates who received at least some local news coverage in either the 2010 or 2014 midterms....
>
> Coders read the full text of each article and recorded several pieces of information. First, they tracked the number of times a candidate's sex or gender was mentioned.... Second, we recorded the number of explicit references to candidate traits, both positive and negative (e.g., "capable" and "ineffective")....
>
> Third, we tracked every time an issue was mentioned in connection with a candidate.... We then classified issues in two ways:

(1) We assigned each issue to one of the eight broad categories...
and (2) we classified a subset of the topics as "women's" or "men's"
issues.

DANNY HAYES AND JENNIFER L. LAWLESS, *Women on the Run:*
*Gender, Media, and Political Campaigns in a Polarized Era*

Hayes and Lawless explain how they collected their data—local
newspaper coverage of congressional candidates—and explain
how they coded and classified the coverage to allow them to
perform statistical analysis of the news pieces. While you probably won't collect 10,000+ news items for a class project, you
could collect information (such as media coverage, interview
responses, or legal briefs) and analyze and sort them to identify
patterns such as repeated words and ideas.

If your data are quantitative, you also need to explain
them. Sociologist Jonathan Horowitz's research concludes
that job quality influences personal assessments of well-being
by "improving social life, altering class identification, affecting
physical health, and increasing amounts of leisure time." See
how he introduces the data he analyzes:

In this study, I use data from the General Social Survey (GSS) and
structural equation modeling to test relationships between job quality and subjective wellbeing. The GSS is a nationally representative
sample of adults in the United States that asks a large number of
questions about experiences at work (Smith et al. 2010). In particular, the GSS introduced a new battery of questions titled "Quality
of Working Life" in 2002 (and repeated in 2006 and 2010) which
includes multiple questions about several job quality dimensions.

JONATHAN HOROWITZ, "Dimensions of Job Quality,
Mechanisms, and Subjective Well-Being in the United States,"
*Sociological Forum*

Here are some templates for discussing data:

▸ In order to test the hypothesis that _____, we assessed _____. Our calculations suggest _____.

▸ I used _____ to investigate _____. The results of this investigation indicate _____.

## "But Others May Object . . ."

No matter how strongly your data support your argument, there are almost surely other perspectives (and thus other data) that you need to acknowledge. By considering possible objections to your argument and taking them seriously, you demonstrate that you've done your work and that you're aware of other perspectives—and most important, you present your own argument as part of an ongoing conversation.

See how law professor Michelle Alexander acknowledges that there may be objections to her argument describing trends in mass incarceration as "the new Jim Crow." See p. 261 for a selection from *The New Jim Crow*.

> Some might argue that as disturbing as this system appears to be, there is nothing particularly new about mass incarceration; it is merely a continuation of past drug wars and biased law enforcement practices. Racial bias in our criminal justice system is simply an old problem that has gotten worse, and the social excommunication of "criminals" has a long history; it is not a recent invention. There is some merit to this argument.
>
> MICHELLE ALEXANDER, *The New Jim Crow: Mass Incarceration in the Age of Colorblindness*

Alexander imagines a conversation with people who might be skeptical about her argument, particularly her claim that this represents a "new" development. And she responds that they are correct, to a point. After acknowledging her agreement with the assessment of historical racial bias in the criminal justice system, she goes on in the rest of her chapter to explain that the expanded scope and consequences of contemporary mass incarceration have caused dramatic differences in society.

Someone may object because there are related phenomena that your analysis does not explain or because you do not have the right data to investigate a particular question. Or perhaps someone may object to assumptions underlying your argument or how you handled your data. Here are some templates for considering naysayers:

▶ _____ might object that _____.

▶ Is my claim realistic? I have argued _____, but readers may question _____.

▶ My explanation accounts for _____ but does not explain _____. This is because _____.

## "Why Should We Care?"

Who should care about your research, and why? Since the social sciences attempt to explain human behavior, it is important to consider how your research affects the assumptions we make about human behavior. In addition, you might offer recommendations for how other social scientists might continue to explore an issue, or what actions policymakers should take.

In the following example, sociologist Devah Pager identifies the implications of her study of the way having a criminal record affects a person applying for jobs.

> [I]n terms of policy implications, this research has troubling conclusions. In our frenzy of locking people up, our "crime control"

policies may in fact exacerbate the very conditions that lead to crime in the first place. Research consistently shows that finding quality steady employment is one of the strongest predictors of desistance from crime (Shover 1996; Sampson and Laub 1993; Uggen 2000). The fact that a criminal record severely limits employment opportunities—particularly among blacks—suggests that these individuals are left with few viable alternatives.

DEVAH PAGER, "The Mark of a Criminal Record,"
*The American Journal of Sociology*

Pager's conclusion that a criminal record negatively affects employment chances creates a vicious circle, she says: steady employment discourages recidivism, but a criminal record makes it harder to get a job.

In answering the "so what?" question, you need to explain why your readers should care. Although sometimes the implications of your work may be so broad that they would be of interest to almost anyone, it's never a bad idea to identify explicitly any groups of people who will find your work important.

Templates for establishing why your claims matter:

▸ **X is important because _____ .**

▸ **Ultimately, what is at stake here is _____ .**

▸ **The finding that _____ should be of interest to _____ because _____ .**

As noted at the beginning of this chapter, the complexity of people allows us to look at their behavior from many different viewpoints. Much has been, and will be, said about how and why people do the things they do. As a result, we can look at writing in the social sciences as an ongoing conversation. When you join this conversation, the "they say / I say" framework will help you figure out what has already been said (they say) and what you can add (I say). The components of social science writing presented in this chapter are tools to help you join that conversation.

# READINGS

# Don't Blame the Eater

## DAVID ZINCZENKO

—▭—

IF EVER THERE WERE a newspaper headline custom-made for
Jay Leno's monologue, this was it. Kids taking on McDonald's
this week, suing the company for making them fat. Isn't that
like middle-aged men suing Porsche for making them get speeding tickets? Whatever happened to personal responsibility?

I tend to sympathize with these portly fast-food patrons,
though. Maybe that's because I used to be one of them.

I grew up as a typical mid-1980s latchkey kid. My parents
were split up, my dad off trying to rebuild his life, my mom
working long hours to make the monthly bills. Lunch and din-
ner, for me, was a daily choice between McDonald's, Taco Bell,
Kentucky Fried Chicken, or Pizza Hut. Then as now, these
were the only available options for an American kid to get an
affordable meal. By age 15, I had packed 212 pounds of torpid
teenage tallow on my once lanky 5-foot-10 frame.

Then I got lucky. I went to college, joined the Navy Reserves
and got involved with a health magazine. I learned how to

———

DAVID ZINCZENKO, who was for many years the editor-in-chief of
the fitness magazine *Men's Health*, is president of Galvanized Brands,
a global health and wellness media company. This piece was first published on the op-ed page of the *New York Times* on November 23, 2002.

manage my diet. But most of the teenagers who live, as I once did, on a fast-food diet won't turn their lives around: they've crossed under the golden arches to a likely fate of lifetime obesity. And the problem isn't just theirs—it's all of ours.

Before 1994, diabetes in children was generally caused by a genetic disorder—only about 5 percent of childhood cases were obesity-related, or Type 2, diabetes. Today, according to the National Institutes of Health, Type 2 diabetes accounts for at least 30 percent of all new childhood cases of diabetes in this country.

For tips on saying why it matters, see Chapter 7.

Not surprisingly, money spent to treat diabetes has skyrocketed, too. The Centers for Disease Control and Prevention estimate that diabetes accounted for $2.6 billion in health care costs in 1969. Today's number is an unbelievable $100 billion a year.

Shouldn't we know better than to eat two meals a day in fast-food restaurants? That's one argument. But where, exactly, are consumers—particularly teenagers—supposed to find alternatives? Drive down any thoroughfare in America, and I guarantee you'll see one of our country's more than 13,000 McDonald's restaurants. Now, drive back up the block and try to find someplace to buy a grapefruit.

Complicating the lack of alternatives is the lack of information about what, exactly, we're consuming. There are no calorie information charts on fast-food packaging, the way there are on grocery items. Advertisements don't carry warning labels the way tobacco ads do. Prepared foods aren't covered under Food and Drug Administration labeling laws. Some fast-food purveyors will provide calorie information on request, but even that can be hard to understand.

For example, one company's Web site lists its chicken salad as containing 150 calories; the almonds and noodles that come with it (an additional 190 calories) are listed separately. Add a serving of the 280-calorie dressing, and you've got a healthy lunch alternative that comes in at 620 calories. But that's not all. Read the small print on the back of the dressing packet and you'll realize it actually contains 2.5 servings. If you pour what you've been served, you're suddenly up around 1,040 calories, which is half of the government's recommended daily calorie intake. And that doesn't take into account that 450-calorie super-size Coke.

Make fun if you will of these kids launching lawsuits against 10 the fast-food industry, but don't be surprised if you're the next plaintiff. As with the tobacco industry, it may be only a matter of time before state governments begin to see a direct line between the $1 billion that McDonald's and Burger King spend each year on advertising and their own swelling health care costs.

And I'd say the industry is vulnerable. Fast-food companies are marketing to children a product with proven health hazards and no warning labels. They would do well to protect themselves, and their customers, by providing the nutrition information people need to make informed choices about their products. Without such warnings, we'll see more sick, obese children and more angry, litigious parents. I say, let the deep-fried chips fall where they may.

# Hidden Intellectualism

## GERALD GRAFF

———🔲———

EVERYONE KNOWS SOME YOUNG PERSON who is impressively "street smart" but does poorly in school. What a waste, we think, that one who is so intelligent about so many things in life seems unable to apply that intelligence to academic work. What doesn't occur to us, though, is that schools and colleges might be at fault for missing the opportunity to tap into such street smarts and channel them into good academic work.

Nor do we consider one of the major reasons why schools and colleges overlook the intellectual potential of street smarts: the fact that we associate those street smarts with anti-intellectual concerns. We associate the educated life, the life of the mind, too narrowly and exclusively with subjects and texts that we consider inherently weighty and academic. We assume

———

GERALD GRAFF, the coauthor of this book, is a professor emeritus of English and education at the University of Illinois at Chicago. He is a past president of the Modern Language Association, the world's largest professional association of university scholars and teachers. This essay is adapted from his 2003 book *Clueless in Academe: How Schooling Obscures the Life of the Mind*.

that it's possible to wax intellectual about Plato, Shakespeare, the French Revolution, and nuclear fission, but not about cars, dating, fashion, sports, TV, or video games.

The trouble with this assumption is that no neces- See pp. 56–59 for tips on disagreeing, with reasons. sary connection has ever been established between any text or subject and the educational depth and weight of the discussion it can generate. Real intellectuals turn any subject, however lightweight it may seem, into grist for their mill through the thoughtful questions they bring to it, whereas a dullard will find a way to drain the interest out of the richest subject. That's why a George Orwell writing on the cultural meanings of penny postcards is infinitely more substantial than the cogitations of many professors on Shakespeare or globalization (104–16).

Students do need to read models of intellectually challenging writing—and Orwell is a great one—if they are to become intellectuals themselves. But they would be more prone to take on intellectual identities if we encouraged them to do so at first on subjects that interest them rather than ones that interest us.

I offer my own adolescent experience as a case in point. 5 Until I entered college, I hated books and cared only for sports. The only reading I cared to do or could do was sports magazines, on which I became hooked, becoming a regular reader of *Sport* magazine in the late forties, *Sports Illustrated* when it began publishing in 1954, and the annual magazine guides to professional baseball, football, and basketball. I also loved the sports novels for boys of John R. Tunis and Clair Bee and autobiographies of sports stars like Joe DiMaggio's *Lucky to Be a Yankee* and Bob Feller's *Strikeout Story*. In short, I was your typical teenage anti-intellectual—or so I believed for a long time. I have recently come to think, however, that my preference for sports over schoolwork was not anti-intellectualism so much as intellectualism by other means.

In the Chicago neighborhood I grew up in, which had become a melting pot after World War II, our block was solidly middle class, but just a block away—doubtless concentrated there by the real estate companies—were African Americans, Native Americans, and "hillbilly" whites who had recently fled postwar joblessness in the South and Appalachia. Negotiating this class boundary was a tricky matter. On the one hand, it was necessary to maintain the boundary between "clean-cut" boys like me and working-class "hoods," as we called them, which meant that it was good to be openly smart in a book-ish sort of way. On the other hand, I was desperate for the approval of the hoods, whom I encountered daily on the play-ing field and in the neighborhood, and for this purpose it was not at all good to be book-smart. The hoods would turn on you if they sensed you were putting on airs over them: "Who you lookin' at, smart ass?" as a leather-jacketed youth once said to me as he relieved me of my pocket change along with my self-respect.

I grew up torn, then, between the need to prove I was smart and the fear of a beating if I proved it too well; between the need not to jeopardize my respectable future and the need to impress the hoods. As I lived it, the conflict came down to a choice between being physically tough and being verbal. For a boy in my neighborhood and elementary school, only being "tough" earned you complete legitimacy. I still recall endless, complicated debates in this period with my closest pals over who was "the toughest guy in the school." If you were less than negligible as a fighter, as I was, you settled for the next best thing, which was to be inarticulate, carefully hiding telltale marks of literacy like correct grammar and pronunciation.

In one way, then, it would be hard to imagine an adolescence more thoroughly anti-intellectual than mine. Yet in retrospect, I see that it's more complicated, that I and the 1950s themselves were not simply hostile toward intellectualism, but divided and ambivalent. When Marilyn Monroe married the playwright Arthur Miller in 1956 after divorcing the retired baseball star Joe DiMaggio, the symbolic triumph of geek over jock suggested the way the wind was blowing. Even Elvis, according to his biographer Peter Guralnick, turns out to have supported Adlai over Ike in the presidential election of 1956. "I don't dig the intellectual bit," he told reporters. "But I'm telling you, man, he knows the most" (327).

Though I too thought I did not "dig the intellectual bit," I see now that I was unwittingly in training for it. The germs had actually been planted in the seemingly philistine debates about which boys were the toughest. I see now that in the interminable analysis of sports teams, movies, and toughness that my friends and I engaged in—a type of analysis, needless to say, that the real toughs would never have stooped to—I was already betraying an allegiance to the egghead world. I was practicing being an intellectual before I knew that was what I wanted to be.

It was in these discussions with friends about toughness and sports, I think, and in my reading of sports books and magazines, that I began to learn the rudiments of the intellectual life: how to make an argument, weigh different kinds of evidence, move between particulars and generalizations, summarize the views of others, and enter a conversation about ideas. It was in reading and arguing about sports and toughness that

I experienced what it felt like to propose a generalization, restate and respond to a counterargument, and perform other intellectualizing operations, including composing the kind of sentences I am writing now.

Only much later did it dawn on me that the sports world was more compelling than school because it was *more intellectual than school*, not less. Sports after all was full of challenging arguments, debates, problems for analysis, and intricate statistics that you could care about, as school conspicuously was not. I believe that street smarts beat out book smarts in our culture not because street smarts are nonintellectual, as we generally suppose, but because they satisfy an intellectual thirst more thoroughly than school culture, which seems pale and unreal.

They also satisfy the thirst for community. When you entered sports debates, you became part of a community that was not limited to your family and friends, but was national and public. Whereas schoolwork isolated you from others, the pennant race or Ted Williams's .400 batting average was something you could talk about with people you had never met. Sports introduced you not only to a culture steeped in argument, but to a public argument culture that transcended the personal. I can't blame my schools for failing to make intellectual culture resemble the Super Bowl, but I do fault them for failing to learn anything from the sports and entertainment worlds about how to organize and represent intellectual culture, how to exploit its gamelike element and turn it into arresting public spectacle that might have competed more successfully for my youthful attention.

For here is another thing that never dawned on me and is still kept hidden from students, with tragic results: that the real intellectual world, the one that existed in the big world beyond school, is organized very much like the world of team sports, with rival texts, rival interpretations and evaluations of texts, rival theories of why they should be read and taught, and elaborate team competitions in which "fans" of writers, intellectual systems, methodologies, and -isms contend against each other.

To be sure, school contained plenty of competition, which became more invidious as one moved up the ladder (and has become even more so today with the advent of high-stakes testing). In this competition, points were scored not by making arguments, but by a show of information or vast reading, by grade-grubbing, or other forms of one-upmanship. School competition, in short, reproduced the less attractive features of sports culture without those that create close bonds and community.

And in distancing themselves from anything as enjoyable 15 and absorbing as sports, my schools missed the opportunity to capitalize on an element of drama and conflict that the intellectual world shares with sports. Consequently, I failed to see the parallels between the sports and academic worlds that could have helped me cross more readily from one argument culture to the other.

Sports is only one of the domains whose potential for literacy training (and not only for males) is seriously underestimated by educators, who see sports as competing with academic development rather than a route to it. But if this argument suggests why it is a good idea to assign readings and topics that are close to students' existing interests, it also suggests the limits of this tactic. For students who get excited about the chance to write about their passion for cars will often write as poorly and unreflectively on that topic as on Shakespeare or Plato. Here is the flip side of what I pointed out before: that there's no necessary relation between the degree of interest a student shows in a text or subject and the quality of thought or expression such a student manifests in writing or talking about it. The challenge, as college professor Ned Laff has put it, "is not simply to exploit students' nonacademic interests, but to get them to see those interests through academic eyes."

To say that students need to see their interests "through academic eyes" is to say that street smarts are not enough. Making students' nonacademic interests an object of academic study is useful, then, for getting students' attention and overcoming their boredom and alienation, but this tactic won't in itself necessarily move them closer to an academically rigorous treatment of those interests. On the other hand, inviting students to write about cars, sports, or clothing fashions does not have to be a pedagogical cop-out as long as students are required to see these interests "through academic eyes," that is, to think and write about cars, sports, and fashions in a reflective, analytical way, one that sees them as microcosms of what is going on in the wider culture.

If I am right, then schools and colleges are missing an opportunity when they do not encourage students to take their nonacademic interests as objects of academic study. It is self-defeating to decline to introduce any text or subject that figures to engage students who will otherwise tune out academic work entirely. If a student cannot get interested in Mill's *On Liberty* but will read *Sports Illustrated* or *Vogue* or the hip-hop magazine *The Source* with absorption, this is a strong argument for assigning the magazines over the classic. It's a good bet that if students get hooked on reading and writing by doing term papers on *The Source*, they will eventually get to *On Liberty*. But even if they don't, the magazine reading will make them more literate and reflective than they would be otherwise. So it makes pedagogical sense to develop classroom units on sports, cars, fashions, rap music, and other such topics. Give me the student anytime who writes a sharply argued, sociologically acute analysis of an issue in *The Source* over the student who writes a lifeless explication of *Hamlet* or Socrates' *Apology*.

## Works Cited

Cramer, Richard Ben. *Joe DiMaggio: The Hero's Life*. Simon & Schuster, 2000.

DiMaggio, Joe. *Lucky to Be a Yankee*. Bantam, 1949.

Feller, Bob. *Strikeout Story*. Bantam, 1948.

Guralnick, Peter. *Last Train to Memphis: The Rise of Elvis Presley*. Little, Brown, 1994.

Orwell, George. *A Collection of Essays*. Harcourt, 1953.

# "Rise of the Machines" Is Not a Likely Future

## MICHAEL LITTMAN

—◻—

EVERY NEW TECHNOLOGY BRINGS its own nightmare scenarios. Artificial intelligence (AI) and robotics are no exceptions. Indeed, the word "robot" was coined for a 1920 play that dramatized just such a doomsday for humanity.

Recently, an open letter about the future of AI, signed by a number of high-profile scientists and entrepreneurs, spurred a new round of harrowing headlines like "Top Scientists Have an Ominous Warning about Artificial Intelligence," and "Artificial Intelligence Experts Sign Open Letter to Protect Mankind from Machines." The implication is that the machines will one day displace humanity.

Let's get one thing straight: a world in which humans are enslaved or destroyed by superintelligent machines of our

———

MICHAEL LITTMAN is a professor of computer science at Brown University. He is also codirector of the Humanity Centered Robotics Initiative at Brown, a group dedicated to advancing robotics and studying the impact of these advancements on society. This piece was originally published in *Live Science* on January 28, 2015.

own creation is purely science fiction. Like every other technology, AI has risks and benefits, but we cannot let fear dominate the conversation or guide AI research. Nevertheless, the idea of dramatically changing the AI research agenda to focus on AI "safety" is the primary message of a group calling itself the Future of Life Institute (FLI). FLI includes a handful of deep thinkers and public figures such as Elon Musk and Stephen Hawking and worries about the day in which humanity is steamrolled by powerful programs run amuck.

As eloquently described in the book *Superintelligence: Paths, Dangers, Strategies* by FLI advisory board member and Oxford-based philosopher Nick Bostrom, the plot unfolds in three parts. In the first part—roughly where we are now—computational power and intelligent software develops at an increasing pace through the toil of scientists and engineers. Next, a breakthrough is made: programs are created that possess intelligence on par with humans. These programs, running on increasingly fast computers, improve themselves extremely rapidly, resulting in a runaway "intelligence explosion." In the third and final act, a singular super-intelligence takes hold—outsmarting, outmaneuvering, and ultimately outcompeting the entirety of humanity and perhaps life itself. End scene.

Let's take a closer look at this apocalyptic storyline. Of the three parts, the first is indeed happening now and Bostrom provides cogent and illuminating glimpses into current and near-future technology. The third part is a philosophical romp exploring the consequences of supersmart machines. It's that second part—the intelligence explosion—that demonstrably violates what we know of computer science and natural intelligence.

## Runaway Intelligence?

See Chapter 16 for tips on presenting the prevailing theories. The notion of the intelligence explosion arises from Moore's Law, the observation that the speed of computers has been increasing exponentially since the 1950s. Project this trend forward and we'll see computers with the computational power of the entire human race within the next few decades. It's a leap to go from this idea to unchecked growth of machine intelligence, however.

First, ingenuity is not the sole bottleneck to developing faster computers. The machines need to actually be built, which requires real-world resources. Indeed, Moore's law comes with exponentially increasing production costs as well—mass production of precision electronics does not come cheap. Further, there are fundamental physical laws—quantum limits—that bound how quickly a transistor can do its work. Non-silicon technologies may overcome those limits, but such devices remain highly speculative.

In addition to physical laws, we know a lot about the fundamental nature of computation and its limits. For example, some computational puzzles, like figuring out how to factor a number and thereby crack online cryptography schemes, are generally believed to be unsolvable by any fast program. They are part of a class of mathematically defined problems that are "NP-complete," meaning that they are exactly as hard as any problem that can be solved non-deterministically (N) in polynomial time (P), and they have resisted any attempt at scalable solution. As it turns out, most computational problems that we associate with human intelligence are known to be in this class.

See Chapter 6 for tips on anticipating objections. Wait a second, you might say. How does the human mind manage to solve mathematical problems that computer scientists believe can't be solved? We don't. By and large, we cheat. We build a cartoonish mental model of the elements of the world that we're interested in and then probe the behavior of this invented miniworld. There's a trade-off between completeness and tractability in these imagined microcosms. Our ability to propose and ponder and project credible futures comes at the cost of accuracy. Even allowing for the possibility of the existence of considerably faster computers than we have today, it is a logical impossibility that these computers would be able to accurately simulate reality faster than reality itself.

## Countering the Anti-AI Cause

In the face of general skepticism in the AI and computer science 10 communities about the possibility of an intelligence explosion, FLI still wants to win support for its cause. The group's letter calls for increased attention to maximizing the societal benefits of developing AI. Many of my esteemed colleagues signed the letter to show their support for the importance of avoiding potential pitfalls of the technology. But a few key phrases in the letter such as "our AI systems must do what we want them to do" (Tegmark) are taken by the press as an admission that AI researchers believe they might be creating something that cannot be controlled. It also implies that AI researchers are asleep at the wheel, oblivious to the ominous possibilities, which is simply untrue.

To be clear, there are indeed concerns about the near-term future of AI—algorithmic traders crashing the economy, or sensitive power grids overreacting to fluctuations and shutting down electricity for large swaths of the population. There's also a concern that systemic biases within academia and industry prevent underrepresented minorities from participating and helping to steer the growth of information technology. These worries should play a central role in the development and deployment of new ideas. But dread predictions of computers suddenly waking up and turning on us are simply not realistic.

I welcome an open discussion about how AI can be made robust and beneficial, and how we can engineer intelligent machines and systems that make society better. But, let's please keep the discussion firmly within the realm of reason and leave the robot uprisings to Hollywood screenwriters.

## Works Cited

Bostrom, Nick. *Superintelligence: Paths, Dangers, Strategies*. Oxford UP, 2014.

Čapek, Karel. *R. U. R.* Translated by David Wyllie, The University of Adelaide, 2014. eBooks@Adelaide, https://ebooks.adelaide.edu.au/c/capek/karel/rur/index.html. Accessed 9 June 2017.

Sparkes, Matthew. "Top Scientists Have an Ominous Warning about Artificial Intelligence." *Business Insider*, 13 Jan. 2015, http://www.businessinsider.com/top-scientists-have-an-ominous-warning-about-artificial-intelligence-2015-1. Accessed 9 June 2017.

Statt, Nick. "Artificial intelligence experts sign open letter to protect mankind from machines." *CNET*, 11 Jan. 2015, https://www.cnet.com/news/artificial-intelligence-experts-sign-open-letter-to-protect-mankind-from-machines/. Accessed 9 June 2017.

Tegmark, Max, et al. "An Open Letter: Research Priorities for Robust and Beneficial Artificial Intelligence." *Future of Life Institute*, 2015, https://futureoflife.org/ai-open-letter. Accessed 9 June 2017.

# The New Jim Crow: Mass Incarceration in the Age of Colorblindness

## MICHELLE ALEXANDER

—◻—

JARVIOUS COTTON CANNOT VOTE. Like his father, grandfather, great-grandfather, and great-great-grandfather, he has been denied the right to participate in our electoral democracy. Cotton's family tree tells the story of several generations of black men who were born in the United States but who were denied the most basic freedom that democracy promises—the freedom to vote for those who will make the rules and laws that govern one's life. Cotton's great-great-grandfather could not vote as a slave. His great-grandfather was beaten to death by the Ku Klux Klan for attempting to vote. His grandfather was prevented from voting by Klan intimidation. His father

———

MICHELLE ALEXANDER is a professor, civil rights advocate, and legal scholar. In 2016, she became a visiting professor and a student at Union Theological Seminary. In the past she has held positions at the ACLU, Stanford Law School, and the law firm Saperstein, Goldstein, Demchak & Bailer. This essay is adapted from her 2010 best-selling book *The New Jim Crow: Mass Incarceration in the Age of Colorblindness*.

was barred from voting by poll taxes and literacy tests. Today, Jarvious Cotton cannot vote because he, like many black men in the United States, has been labeled a felon and is currently on parole.[1]

Cotton's story illustrates, in many respects, the old adage "The more things change, the more they remain the same." In each generation, new tactics have been used for achieving the same goals—goals shared by the Founding Fathers. Denying African Americans citizenship was deemed essential to the formation of the original union. Hundreds of years later, America is still not an egalitarian democracy. The arguments and rationalizations that have been trotted out in support of racial exclusion and discrimination in its various forms have changed and evolved, but the outcome has remained largely the same. An extraordinary percentage of black men in the United States are legally barred from voting today, just as they have been throughout most of American history. They are also subject to legalized discrimination in employment, housing, education, public benefits, and jury service, just as their parents, grandparents, and great-grandparents once were.

What has changed since the collapse of Jim Crow has less to do with the basic structure of our society than with the language we use to justify it. In the era of colorblindness, it is no longer socially permissible to use race, explicitly, as a justification for discrimination, exclusion, and social contempt. So we don't. Rather than rely on race, we use our criminal justice system to label people of color "criminals" and then engage in all the practices we supposedly left behind. Today it is perfectly legal to discriminate against criminals in nearly all the ways that it was once legal to discriminate against African Americans. Once you're labeled a felon, the old forms of discrimination—employment discrimination, housing discrimination, denial of the right to vote, denial of educational opportunity, denial of food stamps and other public benefits, and exclusion from jury service—are suddenly legal. As a criminal, you have scarcely more rights, and arguably less respect, than a black man living in Alabama at the height of Jim Crow. We have not ended racial caste in America; we have merely redesigned it.

I reached the conclusions presented in this book reluctantly. Ten years ago, I would have argued strenuously against the central claim made here—namely, that something akin to a racial caste system currently exists in the United States. Indeed, if Barack Obama had been elected president back then, I would have argued that his election marked the nation's triumph over racial caste—the final nail in the coffin of Jim Crow. My elation would have been tempered by the distance yet to be traveled to reach the promised land of racial justice in America, but my conviction that nothing remotely similar to Jim Crow exists in this country would have been steadfast.

See pp. 24–25 for tips on making what "they say" something you say.

Today my elation over Obama's election is tempered by a far more sobering awareness. As an African American woman, with three young children who will never know a world in which a black man could not be president of the United States, I was beyond thrilled on election night. Yet when I walked out of the election night party, full of hope and enthusiasm, I was immediately reminded of the harsh realities of the New Jim Crow. A black man was on his knees in the gutter, hands cuffed behind his back, as several police officers stood around him talking, joking, and ignoring his human existence. People poured out of the building; many stared for a moment at the black man cowering in the street, and then averted their gaze. What did the election of Barack Obama mean for him?

Like many civil rights lawyers, I was inspired to attend law school by the civil rights victories of the 1950s and 1960s. Even in the face of growing social and political opposition to remedial policies such as affirmative action, I clung to the notion that the evils of Jim Crow are behind us and that, while we have a long way to go to fulfill the dream of an egalitarian, multiracial democracy, we have made real progress and are now struggling to hold on to the gains of the past. I thought my job as a civil rights lawyer was to join with the allies of racial progress to resist attacks on affirmative action and to eliminate the vestiges of Jim Crow segregation, including our still separate and unequal system of education. I understood the problems plaguing poor communities of color, including problems associated with crime and rising incarceration rates, to be a function of poverty and lack of access to quality education—the continuing legacy of slavery and Jim Crow. Never did I seriously consider the possibility that a new racial caste system was operating in this country. The new system had been developed and implemented swiftly, and it was largely invisible, even to people, like me, who spent most of their waking hours fighting for justice.

I first encountered the idea of a new racial caste system more than a decade ago, when a bright orange poster caught my eye. I was rushing to catch the bus, and I noticed a sign stapled to a telephone pole that screamed in large bold print: THE DRUG WAR IS THE NEW JIM CROW. I paused for a moment and skimmed the text of the flyer. Some radical group was holding a community meeting about police brutality, the new three-strikes law in California, and the expansion of America's prison system. The meeting was being held at a small community church a few blocks away; it had seating capacity for no more than fifty people. I sighed, and muttered to myself something like, "Yeah, the criminal justice system is racist in many ways, but it really doesn't help to make such an absurd comparison. People will just think you're crazy." I then crossed the street and hopped on the bus. I was headed to my new job, director of the Racial Justice Project of the American Civil Liberties Union (ACLU) in Northern California.

When I began my work at the ACLU, I assumed that the criminal justice system had problems of racial bias, much in the same way that all major institutions in our society are plagued with problems associated with conscious and unconscious bias. As a lawyer who had litigated numerous class-action employment-discrimination cases, I understood well the many ways in which racial stereotyping can permeate subjective decision-making processes at all levels of an organization, with devastating consequences. I was familiar with the challenges associated with reforming institutions in which racial stratification is thought to be normal—the natural consequence of differences in education, culture, motivation, and, some still believe, innate ability. While at the ACLU, I shifted my focus from employment discrimination to criminal justice reform and dedicated myself to the task of working with others to identify and eliminate racial bias whenever and wherever it reared its ugly head.

By the time I left the ACLU, I had come to suspect that I was wrong about the criminal justice system. It was not just another institution infected with racial bias but rather a different beast entirely. The activists who posted the sign on the telephone pole were not crazy; nor were the smattering of lawyers and advocates around the country who were beginning to connect the dots between our current system of mass incarceration and earlier forms of social control. Quite belatedly, I came to see that mass incarceration in the United States had, in fact, emerged as a stunningly comprehensive and well-disguised system of racialized social control that functions in a manner strikingly similar to Jim Crow.

In my experience, people who have been incarcerated 10 rarely have difficulty identifying the parallels between these systems of social control. Once they are released, they are often denied the right to vote, excluded from juries, and relegated to a racially segregated and subordinated existence. Through a web of laws, regulations, and informal rules, all of which are powerfully reinforced by social stigma, they are confined to the margins of mainstream society and denied access to the mainstream economy. They are legally denied the ability to obtain employment, housing, and public benefits—much as African Americans were once forced into a segregated, second-class citizenship in the Jim Crow era.

Those of us who have viewed that world from a comfortable distance—yet sympathize with the plight of the so-called underclass—tend to interpret the experience of those caught up in the criminal justice system primarily through the lens of popularized social science, attributing the staggering increase in incarceration rates in communities of color to the predictable, though unfortunate, consequences of poverty, racial segregation, unequal educational opportunities, and the presumed realities of the drug market, including the mistaken belief that most drug dealers are black or brown. Occasionally, in the course of my work, someone would make a remark suggesting that perhaps the War on Drugs is a racist conspiracy to put blacks back in their place. This type of remark was invariably accompanied by nervous laughter, intended to convey the impression that although the idea had crossed their minds, it was not an idea a reasonable person would take seriously.

Most people assume the War on Drugs was launched in response to the crisis caused by crack cocaine in inner-city neighborhoods. This view holds that the racial disparities in drug convictions and sentences, as well as the rapid explosion of the prison population, reflect nothing more than the government's zealous—but benign—efforts to address rampant drug crime in poor, minority neighborhoods. This view, while understandable, given the sensational media coverage of crack in the 1980s and 1990s, is simply wrong.

While it is true that the publicity surrounding crack cocaine led to a dramatic increase in funding for the drug war (as well as to sentencing policies that greatly exacerbated racial disparities in incarceration rates), there is See p. 88 for tips on making concessions while still standing your ground. no truth to the notion that the War on Drugs was launched in response to crack cocaine. President Ronald Reagan officially announced the current drug war in 1982, before crack became an issue in the media or a crisis in poor black neighborhoods. A few years after the drug war was declared, crack began to spread rapidly in the poor black neighborhoods of Los Angeles and later emerged in cities across the country.[2] The Reagan administration hired staff to publicize the emergence of crack cocaine in 1985 as part of a strategic effort to build public and legislative support for the war. The media campaign was an extraordinary success. Almost overnight, the media was saturated with images of black "crack whores," "crack dealers," and "crack babies"—images that seemed to confirm the worst negative racial stereotypes about impoverished inner-city residents. The media bonanza surrounding the "new demon drug" helped to catapult the War on Drugs from an ambitious federal policy to an actual war.

The timing of the crack crisis helped to fuel conspiracy theories and general speculation in poor black communities that the War on Drugs was part of a genocidal plan by the government to destroy black people in the United States. From the outset, stories circulated on the street that crack and other drugs were being brought into black neighborhoods by the CIA. Eventually, even the Urban League came to take the claims of genocide seriously. In its 1990 report "The State of Black America," it stated: "There is at least one concept that must be recognized if one is to see the pervasive and insidious nature of the drug problem for the African American community. Though difficult to accept, that is the concept of genocide."[3] While the conspiracy theories were initially dismissed as far-fetched, if not downright loony, the word on the street turned out to be right, at least to a point. The CIA admitted in 1998 that guerrilla armies it actively supported in Nicaragua were smuggling illegal drugs into the United States—drugs that were making their way onto the streets of inner-city black neighborhoods in the form of crack cocaine. The CIA also admitted that, in the midst of the War on Drugs, it blocked law enforcement efforts to investigate illegal drug networks that were helping to fund its covert war in Nicaragua.[4]

It bears emphasis that the CIA never admitted (nor has any evidence been revealed to support the claim) that it intentionally sought the destruction of the black community by allowing illegal drugs to be smuggled into the United States. Nonetheless, conspiracy theorists surely must be forgiven for their bold accusation of genocide, in light of the devastation wrought by crack cocaine and the drug war, and the odd coincidence that an illegal drug crisis suddenly appeared in the black community after—not before—a drug war had been declared. In fact, the War on Drugs began at a time when illegal drug use was on the decline.[5] During this same time period, however, a war was declared, causing arrests and convictions for drug offenses to skyrocket, especially among people of color.

The impact of the drug war has been astounding. In less than thirty years, the US penal population exploded from around 300,000 to more than 2 million, with drug convictions accounting for the majority of the increase.[6] The United States now has the highest rate of incarceration in the world, dwarfing the rates of nearly every developed country, even surpassing those in highly repressive regimes like Russia, China, and Iran. In Germany, 93 people are in prison for every 100,000 adults and children. In the United States, the rate is roughly eight times that, or 750 per 100,000.[7]

The racial dimension of mass incarceration is its most striking feature. No other country in the world imprisons so many of its racial or ethnic minorities. The United States imprisons a larger percentage of its black population than South Africa did at the height of apartheid. In Washington, DC, our nation's capital, it is estimated that three out of four young black men (and nearly all those in the poorest neighborhoods) can expect to serve time in prison.[8] Similar rates of incarceration can be found in black communities across America.

These stark racial disparities cannot be explained by rates of drug crime. Studies show that people of all colors *use and sell* illegal drugs at remarkably similar rates.[9] If there are significant differences in the surveys to be found, they frequently suggest that whites, particularly white youth, are more likely to engage in drug crime than people of color.[10] That is not what one would guess, however, when entering our nation's prisons and jails, which are overflowing with black and brown drug offenders. In some states, black men have been admitted to prison on drug charges at rates twenty to fifty times greater than those of white men.[11] And in major cities wracked by the drug war, as many as 80 percent of young African American men now have criminal records and are thus subject to legalized discrimination for the rest of their lives.[12] These young men are part of a growing undercaste, permanently locked up and locked out of mainstream society.

. . .

The language of caste may well seem foreign or unfamiliar to some. Public discussions about racial caste in America are relatively rare. We avoid talking about caste in our society because we are ashamed of our racial history. We also avoid talking about race. We even avoid talking about class. Conversations about class are resisted in part because there is a tendency to imagine that one's class reflects upon one's character. What is key to America's understanding of class is the persistent belief—despite all evidence to the contrary—that anyone, with the proper discipline and drive, can move from a lower class to a higher class. We recognize that mobility may be difficult, but the key to our collective self-image is the assumption that mobility is always possible, so failure to move up reflects on one's character. By extension, the failure of a race or ethnic group to move up reflects very poorly on the group as a whole.

What is completely missed in the rare public debates today 20 about the plight of African Americans is that a huge percentage of them are not free to move up at all. It is not just that they lack opportunity, attend poor schools, or are plagued by poverty. They are barred by law from doing so. And the major institutions with which they come into contact are designed to prevent their mobility. To put the matter starkly: the current system of control permanently locks a huge percentage of the African American community out of the mainstream society and economy. The system operates through our criminal justice institutions, but it functions more like a caste system than a system of crime control. Viewed from this perspective, the so-called underclass is better understood as an *undercaste*—a lower caste of individuals who are permanently barred by law and custom from mainstream society. Although this new system of racialized social control purports to be colorblind, it creates and maintains racial hierarchy much as earlier systems of control did. Like Jim Crow (and slavery), mass incarceration operates as a tightly networked system of laws, policies, customs, and institutions that operate collectively to ensure the subordinate status of a group defined largely by race.

. . .

Skepticism about the claims made here is warranted. There are important differences, to be sure, among mass incarceration, Jim Crow, and slavery—the three major racialized systems of control adopted in the United States to date. Failure to acknowledge the relevant differences, as well as their implications, would be a disservice to racial justice discourse. Many of the differences are not as dramatic as they initially appear, however; others serve to illustrate the ways in which systems of racialized social control have managed to morph, evolve, and adapt to changes in the political, social, and legal context over time. Ultimately, I believe that the similarities between these systems of control overwhelm the differences and that mass incarceration, like its predecessors, has been largely immunized from legal challenge. If this claim is substantially correct, the implications for racial justice advocacy are profound.

See Chapter 7 for tips on establishing why your claim matters.

With the benefit of hindsight, surely we can see that piecemeal policy reform or litigation alone would have been a futile approach to dismantling Jim Crow segregation. While those strategies certainly had their place, the Civil Rights Act of 1964 and the concomitant cultural shift would never have occurred without the cultivation of a critical political consciousness in the African American community and the widespread, strategic activism that flowed from it. Likewise, the notion that the *New* Jim Crow can ever be dismantled through traditional litigation and policy-reform strategies that are wholly disconnected from a major social movement seems fundamentally misguided.

Such a movement is impossible, though, if those most committed to abolishing racial hierarchy continue to talk and behave as if a state-sponsored racial caste system no longer exists. If we continue to tell ourselves the popular myths about racial progress or, worse yet, if we say to ourselves that the problem of mass incarceration is just too big, too daunting for us to do anything about and that we should instead direct our energies to battles that might be more easily won, history will judge us harshly. A human rights nightmare is occurring on our watch.

A new social consensus must be forged about race and the role of race in defining the basic structure of our society, if we hope ever to abolish the New Jim Crow. This new consensus must begin with dialogue, a conversation that fosters a critical consciousness, a key prerequisite to effective social action. My writing is an attempt to ensure that the conversation does not end with nervous laughter.

## Notes

1. Jarvious Cotton was a plaintiff in *Cotton v. Fordice*, 157 F.3d 388 (5th Cir. 1998), which held that Mississippi's felon disenfranchisement provision had lost its racially discriminatory taint. The information regarding Cotton's family tree was obtained by Emily Bolton on March 29, 1999, when she interviewed Cotton at Mississippi State Prison. Jarvious Cotton was released on parole in Mississippi, a state that denies voting rights to parolees.

2. The *New York Times* made the national media's first specific reference to crack in a story published in late 1985. Crack became known in a few impoverished neighborhoods in Los Angeles, New York, and Miami in early 1986. See Craig Reinarman and Harry Levine, "The Crack Attack: America's Latest Drug Scare, 1986–1992," in *Images of Issues: Typifying Contemporary Social Problems* (New York: Aldine De Gruyter, 1995), 152.

3. Clarence Page, "'The Plan': A Paranoid View of Black Problems," *Dover* (Delaware) *Herald*, Feb. 23, 1990. See also Manning Marable, *Race, Reform, and Rebellions: The Second Reconstruction in Black America, 1945–1990* (Jackson: University Press of Mississippi, 1991), 212–13.

4. See Alexander Cockburn and Jeffrey St. Clair, *Whiteout: The CIA, Drugs, and the Press* (New York: Verso, 1999). See also Nick Shou, "The Truth in 'Dark Alliance,'" *Los Angeles Times,* Aug. 18, 2006; Peter Kornbluh, "CIA's Challenge in South Central," *Los Angeles Times* (Washington edition), Nov. 15, 1996; and Alexander Cockburn, "Why They Hated Gary Webb," *The Nation*, Dec. 16, 2004.

5. Katherine Beckett and Theodore Sasson, *The Politics of Injustice: Crime and Punishment in America* (Thousand Oaks, CA: Sage Publications, 2004), 163.

6. Marc Mauer, *Race to Incarcerate*, rev. ed. (New York: The New Press, 2006), 33.

7. PEW Center on the States, *One in 100: Behind Bars in America 2008* (Washington, DC: PEW Charitable Trusts, 2008), 5.

8. Donald Braman, *Doing Time on the Outside: Incarceration and Family Life in Urban America* (Ann Arbor: University of Michigan Press, 2004), 3, citing D.C. Department of Corrections data for 2000.

9. See, e.g., U.S. Department of Health and Human Services, Substance Abuse and Mental Health Services Administration, *Summary of Findings from the 2000 National Household Survey on Drug Abuse*, NHSDA series H-13, DHHS pub. no. SMA 01-3549 (Rockville, MD: 2001), reporting that 6.4 percent of whites, 6.4 percent of blacks, and 5.3 percent of Hispanics were current users of illegal drugs in 2000; *Results from the 2002 National Survey on Drug Use and Health: National Findings*, NHSDA series H-22, DHHS pub. no. SMA 03-3836 (2003), revealing nearly identical rates of illegal drug use among whites and blacks, only a single percentage point between them; and *Results from the 2007 National Survey on Drug Use and Health: National Findings*, NSDUH series H-34, DHHS pub. no. SMA 08-4343 (2007), showing essentially the same finding. See also Marc Mauer and Ryan S. King, *A 25-Year Quagmire: The "War on Drugs" and Its Impact on American Society* (Washington, DC: Sentencing Project, 2007), 19, citing a study suggesting that African Americans have slightly higher rates of illegal drug use than whites.

10. See, e.g., Howard N. Snyder and Melissa Sickman, *Juvenile Offenders and Victims: 2006 National Report*, U.S. Department of Justice, Office of Justice Programs, Office of Juvenile Justice and Delinquency Prevention (Washington,

DC: U.S. Department of Justice, 2006), reporting that white youth are more likely than black youth to engage in illegal drug sales. See also Lloyd D. Johnson, Patrick M. O'Malley, Jerald G. Bachman, and John E. Schulenberg, *Monitoring the Future, National Survey Results on Drug Use, 1975–2006*, vol. 1, *Secondary School Students*, U.S. Department of Health and Human Services, National Institute on Drug Abuse, NIH pub. no. 07-6205 (Bethesda, MD: 2007), 32, "African American 12th graders have consistently shown lower usage rates than White 12th graders for most drugs, both licit and illicit"; and Lloyd D. Johnston, Patrick M. O'Malley, and Jerald G. Bachman, *Monitoring the Future: National Results on Adolescent Drug Use: Overview of Key Findings 2002*, U.S. Department of Health and Human Services, National Institute on Drug Abuse, NIH pub. no. 03-5374 (Bethesda, MD: 2003), presenting data showing that African American adolescents have slightly lower rates of illicit drug use than their white counterparts.

11. Human Rights Watch, *Punishment and Prejudice: Racial Disparities in the War on Drugs*, HRW Reports, vol. 12, no. 2 (New York, 2000).

12. See, e.g., Paul Street, *The Vicious Circle: Race, Prison, Jobs, and Community in Chicago, Illinois, and the Nation* (Chicago: Chicago Urban League, Department of Research and Planning, 2002).

# Everything That Rises Must Converge

## FLANNERY O'CONNOR

HER DOCTOR HAD TOLD JULIAN'S MOTHER that she must lose twenty pounds on account of her blood pressure, so on Wednesday nights Julian had to take her downtown on the bus for a reducing class at the Y. The reducing class was designed for working girls over fifty, who weighed from 165 to 200 pounds. His mother was one of the slimmer ones, but she said ladies did not tell their age or weight. She would not ride the buses by herself at night since they had been integrated, and because the reducing class was one of her few pleasures, necessary for her health, and *free*, she said Julian could at least put himself out to take her, considering all she did for him. Julian did not

FLANNERY O'CONNOR (1925–1964) was an American writer and essayist. Born in Savannah, Georgia, she authored two novels and over thirty short stories. "Everything That Rises Must Converge" comes from her second short story collection, published posthumously in 1965. Her style is frequently associated with the Southern Gothic, a genre of stories set in the American South in which characters often find themselves in ominous situations.

like to consider all she did for him, but every Wednesday night he braced himself and took her.

She was almost ready to go, standing before the hall mirror, putting on her hat, while he, his hands behind him, appeared pinned to the door frame, waiting like Saint Sebastian for the arrows to begin piercing him. The hat was new and had cost her seven dollars and a half. She kept saying, "Maybe I shouldn't have paid that for it. No, I shouldn't have. I'll take it off and return it tomorrow. I shouldn't have bought it."

Julian raised his eyes to heaven. "Yes, you should have bought it," he said. "Put it on and let's go." It was a hideous hat. A purple velvet flap came down on one side of it and stood up on the other; the rest of it was green and looked like a cushion with the stuffing out. He decided it was less comical than jaunty and pathetic. Everything that gave her pleasure was small and depressed him.

She lifted the hat one more time and set it down slowly on top of her head. Two wings of gray hair protruded on either side of her florid face, but her eyes, sky-blue, were as innocent and untouched by experience as they must have been when she was ten. Were it not that she was a widow who had struggled fiercely to feed and clothe and put him through school and who was supporting him still, "until he got on his feet," she might have been a little girl that he had to take to town.

"It's all right, it's all right," he said. "Let's go." He opened the ⁵ door himself and started down the walk to get her going. The sky was a dying violet and the houses stood out darkly against it, bulbous liver-colored monstrosities of a uniform ugliness though no two were alike. Since this had been a fashionable neighborhood forty years ago, his mother persisted in thinking they did well to have an apartment in it. Each house had a narrow collar of dirt around it in which sat, usually, a grubby child.

Julian walked with his hands in his pockets, his head down and thrust forward and his eyes glazed with the determination to make himself completely numb during the time he would be sacrificed to her pleasure.

The door closed and he turned to find the dumpy figure, surmounted by the atrocious hat, coming toward him. "Well," she said, "you only live once and paying a little more for it, I at least won't meet myself coming and going."

"Some day I'll start making money," Julian said gloomily— he knew he never would—"and you can have one of those jokes whenever you take the fit." But first they would move. He visualized a place where the nearest neighbors would be three miles away on either side.

"I think you're doing fine," she said, drawing on her gloves. "You've only been out of school a year. Rome wasn't built in a day."

She was one of the few members of the Y reducing class who arrived in hat and gloves and who had a son who had been to college. "It takes time," she said, "and the world is in such a mess. This hat looked better on me than any of the others, though when she brought it out I said, 'Take that thing back. I wouldn't have it on my head,' and she said, 'Now wait till you see it on,' and when she put it on me, I said, 'We-ull,' and she said, 'If you ask me, that hat does something for you and you do something for the hat, and besides,' she said, 'with that hat, you won't meet yourself coming and going.'"

Julian thought he could have stood his lot better if she had 10 been selfish, if she had been an old hag who drank and screamed at him. He walked along, saturated in depression, as if in the midst of his martyrdom he had lost his faith. Catching sight of his long, hopeless, irritated face, she stopped suddenly with a grief-stricken look, and pulled back on his arm. "Wait on me," she said. "I'm going back to the house and take this thing off and tomorrow I'm going to return it. I was out of my head. I can pay the gas bill with that seven-fifty."

He caught her arm in a vicious grip. "You are not going to take it back," he said. "I like it."

"Well," she said, "I don't think I ought . . ."

"Shut up and enjoy it," he muttered, more depressed than ever.

"With the world in the mess it's in," she said, "it's a wonder we can enjoy anything. I tell you, the bottom rail is on the top."

Julian sighed. 15

"Of course," she said, "if you know who you are, you can go anywhere." She said this every time he took her to the reducing class. "Most of them in it are not our kind of people," she said, "but I can be gracious to anybody. I know who I am."

"They don't give a damn for your graciousness," Julian said savagely. "Knowing who you are is good for one generation only. You haven't the foggiest idea where you stand now or who you are."

She stopped and allowed her eyes to flash at him. "I most certainly do know who I am," she said, "and if you don't know who you are, I'm ashamed of you."

"Oh hell," Julian said.

"Your great-grandfather was a former governor of this state," 20 she said. "Your grandfather was a prosperous landowner. Your grandmother was a Godhigh."

"Will you look around you," he said tensely, "and see where you are now?" and he swept his arm jerkily out to indicate the neighborhood, which the growing darkness at least made less dingy.

"You remain what you are," she said. "Your great-grandfather had a plantation and two hundred slaves."

"There are no more slaves," he said irritably.

"They were better off when they were," she said. He groaned to see that she was off on that topic. She rolled onto it every few days like a train on an open track. He knew every stop, every junction, every swamp along the way, and knew the exact point at which her conclusion would roll majestically into the station: "It's ridiculous. It's simply not realistic. They should rise, yes, but on their own side of the fence."

"Let's skip it," Julian said.   25

"The ones I feel sorry for," she said, "are the ones that are half white. They're tragic."

"Will you skip it?"

"Suppose we were half white. We would certainly have mixed feelings."

"I have mixed feelings now," he groaned.

"Well let's talk about something pleasant," she said.   30 "I remember going to Grandpa's when I was a little girl. Then the house had double stairways that went up to what was really the second floor—all the cooking was done on the first. I used to like to stay down in the kitchen on account of the way the walls smelled. I would sit with my nose pressed against the plaster and take deep breaths. Actually the place belonged to the Godhighs but your grandfather Chestny paid the mortgage and saved it for them. They were in reduced circumstances," she said, "but reduced or not, they never forgot who they were."

"Doubtless that decayed mansion reminded them," Julian muttered. He never spoke of it without contempt or thought of it without longing. He had seen it once when he was a child before it had been sold. The double stairways had rotted and been torn down. Negroes were living in it. But it remained in his mind as his mother had known it. It appeared in his dreams regularly. He would stand on the wide porch, listening to the rustle of oak leaves, then wander through the high-ceilinged hall into the parlor that opened onto it and gaze at the worn rugs and faded draperies. It occurred to him that it was he, not she, who could have appreciated it. He preferred its threadbare elegance to anything he could name and it was because of it that all the neighborhoods they had lived in had been a torment to him—whereas she had hardly known the difference. She called her insensitivity "being adjustable."

"And I remember the old darky who was my nurse, Caroline. There was no better person in the world. I've always had a great respect for my colored friends," she said. "I'd do anything in the world for them and they'd . . ."

"Will you for God's sake get off that subject?" Julian said. When he got on a bus by himself, he made it a point to sit down beside a Negro, in reparation as it were for his mother's sins.

"You're mighty touchy tonight," she said. "Do you feel all right?"

"Yes I feel all right," he said. "Now lay off." 35

She pursed her lips. "Well, you certainly are in a vile humor," she observed. "I just won't speak to you at all."

They had reached the bus stop. There was no bus in sight and Julian, his hands still jammed in his pockets and his head thrust forward, scowled down the empty street. The frustration of having to wait on the bus as well as ride on it began to creep up his neck like a hot hand. The presence of his mother was borne in upon him as she gave a pained sigh. He looked at her bleakly. She was holding herself very erect under the preposterous hat, wearing it like a banner of her imaginary dignity. There was in him an evil urge to break her spirit. He suddenly unloosened his tie and pulled it off and put it in his pocket.

She stiffened. "Why must you look like *that* when you take me to town?" she said. "Why must you deliberately embarrass me?"

"If you'll never learn where you are," he said, "you can at least learn where I am."

"You look like a—thug," she said.                    40

"Then I must be one," he murmured.

"I'll just go home," she said. "I will not bother you. If you can't do a little thing like that for me . . ."

Rolling his eyes upward, he put his tie back on. "Restored to my class," he muttered. He thrust his face toward her and hissed, "True culture is in the mind, the *mind*," he said, and tapped his head, "the mind."

"It's in the heart," she said, "and in how you do things and how you do things is because of who you *are*."

"Nobody in the damn bus cares who you are."          45

"I care who I am," she said icily.

The lighted bus appeared on top of the next hill and as it approached, they moved out into the street to meet it. He put his hand under her elbow and hoisted her up on the creaking step. She entered with a little smile, as if she were going into a drawing room where everyone had been waiting for her. While he put in the tokens, she sat down on one of the broad front seats for three which faced the aisle. A thin woman with protruding teeth and long yellow hair was sitting on the end of it. His mother moved up beside her and left room for Julian beside herself. He sat down and looked at the floor across the aisle where a pair of thin feet in red and white canvas sandals were planted.

His mother immediately began a general conversation meant to attract anyone who felt like talking. "Can it get any hotter?" she said and removed from her purse a folding fan, black with a Japanese scene on it, which she began to flutter before her.

"I reckon it might could," the woman with the protruding teeth said, "but I know for a fact my apartment couldn't get no hotter."

"It must get the afternoon sun," his mother said. She sat forward and looked up and down the bus. It was half filled. Everybody was white. "I see we have the bus to ourselves," she said. Julian cringed.

"For a change," said the woman across the aisle, the owner of the red and white canvas sandals. "I come on one the other day and they were thick as fleas—up front and all through."

"The world is in a mess everywhere," his mother said. "I don't know how we've let it get in this fix."

"What gets my goat is all those boys from good families stealing automobile tires," the woman with the protruding teeth said. "I told my boy, I said you may not be rich but you been raised right and if I ever catch you in any such mess, they can send you on to the reformatory. Be exactly where you belong."

"Training tells," his mother said. "Is your boy in high school?"

"Ninth grade," the woman said.

"My son just finished college last year. He wants to write but he's selling typewriters until he gets started," his mother said.

The woman leaned forward and peered at Julian. He threw her such a malevolent look that she subsided against the seat. On the floor across the aisle there was an abandoned newspaper. He got up and got it and opened it out in front of him. His mother discreetly continued the conversation in a lower tone but the woman across the aisle said in a loud voice, "Well that's nice. Selling typewriters is close to writing. He can go right from one to the other."

"I tell him," his mother said, "that Rome wasn't built in a day."

Behind the newspaper Julian was withdrawing into the inner compartment of his mind where he spent most of his time. This was a kind of mental bubble in which he established himself when he could not bear to be a part of what was going on around him. From it he could see out and judge but in it he was safe from any kind of penetration from without. It was the only place where he felt free of the general idiocy of his fellows. His mother had never entered it but from it he could see her with absolute clarity.

The old lady was clever enough and he thought that if she had started from any of the right premises, more might have been expected of her. She lived according to the laws of her own fantasy world outside of which he had never seen her set foot. The law of it was to sacrifice herself for him after she had first created the necessity to do so by making a mess of things. If he had permitted her sacrifices, it was only because her lack of foresight had made them necessary. All of her life had been a struggle to act like a Chestny without the Chestny goods, and to give him everything she thought a Chestny ought to have; but since, said she, it was fun to struggle, why complain? And when you had won, as she had won, what fun to look back on the hard times! He could not forgive her that she had enjoyed the struggle and that she thought *she* had won.

What she meant when she said she had won was that she had brought him up successfully and had sent him to college and that he had turned out so well—good looking (her teeth had gone unfilled so that his could be straightened), intelligent (he realized he was too intelligent to be a success), and with a future ahead of him (there was of course no future ahead of him). She excused his gloominess on the grounds that he was still growing up and his radical ideas on his lack of practical experience. She said he didn't yet know a thing about "life," that he hadn't even entered the real world—when already he was as disenchanted with it as a man of fifty.

The further irony of all this was that in spite of her, he had turned out so well. In spite of going to only a third-rate college, he had, on his own initiative, come out with a first-rate education; in spite of growing up dominated by a small mind, he had ended up with a large one; in spite of all her foolish views, he was free of prejudice and unafraid to face facts. Most miraculous of all, instead of being blinded by love for her as she was for him, he had cut himself emotionally free of her and could see her with complete objectivity. He was not dominated by his mother.

The bus stopped with a sudden jerk and shook him from his meditation. A woman from the back lurched forward with little steps and barely escaped falling in his newspaper as she righted herself. She got off and a large Negro got on. Julian kept his paper lowered to watch. It gave him a certain satisfaction to see injustice in daily operation. It confirmed his view that with a few exceptions there was no one worth knowing within a radius of three hundred miles. The Negro was well dressed and carried a briefcase. He looked around and then sat down on the other end of the seat where the woman with the red and white canvas sandals was sitting. He immediately unfolded a newspaper and obscured himself behind it. Julian's mother's elbow at once prodded insistently into his ribs. "Now you see why I won't ride on these buses by myself," she whispered.

The woman with the red and white canvas sandals had risen at the same time the Negro sat down and had gone further back in the bus and taken the seat of the woman who had got off. His mother leaned forward and cast her an approving look.

Julian rose, crossed the aisle, and sat down in the place of the 65
woman with the canvas sandals. From this position, he looked
serenely across at his mother. Her face had turned an angry
red. He stared at her, making his eyes the eyes of a stranger.
He felt his tension suddenly lift as if he had openly declared
war on her.

He would have liked to get in conversation with the Negro
and to talk with him about art or politics or any subject that
would be above the comprehension of those around them, but
the man remained entrenched behind his paper. He was either
ignoring the change of seating or had never noticed it. There
was no way for Julian to convey his sympathy.

His mother kept her eyes fixed reproachfully on his face. The
woman with the protruding teeth was looking at him avidly as
if he were a type of monster new to her.

"Do you have a light?" he asked the Negro.

Without looking away from his paper, the man reached in
his pocket and handed him a packet of matches.

"Thanks," Julian said. For a moment he held the matches 70
foolishly. A NO SMOKING sign looked down upon him from over
the door. This alone would not have deterred him; he had no
cigarettes. He had quit smoking some months before because
he could not afford it. "Sorry," he muttered and handed back
the matches. The Negro lowered the paper and gave him an
annoyed look. He took the matches and raised the paper again.

His mother continued to gaze at him but she did not take
advantage of his momentary discomfort. Her eyes retained their
battered look. Her face seemed to be unnaturally red, as if her
blood pressure had risen. Julian allowed no glimmer of sympathy
to show on his face. Having got the advantage, he wanted desperately to keep it and carry it through. He would have liked to
teach her a lesson that would last her a while, but there seemed

no way to continue the point. The Negro refused to come out from behind his paper.

Julian folded his arms and looked stolidly before him, facing her but as if he did not see her, as if he had ceased to recognize her existence. He visualized a scene in which, the bus having reached their stop, he would remain in his seat and when she said, "Aren't you going to get off?" he would look at her as at a stranger who had rashly addressed him. The corner they got off on was usually deserted, but it was well lighted and it would not hurt her to walk by herself the four blocks to the Y. He decided to wait until the time came and then decide whether or not he would let her get off by herself. He would have to be at the Y at ten to bring her back, but he could leave her wondering if he was going to show up. There was no reason for her to think she could always depend on him.

He retired again into the high-ceilinged room sparsely set-tled with large pieces of antique furniture. His soul expanded momentarily but then he became aware of his mother across from him and the vision shriveled. He studied her coldly. Her feet in little pumps dangled like a child's and did not quite reach the floor. She was training on him an exaggerated look of reproach. He felt completely detached from her. At that moment he could with pleasure have slapped her as he would have slapped a particularly obnoxious child in his charge.

He began to imagine various unlikely ways by which he could teach her a lesson. He might make friends with some distinguished Negro professor or lawyer and bring him home to spend the evening. He would be entirely justified but her blood pressure would rise to 300. He could not push her to the extent of making her have a stroke, and moreover, he had never been successful at making any Negro friends. He had tried to strike up an acquaintance on the bus with some of the better types, with ones that looked like professors or ministers or lawyers. One morning he had sat down next to a distinguished-looking dark brown man who had answered his questions with a sonorous solemnity but who had turned out to be an undertaker. Another day he had sat down beside a cigar-smoking Negro with a diamond ring on his finger, but after a few stilted pleasantries, the Negro had rung the buzzer and risen, slipping two lottery tickets into Julian's hand as he climbed over him to leave.

He imagined his mother lying desperately ill and his being 75 able to secure only a Negro doctor for her. He toyed with that idea for a few minutes and then dropped it for a momentary vision of himself participating as a sympathizer in a sit-in demonstration. This was possible but he did not linger with it. Instead, he approached the ultimate horror. He brought home a beautiful suspiciously Negroid woman. Prepare yourself, he said. There is nothing you can do about it. This is the woman I've chosen. She's intelligent, dignified, even good, and she's suffered and she hasn't thought it *fun*. Now persecute us, go ahead and persecute us. Drive her out of here, but remember, you're driving me too. His eyes were narrowed and through the indignation he had generated, he saw his mother across the aisle, purple-faced, shrunken to the dwarf-like proportions of her moral nature, sitting like a mummy beneath the ridiculous banner of her hat.

He was tilted out of his fantasy again as the bus stopped. The door opened with a sucking hiss and out of the dark a large, gaily dressed, sullen-looking colored woman got on with a little boy. The child, who might have been four, had on a short plaid suit and a Tyrolean hat with a blue feather in it. Julian hoped that he would sit down beside him and that the woman would push in beside his mother. He could think of no better arrangement.

As she waited for her tokens, the woman was surveying the seating possibilities—he hoped with the idea of sitting where she was least wanted. There was something familiar-looking about her but Julian could not place what it was. She was a giant of a woman. Her face was set not only to meet opposition but to seek it out. The downward tilt of her large lower lip was like a warning sign: DON'T TAMPER WITH ME. Her bulging figure was encased in a green crepe dress and her feet overflowed in red shoes. She had on a hideous hat. A purple velvet flap came down on one side of it and stood up on the other; the rest of it was green and looked like a cushion with the stuffing out. She carried a mammoth red pocketbook that bulged throughout as if it were stuffed with rocks.

To Julian's disappointment, the little boy climbed up on the empty seat beside his mother. His mother lumped all children, black and white, into the common category, "cute," and she thought little Negroes were on the whole cuter than little white children. She smiled at the little boy as he climbed on the seat.

Meanwhile the woman was bearing down upon the empty seat beside Julian. To his annoyance, she squeezed herself into it. He saw his mother's face change as the woman settled herself next to him and he realized with satisfaction that this was more objectionable to her than it was to him. Her face seemed almost gray and there was a look of dull recognition in her eyes, as if suddenly she had sickened at some awful confrontation. Julian saw that it was because she and the woman had, in a sense, swapped sons. Though his mother would not realize the symbolic significance of this, she would feel it. His amusement showed plainly on his face.

The woman next to him muttered something unintelligible to herself. He was conscious of a kind of bristling next to him, 80

288

muted growling like that of an angry cat. He could not see anything but the red pocketbook upright on the bulging green thighs. He visualized the woman as she had stood waiting for her tokens—the ponderous figure, rising from the red shoes upward over the solid hips, the mammoth bosom, the haughty face, to the green and purple hat.

His eyes widened.

The vision of the two hats, identical, broke upon him with the radiance of a brilliant sunrise. His face was suddenly lit with joy. He could not believe that Fate had thrust upon his mother such a lesson. He gave a loud chuckle so that she would look at him and see that he saw. She turned her eyes on him slowly. The blue in them seemed to have turned a bruised purple. For a moment he had an uncomfortable sense of her innocence, but it lasted only a second before principle rescued him. Justice entitled him to laugh. His grin hardened until it said to her as plainly as if he were saying aloud: Your punishment exactly fits your pettiness. This should teach you a permanent lesson.

Her eyes shifted to the woman. She seemed unable to bear looking at him and to find the woman preferable. He became conscious again of the bristling presence at his side. The woman was rumbling like a volcano about to become active. His mother's mouth began to twitch slightly at one corner. With a sinking heart, he saw incipient signs of recovery on her face and realized that this was going to strike her suddenly as funny and was going to be no lesson at all. She kept her eyes on the woman and an amused smile came over her face as if the woman were a monkey that had stolen her hat. The little Negro was looking up at her with large fascinated eyes. He had been trying to attract her attention for some time.

"Carver!" the woman said suddenly. "Come heah!"

When he saw that the spotlight was on him at last, Carver 85 drew his feet up and turned himself toward Julian's mother and giggled.

"Carver!" the woman said. "You heah me? Come heah!"

Carver slid down from the seat but remained squatting with his back against the base of it, his head turned slyly around toward Julian's mother, who was smiling at him. The woman reached a hand across the aisle and snatched him to her. He righted himself and hung backwards on her knees, grinning at Julian's mother. "Isn't he cute?" Julian's mother said to the woman with the protruding teeth.

"I reckon he is," the woman said without conviction.

The Negress yanked him upright but he eased out of her grip and shot across the aisle and scrambled, giggling wildly, onto the seat beside his love.

"I think he likes me," Julian's mother said, and smiled at 90 the woman. It was the smile she used when she was being particularly gracious to an inferior. Julian saw everything lost. The lesson had rolled off her like rain on a roof.

The woman stood up and yanked the little boy off the seat as if she were snatching him from contagion. Julian could feel the rage in her at having no weapon like his mother's smile. She gave the child a sharp slap across his leg. He howled once and then thrust his head into her stomach and kicked his feet against her shins. "Behave," she said vehemently.

The bus stopped and the Negro who had been reading the newspaper got off. The woman moved over and set the little boy down with a thump between herself and Julian. She held him firmly by the knee. In a moment he put his hands in front of his face and peeped at Julian's mother through his fingers.

"I see yoooooooo!" she said and put her hand in front of her face and peeped at him.

The woman slapped his hand down. "Quit yo' foolishness," she said, "before I knock the living Jesus out of you!"

Julian was thankful that the next stop was theirs. He reached 95 up and pulled the cord. The woman reached up and pulled it at the same time. Oh my God, he thought. He had the terrible intuition that when they got off the bus together, his mother would open her purse and give the little boy a nickel. The gesture would be as natural to her as breathing. The bus stopped and the woman got up and lunged to the front, dragging the child, who wished to stay on, after her. Julian and his mother got up and followed. As they neared the door, Julian tried to relieve her of her pocketbook.

"No," she murmured, "I want to give the little boy a nickel."

"No!" Julian hissed. "No!"

She smiled down at the child and opened her bag. The bus door opened and the woman picked him up by the arm and descended with him, hanging at her hip. Once in the street she set him down and shook him.

Julian's mother had to close her purse while she got down the bus step but as soon as her feet were on the ground, she opened it again and began to rummage inside. "I can't find but a penny," she whispered, "but it looks like a new one."

"Don't do it!" Julian said fiercely between his teeth. There 100 was a streetlight on the corner and she hurried to get under it so that she could better see into her pocketbook. The woman was heading off rapidly down the street with the child still hanging backward on her hand.

"Oh little boy!" Julian's mother called and took a few quick steps and caught up with them just beyond the lamppost. "Here's a bright new penny for you," and she held out the coin, which shone bronze in the dim light.

The huge woman turned and for a moment stood, her shoulders lifted and her face frozen with frustrated rage, and stared at Julian's mother. Then all at once she seemed to explode like a piece of machinery that had been given one ounce of pressure too much. Julian saw the black fist swing out with the red pocketbook. He shut his eyes and cringed as he heard the woman shout, "He don't take nobody's pennies!" When he opened his eyes, the woman was disappearing down the street with the little boy staring wide-eyed over her shoulder. Julian's mother was sitting on the sidewalk.

"I told you not to do that," Julian said angrily. "I told you not to do that!"

He stood over her for a minute, gritting his teeth. Her legs were stretched out in front of her and her hat was on her lap. He squatted down and looked her in the face. It was totally expressionless. "You got exactly what you deserved," he said. "Now get up."

He picked up her pocketbook and put what had fallen out 105 back in it. He picked the hat up off her lap. The penny caught his eye on the sidewalk and he picked that up and let it drop before her eyes into the purse. Then he stood up and leaned over and held his hands out to pull her up. She remained immobile. He sighed. Rising above them on either side were black apartment buildings, marked with irregular rectangles of light. At the end of the block a man came out of a door and walked off in the opposite direction. "All right," he said, "suppose somebody happens by and wants to know why you're sitting on the sidewalk?"

She took the hand and, breathing hard, pulled heavily up on it and then stood for a moment, swaying slightly as if the spots of light in the darkness were circling around her. Her eyes, shadowed and confused, finally settled on his face. He did not try to conceal his irritation. "I hope this teaches you a lesson," he said. She leaned forward and her eyes raked his face. She seemed trying to determine his identity. Then, as if she found nothing familiar about him, she started off with a headlong movement in the wrong direction.

"Aren't you going on to the Y?" he asked.

"Home," she muttered.

"Well, are we walking?"

For answer she kept going. Julian followed along, his hands behind him. He saw no reason to let the lesson she had had go without backing it up with an explanation of its meaning. She might as well be made to understand what had happened to her. "Don't think that was just an uppity Negro woman," he said. "That was the whole colored race which will no longer take your condescending pennies. That was your black double. She can wear the same hat as you, and to be sure," he added gratuitously (because he thought it was funny), "it looked better on her than it did on you. What all this means," he said, "is that the old world is gone. The old manners are obsolete and your graciousness is not worth a damn." He thought bitterly of the house that had been lost for him. "You aren't who you think you are," he said.

She continued to plow ahead, paying no attention to him. Her hair had come undone on one side. She dropped her pocketbook and took no notice. He stooped and picked it up and handed it to her but she did not take it.

"You needn't act as if the world had come to an end," he said, "because it hasn't. From now on you've got to live in a new world and face a few realities for a change. Buck up," he said, "it won't kill you."

She was breathing fast.

"Let's wait on the bus," he said.

"Home," she said thickly.

"I hate to see you behave like this," he said. "Just like a child. I should be able to expect more of you." He decided to stop where he was and make her stop and wait for a bus. "I'm not going any farther," he said, stopping. "We're going on the bus."

She continued to go on as if she had not heard him. He took a few steps and caught her arm and stopped her. He looked into her face and caught his breath. He was looking into a face he had never seen before. "Tell Grandpa to come get me," she said.

He stared, stricken.

"Tell Caroline to come get me," she said.

Stunned, he let her go and she lurched forward again, walk- ing as if one leg were shorter than the other. A tide of darkness seemed to be sweeping her from him. "Mother!" he cried. "Darling, sweetheart, wait!" Crumpling, she fell to the pavement. He dashed forward and fell at her side, crying, "Mamma, Mamma!" He turned her over. Her face was fiercely distorted. One eye, large and staring, moved slightly to the left as if it had become unmoored. The other remained fixed on him, raked his face again, found nothing and closed.

"Wait here, wait here!" he cried and jumped up and began to run for help toward a cluster of lights he saw in the distance ahead of him. "Help, help!" he shouted, but his voice was thin, scarcely a thread of sound. The lights drifted farther away the faster he ran and his feet moved numbly as if they carried him nowhere. The tide of darkness seemed to sweep him back to her, postponing from moment to moment his entry into the world of guilt and sorrow.

# GLOSSARY

The following is a list of terms relating to academic writing for which we thought definitions would be useful. In providing these definitions, we have sometimes highlighted the conversational aspects of writing that our book aims to help students master.

**academic writing** Writing done for a school assignment or scholarly publication. At its best, it makes an argument in response to the ideas of others, defends its argument with reasons and evidence, acknowledges counterarguments from multiple perspectives, and indicates why its argument matters.

**allusion** An indirect reference—for example, to a person, literary work, or historical event. Not to be confused with "illusion."

**analogy** A comparison that explains something unfamiliar by referring to something familiar.

**analysis** A methodical examination that breaks something down into its parts and explains how they work together.

**anecdote** A brief story or narrative often used to support an argument.

**annotation** A commentary on a text that highlights key words, phrases, or sentences, points out connections, and offers comments or questions in the margin.

**argument** A position taken in response to others' views on the same subject, in which the writer first identifies these alternative or opposing views, then responds to them by stating, explaining, and supporting his or her own views.

**assumption** A belief either stated or unstated that is regarded as true, upon which other claims are based.

**audience** The actual or intended readers of a piece of writing.

**authority** A person or text cited as support for an argument. A quality of writing that indicates that a writer knows what he or she is talking about.

**cause and effect** A strategy of analyzing why something occurred or speculating about what its consequences will be. Cause and effect can serve as the organizing principle for a whole text.

**chronological order** A way of organizing text that proceeds from the beginning of an event to the end. Reverse chronological order proceeds in the other direction, from the end to the beginning.

**citation** In a text, the act of giving information from a source. A citation and its corresponding parenthetical documentation, footnote, or endnote provide minimal information about the source; complete bibliographic information appears in a list of works cited or references at the end of the text.

**claim** A statement about a belief or position on a subject which the writer must support with reasons and evidence. Some use the words "claim" and "thesis" interchangeably. A paper, however, can only have one thesis, but may include multiple claims that support the author's thesis or main argument.

**classifying and dividing** A strategy that either groups (classifies) numerous individual items into categories by their similarities (for example, classifying cereal, bread, butter, chicken, cheese, cream, eggs, and oil as carbohydrates, proteins, and fats) or breaks (divides) one large category into small categories (for example, dividing food into carbohydrates, proteins, and fats). Classification and/or division can serve as the organizing principle for a whole text.

**cliché** An expression used so frequently that it becomes trite and so is no longer fresh: *busy as a bee, live and learn.*

**coherence** Unity or cohesion in a piece of writing, usually achieved by making sure that all claims revolve around one and only one overarching argument. The quality that allows an audience to follow a text and to see the connections among ideas, sentences, and paragraphs.

**colloquial language** Informal, relaxed language characteristic of everyday conversations.

**common ground** Shared values. Writers build common ground with readers by acknowledging others' points of view, seeking areas of compromise, and using language that includes, rather than excludes, those they aim to reach.

**conflict** In literary works, the central conflict, which drives the narrative, sometimes represented in an actual debate among characters. These conflicts often reflect larger questions in a society or historical era and are sometimes located within a character.

**counterargument** In argument, an alternative position or objection to the writer's position. The writer of an argument should not only acknowledge counterarguments but also be able to answer them.

**credibility** The sense of trustworthiness that a writer conveys through his or her text.

**criteria** The standards against which something is judged. When evaluating something—a piece of literature, an idea, a performance, a candidate—we develop our own standards or adopt those of others to help us determine the quality or value. Teachers establish the criteria for different grades on papers; voters may come up with their own criteria for electing a candidate; students and parents may have different criteria for choosing which colleges to apply to or attend.

**critique** A detailed analysis or evaluation of something—such as a theory, an argument, a work of art.

**data** Facts, statistics, and other information; the plural of *datum*. Technically, writers should use a plural verb when referring to *data* (*The data arrive from many sources*), but some writers treat it as singular (*The data is persuasive*).

**debate** A competitive exchange of ideas.

**definition** A strategy that says what something is. *Formal definitions* identify the category that something belongs to and tell what distinguishes it from other things in that category: a worm as an invertebrate (a category) with a long, rounded body and no appendages (distinguishing features). *Extended definitions* go into more detail: a paragraph or even an essay explaining why a character in a story is tragic. *Stipulative definitions* explain a writer's distinctive use of a term, one not found in a dictionary. Definition can serve as the organizing principle for a whole text.

**description** A strategy that tells how something looks, sounds, smells, feels, or tastes. Effective description creates a clear, dominant impression built from specific details. Description can be objective, subjective, or both. Description can serve as the organizing principle for a whole text.

**design** The way a text is arranged and presented visually. Elements of design include font, color, illustration, layout, and white space. As an important component of rhetorical situation, design determines how well a text reaches its audience and achieves its purpose.

**dialogue** A less competitive exchange of ideas than debate, dialogue usually seeks to reconcile differences and reach agreement. Also, the representation in writing of a conversation between two or more parties.

**diction** The words and phrases a writer chooses, and how he or she uses them. Diction may be described in terms of various qualities, such as the degree to which it is formal or colloquial, abstract or concrete, literal or figurative.

**documentation** Publication information about the sources cited in a text. The documentation usually appears in an abbreviated form in parentheses at the point of citation or in an endnote or a footnote. Complete documentation usually appears in a list of works cited or references at the end of the text. Documentation styles vary by discipline. For example, Modern Language Association (MLA) style requires an author's complete first name if it appears in a source, whereas American Psychological Association (APA) style requires only the initial of an author's first name.

**either/or argument** An argument that oversimplifies the subject by suggesting that only two possible positions exist on a complex issue.

**emotional appeal** In argument, an appeal to readers' feelings. Emotional appeals should be used carefully in academic writing, where arguments are often expected to emphasize logical reasons and evidence more than emotion.

**evaluation** A writing genre that makes a judgment about an object—a source, poem, trend, film, or restaurant—based on certain criteria.

**evidence** The statistics, calculations, examples, facts, anecdotes, quotations, case studies, or anything else used to support a writer's argument. Evidence should be sufficient (enough to show that the reasons have merit) and relevant (appropriate to the argument being made).

**explaining a process** A strategy for telling how something is done or how to do something. An explanation of a process can serve as the organizing principle for a whole text.

**genre** A kind of writing that follows certain pre-established formal conventions: the short story, novel, poem, love letter, memo, lab report, literary analysis, and so forth.

**hypothesis** A working belief used as a basis for further research; an assumption to be tested as one's work unfolds.

**inference** A logical conclusion deduced from facts and evidence.

**interpretation** The act of making sense of something or explaining what it means.

**jargon** Specialized vocabulary used by insiders in a profession, trade, or field.

**literature** Literary works, including fiction, poetry, drama, and some nonfiction; also, the body of written work produced in a field.

**logical appeal** In argument, an appeal to readers based on the use of logical reasoning and of evidence such as facts, statistics, and statements from authorities on the subject.

**medium** The means or vehicle used to communicate—print, audio, and video, or some combination of these in, for example, slide presentation, blog, or website.

**metacommentary** Parts of a text when writers comment on or re-explain their claims and tell their reader how—and how *not*—to understand those claims.

**metaphor** A figure of speech that makes a comparison without using the word *like* or *as*: "All the world's a stage / And all the men and women merely players" (Shakespeare, *As You Like It* 2.7.138–39).

**narration** A strategy for presenting information as a story, for telling "what happened." It is a pattern most often associated with fiction, but it shows up in all kinds of writing. When used in academic writing, narration is used to support a point—not merely to tell an interesting story for its own sake. It must also present events in some kind of sequence and include only pertinent details.

**parallelism** A writing technique that puts similar items into the same grammatical category. For example, every item on a to-do list might begin with a command: *clean, wash, buy*; or a discussion of favorite hobbies might name each as a gerund: *running, playing basketball, writing poetry.*

**paraphrase** A rewording of someone else's text that explains what it says in one's own words. Paraphrasing is generally called for when writers want to identify the gist of an argument without including supporting details. Like a quotation or summary, a paraphrase needs to be credited to its source and documented.

**persuasion** The act of convincing others to accept what you say as true, or of moving them to do something.

**plagiarism** The use of another person's words or ideas without appropriately crediting and including documentation of the source. Plagiarism is a serious breach of ethics.

**point of view** The vantage point, lens, outlook, or perspective from which a writer presents information; it can be in the first person (*I, we*), the second person (*you*), or the third person (*he, she, it, they, a student, the students*).

**pointing words** Words such as *this, these, such, she,* and *it* that point or refer to something in the previous sentence and enable readers to move effortlessly through it.

**position** A belief or claim. In an argument, a position is usually stated in a thesis or clearly implied, and it requires support with reasons and evidence.

**primary source** A source such as a literary work, historical document, work of art, or performance that a researcher examines first-hand. Primary sources also include experiments and field research. A researcher would likely consider the Declaration of Independence a primary source and a textbook's description of how the document was written a secondary source.

**prose** Spoken or written language without the metrical structure used in poetry; often contrasted with poetry.

**quotation** Placing someone else's words exactly as they were spoken or written into one's own writing. Quoting is most effective when the exact wording is worth repeating or makes a point so well that no rewording will do it justice. Quotations need to be acknowledged with documentation and framed to fit the purpose of the writer using them. There are two main types: *direct quotations* (which require quotation marks around the original writer's exact words) and *indirect quotations* (which do not use quotation marks but, instead, paraphrase what was said).

**reason** Support for a claim or position, requiring its own support in the form of evidence.

**refutation** A rebuttal; the act of showing another's argument to be wrong.

**repetition** A strategy for connecting the parts of an argument by repeating key terms or phrases throughout the text.

**revision** The process of making substantive changes, including additions and cuts, to a draft in order to improve it. During revision, writers generally try to sharpen their focus, strengthen their position, remove irrelevancies, and tighten connections.

**rhetoric** The art of using language effectively in speech and writing to persuade people to adopt a position or course of action. The term originally belonged to oratory, and it implies the presence of both a speaker or a writer, and a listener or reader.

**rhetorical précis** A genre that summarizes the main ideas of a text (*what* it says) and also analyzes the rhetorical strategies used in the text (*how* it says it). Unlike a plain summary, a précis uses a prescribed format, examining and commenting on the author's technique and how it affects the meaning of his or her message.

**rhetorical situation** Often defined as the context in which writing takes place, including purpose, audience, genre, stance, and medium. The rhetorical situation also includes the conversation, debate, problem, or whatever else motivates a piece of writing.

**satire** A genre of comedy in writing that is directed at ridiculing human foibles and vices, such as vanity, hypocrisy, stupidity, and greed. It differs from pure comedy in that the aim is not simply to evoke laughter, but to expose and censure faults, often with the aim of correcting them.

**secondary source** An analysis or interpretation of a primary source. In writing about the Revolutionary War, a researcher would likely consider the Declaration of Independence a primary source and a textbook's description of how the document was written a secondary source.

**signal phrase** Words used to attribute quoted, paraphrased, or summarized material to a source, as in "he insists," "she claims," "she rejects."

**skeptic** Someone who questions or doubts what others say or think; a naysayer.

**stance** A writer's attitude toward his or her subject—for example, reasonable, neutral, angry, curious. Stance is conveyed through tone.

**stereotype** A caricature that reduces a person or group of people to a simple trait, usually in an offensive way.

**style** In writing, the arrangement of sentences, clauses, phrases, words, and punctuation in a distinctive and recognizable way.

**summary** A condensed restatement of others' ideas in one's own words.

**synthesize** To combine ideas and information from multiple sources—and in writing, to weave the ideas of others in—with your own.

**textual analysis** A writing genre in which a writer looks at what a text says and how it says it. Key features include summary of the text, attention to context, clear interpretation or judgment, and reasonable support for conclusions.

**thesis** A clear statement of the topic and main point in a piece of writing, in which the writer gives readers an idea of what the text will cover and what the writer will say about it. The words "thesis" and "argument" are often confused. In an argument, the writer takes a position on a subject about which people disagree and seeks to persuade them by providing reasons and evidence; a thesis, however, is a sentence in which the writer states his or her argument and explains the means by which it will be supported.

**tone** A writer's attitude toward his or her subject or audience: sympathy, longing, amusement, shock, sarcasm, awe—the range is endless.

**topic sentence** A sentence, often at the beginning of a paragraph, that contains the paragraph's main point. The details in the rest of the paragraph should support the topic sentence.

**transition** A word or phrase that connects sentences and paragraphs to guide readers through a text. Transitions can show comparisons (*also, similarly*); contrasts (*but, instead*); examples (*for instance, in fact*); sequence (*first, second, finally*); time (*at first, meanwhile*); and more.

**vernacular** The informal language spoken in a particular community, country, or region.

**voice markers** Signal phrases that identify for readers whose ideas are being expressed in a text: "Smith's view is . . ."; "I assert . . ."

**works-cited list** A list at the end of a researched text that contains full bibliographic information for all the sources cited in the text.

# INDEX OF TEMPLATES

—▣—

## DISAGREEING WITHOUT BEING DISAGREEABLE
### (pp. 10–11)

▸ While I understand the impulse to _____, my own view is _____.

▸ While I agree with X that _____, I cannot accept her overall conclusion that _____.

▸ While X argues _____, and I argue _____, in a way we're both right.

## THE TEMPLATE OF TEMPLATES
### (p. 11)

▸ In recent discussions of _____, a controversial issue has been whether _____. On the one hand, some argue that _____. From this perspective, _____. On the other hand, however, others argue that _____. In the words of _____, one of this view's main proponents, "_____." According to this view, _____. In sum, then, the issue is whether _____ or _____.

My own view is that _____. Though I concede that _____, I still maintain that _____. For example, _____. Although some might object that _____, I would reply that _____. The issue is important because _____.

## INTRODUCING WHAT "THEY SAY"
(p. 23)

▸ A number of _____ have recently suggested that _____.

▸ It has become common today to dismiss _____.

▸ In their recent work, Y and Z have offered harsh critiques of _____ for _____.

## INTRODUCING "STANDARD VIEWS"
(pp. 23–24)

▸ Americans today tend to believe that _____.

▸ Conventional wisdom has it that _____.

▸ Common sense seems to dictate that _____.

▸ The standard way of thinking about topic X has it that _____.

▸ It is often said that _____.

▸ My whole life I have heard it said that _____.

▸ You would think that _____.

▸ Many people assume that _____.

## Index of Templates

### MAKING WHAT "THEY SAY" SOMETHING *YOU* SAY
(pp. 24–25)

▸ I've always believed that _____ .

▸ When I was a child, I used to think that _____ .

▸ Although I should know better by now, I cannot help thinking that _____ .

▸ At the same time that I believe _____ , I also believe _____ .


### INTRODUCING SOMETHING IMPLIED OR ASSUMED
(p. 25)

▸ Although none of them have ever said so directly, my teachers have often given me the impression that _____ .

▸ One implication of X's treatment of _____ is that _____ .

▸ Although X does not say so directly, she apparently assumes that _____ .

▸ While they rarely admit as much, _____ often take for granted that _____ .


### INTRODUCING AN ONGOING DEBATE
(pp. 25–28)

▸ In discussions of X, one controversial issue has been _____ . On the one hand, _____ argues _____ . On the other hand, _____ contends _____. Others even maintain _____. My own view is _____.

▸ When it comes to the topic of _____, most of us will readily agree that _____. Where this agreement usually ends, however, is on the question of _____. Whereas some are convinced that _____, others maintain that _____.

▸ In conclusion, then, as I suggested earlier, defenders of _____ can't have it both ways. Their assertion that _____ is contradicted by their claim that _____.


## CAPTURING AUTHORIAL ACTION
(pp. 39–41)

▸ X acknowledges that _____.

▸ X agrees that _____.

▸ X argues that _____.

▸ X believes that _____.

▸ X denies/does not deny that _____.

▸ X claims that _____.

▸ X complains that _____.

▸ X concedes that _____.

▸ X demonstrates that _____.

▸ X deplores the tendency to _____.

▸ X celebrates the fact that _____.

▸ X emphasizes that _____.

- ▶ X insists that _____.

- ▶ X observes that _____.

- ▶ X questions whether _____.

- ▶ X refutes the claim that _____.

- ▶ X reminds us that _____.

- ▶ X reports that _____.

- ▶ X suggests that _____.

- ▶ X urges us to _____.

## INTRODUCING QUOTATIONS
### (p. 47)

- ▶ X states, "_____."

- ▶ As the prominent philosopher X puts it, "_____."

- ▶ According to X, "_____."

- ▶ X himself writes, "_____."

- ▶ In her book, _____, X maintains that "_____"

- ▶ Writing in the journal _____, X complains that "_____."

- ▶ In X's view, "_____."

- ▶ X agrees when she writes, "_____."

- ▶ X disagrees when he writes, "_____."

- ▶ X complicates matters further when he writes, "_____."

## EXPLAINING QUOTATIONS

(pp. 47–48)

- ▸ Basically, X is saying _____.

- ▸ In other words, X believes _____.

- ▸ In making this comment, X urges us to _____.

- ▸ X is corroborating the age-old adage that _____.

- ▸ X's point is that _____.

- ▸ The essence of X's argument is that _____.

## DISAGREEING, WITH REASONS

(p. 58)

- ▸ I think X is mistaken because she overlooks _____.

- ▸ X's claim that _____ rests upon the questionable assumption that _____.

- ▸ I disagree with X's view that _____ because, as recent research has shown, _____.

- ▸ X contradicts herself / can't have it both ways. On the one hand, she argues _____. On the other hand, she also says _____.

- ▸ By focusing on _____, X overlooks the deeper problem of _____.

## Index of Templates

### AGREEING—WITH A DIFFERENCE
(pp. 59–62)

▶ I agree that _____ because my experience _____ confirms it.

▶ X surely is right about _____ because, as she may not be aware, recent studies have shown that _____.

▶ X's theory of _____ is extremely useful because it sheds insight on the difficult problem of _____.

▶ Those unfamiliar with this school of thought may be interested to know that it basically boils down to _____.

▶ I agree that _____, a point that needs emphasizing since so many people believe _____.

▶ If group X is right that _____, as I think they are, then we need to reassess the popular assumption that _____.

### AGREEING AND DISAGREEING SIMULTANEOUSLY
(pp. 63–65)

▶ Although I agree with X up to a point, I cannot accept his overall conclusion that _____.

▶ Although I disagree with much that X says, I fully endorse his final conclusion that _____.

▶ Though I concede that _____, I still insist that _____.

▶ Whereas X provides ample evidence that _____, Y and Z's research on _____ and _____ convinces me that _____ instead.

▸ X is right that _____ , but she seems on more dubious ground when she claims that _____ .

▸ While X is probably wrong when she claims that _____ , she is right that _____ .

▸ I'm of two minds about X's claim that _____ . On the one hand, I agree that _____ . On the other hand, I'm not sure if _____ .

▸ My feelings on the issue are mixed. I do support X's position that _____ , but I find Y's argument about _____ and Z's research on _____ to be equally persuasive.

## SIGNALING WHO IS SAYING WHAT
### (pp. 70–72)

▸ X argues _____ .

▸ According to both X and Y, _____ .

▸ Politicians _____ , X argues, should _____ .

▸ Most athletes will tell you that _____ .

▸ My own view, however, is that _____ .

▸ I agree, as X may not realize, that _____ .

▸ But _____ are real and, arguably, the most significant factor in _____ .

▸ But X is wrong that _____ .

▸ However, it is simply not true that _____ .

▸ Indeed, it is highly likely that _____ .

▸ X's assertion that _____ does not fit the facts.

- X is right that _____.

- X is wrong that _____.

- X is both right and wrong that _____.

- Yet a sober analysis of the matter reveals _____.

- Nevertheless, new research shows _____.

- Anyone familiar with _____ should agree that _____.

## EMBEDDING VOICE MARKERS
### (p. 74)

- X overlooks what I consider an important point about _____.

- My own view is that what X insists is a _____ is in fact a _____.

- I wholeheartedly endorse what X calls _____.

- These conclusions, which X discusses in _____, add weight to the argument that _____.

## ENTERTAINING OBJECTIONS
### (p. 81)

- At this point I would like to raise some objections that have been inspired by the skeptic in me. She feels that I have been ignoring _____. "_____," she says to me, "_____."

- Yet some readers may challenge the view that _____.

- Of course, many will probably disagree with this assertion that _____.

## NAMING YOUR NAYSAYERS

(pp. 82–83)

▸ Here many _____ would probably object that _____.

▸ But _____ would certainly take issue with the argument that _____.

▸ _____, of course, may want to question whether _____.

▸ Nevertheless, both followers and critics of _____ will probably argue that _____.

▸ Although not all _____ think alike, some of them will probably dispute my claim that _____.

▸ _____ are so diverse in their views that it's hard to generalize about them, but some are likely to object on the grounds that _____.

## INTRODUCING OBJECTIONS INFORMALLY

(pp. 83–84)

▸ But is my proposal realistic? What are the chances of its actually being adopted?

▸ Yet is it always true that _____? Is it always the case, as I have been suggesting, that _____?

▸ However, does the evidence I've cited prove conclusively that _____?

▸ "Impossible," some will say. "You must be reading the research selectively."

## MAKING CONCESSIONS WHILE STILL
## STANDING YOUR GROUND (p. 88)

▶ Although I grant that _____, I still maintain that _____.

▶ Proponents of X are right to argue that _____. But they exaggerate when they claim that _____.

▶ While it is true that _____, it does not necessarily follow that _____.

▶ On the one hand, I agree with X that _____. But on the other hand, I still insist that _____.

## INDICATING WHO CARES
### (pp. 94–95)

▶ _____ used to think _____. But recently [or within the past few decades] _____ suggests that _____.

▶ These findings challenge the work of earlier researchers, who tended to assume that _____.

▶ Recent studies like these shed new light on _____, which previous studies had not addressed.

▶ Researchers have long assumed that _____. For instance, one eminent scholar of cell biology, _____, assumed in _____, her seminal work on cell structures and functions, that fat cells _____. As _____ herself put it, "_____" (2012). Another leading scientist, _____, argued that fat cells "_____" (2011). Ultimately, when it came to the nature of fat, the basic assumption was that _____.

But a new body of research shows that fat cells are far more complex and that _____.

▸ If sports enthusiasts stopped to think about it, many of them might simply assume that the most successful athletes _____. However, new research shows _____.

▸ These findings challenge neoliberals' common assumptions that _____.

▸ At first glance, teenagers appear to _____. But on closer inspection _____.


## ESTABLISHING WHY YOUR CLAIMS MATTER
(pp. 97–98)

▸ X matters / is important because _____.

▸ Although X may seem trivial, it is in fact crucial in terms of today's concern over _____.

▸ Ultimately, what is at stake here is _____.

▸ These findings have important consequences for the broader domain of _____.

▸ My discussion of X is in fact addressing the larger matter of _____.

▸ These conclusions / This discovery will have significant applications in _____ as well as in _____.

▸ Although X may seem of concern to only a small group of _____, it should in fact concern anyone who cares about _____.

## COMMONLY USED TRANSITIONS
(pp. 104–06)

**ADDITION**

| | |
|---|---|
| also | in fact |
| and | indeed |
| besides | moreover |
| furthermore | so too |
| in addition | |

**ELABORATION**

| | |
|---|---|
| actually | to put it another way |
| by extension | to put it bluntly |
| in short | to put it succinctly |
| that is | ultimately |
| in other words | |

**EXAMPLE**

| | |
|---|---|
| after all | for instance |
| as an illustration | specifically |
| consider | to take a case in point |
| for example | |

**CAUSE AND EFFECT**

| | |
|---|---|
| accordingly | since |
| as a result | so |
| consequently | then |
| hence | therefore |
| it follows, then | thus |

## COMPARISON

| | |
|---|---|
| along the same lines | likewise |
| in the same way | similarly |

## CONTRAST

| | |
|---|---|
| although | nevertheless |
| but | nonetheless |
| by contrast | on the contrary |
| conversely | on the other hand |
| despite | regardless |
| even though | whereas |
| however | while |
| in contrast | yet |

## CONCESSION

| | |
|---|---|
| admittedly | of course |
| although it is true that | naturally |
| granted | to be sure |
| I concede that | |

## CONCLUSION

| | |
|---|---|
| as a result | so |
| consequently | the upshot of all this is that |
| hence | therefore |
| in conclusion, then | thus |
| in short | to sum up |
| in sum, then | to summarize |
| it follows, then | |

## Index of Templates

### TRANSLATION RECIPES
(pp. 120–21)

▸ Scholar X argues, "_____." In other words, _____.

▸ Essentially, X argues _____.

▸ X's point, succinctly put, is that _____.

▸ Plainly put, _____.

### ADDING METACOMMENTARY
(pp. 133–39)

▸ In other words, _____.

▸ What _____ really means by this is _____.

▸ Ultimately, my goal is to demonstrate that _____.

▸ My point is not _____, but _____.

▸ To put it another way, _____.

▸ In sum, then, _____.

▸ My conclusion, then, is that, _____.

▸ In short, _____.

▸ What is more important, _____.

▸ Incidentally, _____.

▸ By the way, _____.

▸ Chapter 2 explores _____, while Chapter 3 examines _____.

▸ Having just argued that _____, let us now turn our attention to _____.

▸ Although some readers may object that _____, I would answer that _____.

# INDEX OF TEMPLATES

## LINKING TO WHAT "THEY SAY"
(p. 171)

- As X mentions in <u>this article,</u> " _____."

- In making <u>this comment,</u> X warns that _____.

- Economists often assume _____; however, <u>new research</u> by X suggests _____.

## STARTING WITH WHAT OTHERS SAY
## ABOUT A LITERARY WORK
(pp. 188–91)

- Critic X complains that Author Y's story is compromised by his _____. While there's some truth to this critique, I argue that Critic X overlooks _____.

- According to Critic A, novel X suggests _____. I agree, but would add that _____.

- Several members of our class have suggested that the final message of play X is _____. I agree up to a point, but I still think that _____.

- On first reading play Z, I thought it was an uncritical celebration of _____. After rereading the play and discussing it in class, however, I see that it is more critical of _____ than I originally thought.

- It might be said that poem Y is chiefly about _____. But the problem with this reading, in my view, is _____.

- Though religious readers might be tempted to analyze poem X as a parable about _____, a closer examination suggests that the poem is in fact about _____.

## RESPONDING TO OTHER INTERPRETATIONS
## OF A LITERARY WORK
(p. 194)

▶ It might be argued that in the clash between character X and Y in play Z, the author wants us to favor character Y, since she is presented as the play's heroine. I contend, however, that _____.

▶ Several critics seem to assume that poem X endorses the values of _____ represented by the image of _____ over those of _____ represented by the image of _____. I agree, but with the following caveat: _____.

## SHOWING EVIDENCE WHEN WRITING
## ABOUT A LITERARY WORK
(pp. 197–99)

▶ Although some might read the metaphor of _____ in this poem as evidence, that for Author X, _____, I see it as _____.

▶ Some might claim that evidence X suggests _____, but I argue that, on the contrary, it suggests _____.

▶ I agree with my classmate _____ that the image of _____ in novel Y is evidence of _____. Unlike _____, however, I think _____.

## EXPLAIN WHAT THE DATA MEAN
(p. 214)

▶ Our data *support / confirm / verify* the work of X by showing that _____.

▶ By demonstrating _____, X's work *extends* the findings of Y.

▶ The results of X *contradict/refute* Y's conclusion that _____.

▶ X's findings *call into question* the widely accepted theory that _____.

▶ Our data *are consistent with* X's hypothesis that _____.

## EXPLAINING AN EXPERIMENTAL RESULT
### (p. 217)

▶ One explanation for X's finding of _____ is that _____. An alternative explanation is _____.

▶ The difference between _____ and _____ is probably due to _____.

## INTRODUCING GAPS IN THE EXISTING RESEARCH
### (p. 232)

▶ Studies of X have indicated _____. It is not clear, however, that this conclusion applies to _____.

▶ _____ often take for granted that _____. Few have investigated this assumption, however.

▶ X's work tells us a great deal about _____. Can this work be generalized to _____?

▶ Our understanding of _____ remains incomplete because previous work has not examined _____.

# CREDITS

## TEXT

**Michelle Alexander:** Excerpt from *The New Jim Crow.* Copyright © 2010, 2012 by Michelle Alexander. Reprinted by permission of The New Press. www.thenewpress.com.

**Christopher J. Ferguson and Patrick Markey:** Excerpt from "Video Games Aren't Addictive," from *The New York Times*, April 1, 2017. Copyright © 2017 The New York Times. All rights reserved. Used by permission and protected by the Copyright Laws of the United States. The printing, copying, redistribution, or retransmission of this Content without express written permission is prohibited.

**Gerald Graff:** "Hidden Intellectualism," adapted from *Clueless in Academe: How Schooling Obscures the Life of the Mind.* Copyright © 2003 Yale University. Reprinted by permission of Yale University Press.

**Michael Littman:** "'Rise of the Machines' Is Not a Likely Future," From LiveScience.com, January 28, 2015. Reprinted by permission of Wright's Media.

**Flannery O'Connor:** "Everything That Rises Must Converge," from *The Complete Stories.* Copyright © 1956, 1957, 1958, 1960, 1961, 1962 Flannery O'Connor. Copyright renewed 1993 by Regina Cline O'Connor. Reprinted by permission of Farrar, Straus and Giroux and the Mary Flannery O' Connor Charitable Trust via Harold Matson Company, Inc.

**Eric Schlosser:** Excerpt from "A People's Democratic Platform," from *The Nation*, August 2, 2004. Copyright © 2004 The Nation. All rights reserved. Used by permission and protected by the Copyright Laws of the United States. The printing, copying, redistribution, or retransmission of this Content without express written permission is prohibited.

CREDITS

David Zinczenko: "Don't Blame the Eater," *The New York Times*, November 23, 2002, p. A31. Reprinted by permission of the author.

## PHOTOGRAPHS

Chapter 11: p. 148: 20th Century Fox/Courtesy Everett Collection; p. 156: 20th Century Fox/Courtesy Everett Collection; Chapter 15: p. 198: Wikimedia; About the Authors: Tricia Koning.

# ACKNOWLEDGMENTS

—◫—

I would like to thank those colleagues who offered us detailed and valuable feedback about the initial versions of the high school materials: Carol Jago, Santa Monica High School; Hayley Shapland, Carondelet High School; Fran Weinberg; Deanna Benjamin, Washington University; and Mary Trachsel, University of Iowa. Also, my fellow senior teacher Melissa Murphy has provided many insights through her comments about how she uses this book in her high school classes. I am grateful to all my students at Burlingame High School for the lessons they have taught me through our use of "They Say / I Say" over the years; especially to Dasha Krayushkina, Inna Nytochka, Alina Utrata, Kyle Cheung, and Isabel Mueller, who returned my drafted material covered in color-coded notes and asked to meet with me so she could explain them all in person. One student, James Han, said only, "THAT book. I mean, teachers, they think it's great and all, but I think it's. . . oh. . . wait. . . it IS great."

Thanks also to the many teachers who reviewed the third edition: Virginia Reischl, Capistrano Unified School District, CA; Josh Dalton, Desert Christian High School, AZ; Debra Robinson, Mt. Pleasant High School, CA; Tara Seale, Bryant High School, AR; Janet Duckham, Ladue Horton Watkins High School, MO; Noah Barfield, Bainbridge High School, WA; Tom Kissick, Beaver Area High School, PA; Danell

## ACKNOWLEDGMENTS

Simons, South Sioux City High School, NE; Amber Myers, South Sioux City High School, NE; Dan Inloes, Wylie E. Groves High School, MI; Lisa Hardey, Sprague High School, OR; Michelle Potson-Peters, Tecumseh High School, OH; Jeffrey Swartwout, Sprague High School, OR.

To the people at Norton, I have the deepest of gratitude for placing their faith in me to help launch their high school division. Without Jenna Barry, I would never have become involved, for it was she who invited me to become part of this project. Roby Harrington took an early and active interest in my work and this project, which proved important at crucial moments. Marilyn Moller gave me the equivalent of a master class in writing, shaping the ideas and voice of all that I wrote. Melissa Atkin joined the project early on and brought to it not only her editorial gifts but also her wisdom as a former high school teacher who showed a keen understanding of classroom dynamics. Of course, the last word must go to Gerald Graff and Cathy Birkenstein themselves for not only welcoming me to this project but also writing this book, which has done so much over the years to improve my understanding and teaching of writing.

Jim Burke

**GERALD GRAFF**, a professor of English and Education at the University of Illinois at Chicago and the 2008 President of the Modern Language Association of America, has had a major impact on teachers through such books as *Professing Literature: An Institutional History*, *Beyond the Culture Wars: How Teaching the Conflicts Can Revitalize American Education*, and, most recently, *Clueless in Academe: How Schooling Obscures the Life of the Mind*. The new Common Core State Standards for K–12 cite his work on the importance of argument literacy for college and career readiness. **CATHY BIRKENSTEIN**, a lecturer at the University of Illinois at Chicago, has published essays on writing, most recently in *College English*, and, with Gerald, in *The Chronicle of Higher Education*, *Academe*, and *College Composition and Communication*. She and Gerald have given over a hundred lectures and workshops at colleges, conferences, and high schools—and are at present working on a book contending that our currently confusing school and college curriculum needs to be clarified by making the practice of argument the common thread across all disciplines.

**JIM BURKE,** an English teacher at Burlingame High School in California, has been teaching for over twenty-five years and is the author of numerous bestselling professional books, including *The English Teacher's Companion*, *The Common Core Companion*, and most recently, *Uncharted Territory: A High School Reader*, published by W. W. Norton & Company in 2017. He has received many awards, including the Distinguished Service Award from the California Association of Teachers of English. In addition to his commitment to his own classroom, Jim served as an advisor for the College Board's Pre-AP® and Advanced Placement® English Language and Literature programs, and as a consultant for the Partnership for Assessment of Readiness for College and Careers (PARCC). For more information, visit his website (www.englishcompanion.com) or follow him on Twitter (@englishcomp).